The Collected Works of Paul Valéry

Edited by Jackson Mathews

VOLUME I

PAUL VALÉRY

POEMS

Translated by
David Paul

ON POETS AND POETRY

Selected and Translated from the
Notebooks
by
James R. Lawler

BOLLINGEN SERIES XLV · I

PRINCETON UNIVERSITY PRESS

THIS IS VOLUME ONE OF THE
COLLECTED WORKS OF PAUL VALÉRY
CONSTITUTING NUMBER XLV IN BOLLINGEN SERIES
SPONSORED BY BOLLINGEN FOUNDATION.
IT IS THE TWELFTH VOLUME OF THE
COLLECTED WORKS TO APPEAR.

ISBN 0-691-09859-X

Library of Congress catalogue card no. 56-9337
Type composed at the University Printing House, Cambridge, England
Printed in the United States of America

DESIGNED BY ANDOR BRAUN

CONTENTS

CONTENTS

CONTENTS

CHARMES
CHARMS

vii

CONTENTS

PIÈCES DIVERSES DE TOUTE ÉPOQUE
VARIOUS POEMS OF ALL PERIODS

CONTENTS

CONTENTS

CONTENTS

CONTENTS

CONTENTS

xiii

CONTENTS

Recollection

by Paul Valéry

IT HAPPENED at certain stages in my life that poetry became a way of cutting myself off from the "world."

By "world" I mean the whole complex of incidents, demands, compulsions, solicitations, of every kind and degree of urgency, which overtake the mind without offering it any inner illuminations, move it only to disturb, and shift it away from the more important toward the less....

It is no bad thing if certain men have the strength of mind to attach more value and significance to determining a remote decimal number, or to the exact placing of a comma, than to the most resounding of news items, the most terrible catastrophe, or even to their own lives.

This leads me to reflect that one of the advantages of observing traditional forms in the construction of verse consists in the extreme attention which is developed by this discipline, conceived as an ordering toward continuous musicality and the charm of sustained perfection which (according to some minds) is what a true poem ought to offer. The result is an absence of prose—a freedom, that is, from any sense of interruption. To outlaw the arbitrary: to shut out accidents, politics, the chaos of events, and the fluctuations of fashion; to attempt to draw from oneself some work more exquisite than one might have hoped for; to find strength in oneself not to be satisfied with less than prolonged struggles, to set about a passionate quest for the solving of problems imperceptible to most people, in defiance of the headlong rush, the distractions (however affecting) that intrude from the outside world—this is something that appeals to me.

I in no way regret the four years spent daily in struggling to resolve the severest problems of versification.

It was a period of universal panic, anxious hearts, heavy brows, minds under strain, dumbfounded or devastated by the news, the suspense, the setbacks, the wildest speculations and rumors. In circumstances so appalling, what could be done except to endure, destitute as one was of any means of action that might cope with the extraordinary commotion of a world gone mad?

Nothing else perhaps would have served than the vainest and most fine-spun research: of the sort that is dedicated to the delicate contriving of the multiple values of language, super-posed on each other, a research designed to excite, as it demands, the whole will, and all possible obstinacy in that will—in order to keep a part of the mind proof against the terrible effects of anxious waiting, the repercussions, the rumors, the imaginings, and the contagion of the ridiculous.

I fashioned myself a poetry void of hope, a poetry that had no other purpose and almost no other law than to establish for me a way of living with myself, for a part of my days. I set no term to it, and I imposed conditions enough to provide matter for labor without end. . . .

This *assumed infinity* taught me a number of things. I knew very well that a work is never completed except by some accident such as weariness, satisfaction, the need to deliver, or death: for, in relation to who or what is making it, it can only be one stage in a series of inner transformations. How often one would like to start on something which one has just regarded as finished. How often I have looked at what I was about to surrender to other eyes as only the necessary foundation for the desired work, only at that point beginning to *see* in it the possibility of its mature form, as the very likely and very desirable fruit of a new spell of concentration, of an act fully outlined within my powers. The finished work then seemed like the mortal body that must give place to the glorious and transfigured one.

Besides all this, in following my regime of *static* recapitulations and developments, I realized the immense benefits of a life of the mind that was cut off from all speculation on other people's tastes. In order to interest me, poetic problems must be such as could be resolved only by observing certain conditions, considered and established in advance, as in the case of geometry. It was this that led me to avoid seeking out "effects" (for instance detachable "fine lines") and to sacrifice them willingly enough whenever they came to mind. I built up a habit of refusal, as well as some others. In particular I found I came to carry out, after a time, a curious reversal in the workings of the creative mind: I would often arrive at determining what the philosophers (right or wrong) call the "content" of a thought (it would be more useful to talk of the content of the expression) by way of considerations of form. I took the thought, as one might say, for the "unknown quantity," and I would approach that "x" by means of as many approximations as were needed, each one nearer than the last.

ALBUM DE VERS ANCIENS

ALBUM OF EARLY VERSE

La Fileuse

Lilia..., neque nent.

Assise, la fileuse au bleu de la croisée
Où le jardin mélodieux se dodeline;
Le rouet ancien qui ronfle l'a grisée.

Lasse, ayant bu l'azur, de filer la câline
Chevelure, à ses doigts si faibles évasive,
Elle songe, et sa tête petite s'incline.

Un arbuste et l'air pur font une source vive
Qui, suspendue au jour, délicieuse arrose
De ses pertes de fleurs le jardin de l'oisive.

Une tige, où le vent vagabond se repose,
Courbe le salut vain de sa grâce étoilée,
Dédiant magnifique, au vieux rouet, sa rose.

Mais la dormeuse file une laine isolée;
Mystérieusement l'ombre frêle se tresse
Au fil de ses doigts longs et qui dorment, filée.

Le songe se dévide avec une paresse
Angélique, et sans cesse, au doux fuseau crédule,
La chevelure ondule au gré de la caresse...

Derrière tant de fleurs, l'azur se dissimule,
Fileuse de feuillage et de lumière ceinte:
Tout le ciel vert se meurt. Le dernier arbre brûle.

The Spinner

Lilies..., neither do they spin.

Seated the spinner in the blue of the windowpane
Where melodious the garden dawdles:
She is dazed by the humming of the ancient spinning wheel.

Sated with azure, weary of threading the wheedling
Hairs that evade fingers grown so feeble,
She is dreaming, and her small head leans.

Between them the pure air and a shrub contrive
A living spring, light-suspended, delectably sprinkling
The idle girl's garden with a squandering of petals.

A stem, where the vagabond wind comes to rest,
Bows with the vain curtsey of its starry grace,
Vowing its splendid rose to the antique spinning wheel.

But the sleeping girl is spinning a lonely thread:
Mysteriously the fragile shadow braids itself
Along the length of her slender sleeping fingers, divided.

The dream goes on unwinding with an angelic
Slowness, and ceaselessly, trustful of the soft spindle,
The hair undulates obedient to the caress....

Behind such throngs of flowers, the blue hides itself,
A spinner engirdled in foliage and light:
All the green sky is dying. The last tree blazes.

3   I-2

Ta sœur, la grande rose où sourit une sainte,
Parfume ton front vague au vent de son haleine
Innocente, et tu crois languir...Tu es éteinte

Au bleu de la croisée où tu filais la laine.

Your sister, the great rose with the smile of a saint,
Scents your vague brow with the wind of her innocent
Breath, and you feel you are fainting. . . . You have faded
    out

In the blue of the window where you were spinning wool.

Hélène

Azur ! c'est moi. . .Je viens des grottes de la mort
Entendre l'onde se rompre aux degrés sonores,
Et je revois les galères dans les aurores
Ressusciter de l'ombre au fil des rames d'or.

Mes solitaires mains appellent les monarques
Dont la barbe de sel amusait mes doigts purs;
Je pleurais. Ils chantaient leurs triomphes obscurs
Et les golfes enfuis aux poupes de leurs barques.

J'entends les conques profondes et les clairons
Militaires rythmer le vol des avirons;
Le chant clair des rameurs enchaîne le tumulte,

Et les Dieux, à la proue héroïque exaltés
Dans leur sourire antique et que l'écume insulte,
Tendent vers moi leurs bras indulgents et sculptés.

Helen

Azure, it is I!...come from the grottoes of death
To hear the wave breaking on the resounding steps,
And again I can see the galleys in the dawns
Resurrected out of shadow on lines of golden oars.

My hands in their loneliness evoke those monarchs
Whose salt beards used to beguile my pure fingers;
I would weep. They would sing their cloudy triumphs,
And the gulfs glided by on the poops of their barks.

I hear the deep conches and the military
Clarions ringing in cadence to the flying oars;
The clear song of the rowers enchains the tumult,

And the Gods, up-raised on the heroic prows
With their archaic smiles assaulted by the foam,
Stretch out towards me their fond and sculptured arms.

Orphée

...Je compose en esprit, sous les myrtes, Orphée
L'Admirable!...Le feu, des cirques purs descend;
Il change le mont chauve en auguste trophée
D'où s'exhale d'un dieu l'acte retentissant.

Si le dieu chante, il rompt le site tout-puissant;
Le soleil voit l'horreur du mouvement des pierres;
Une plainte inouïe appelle éblouissants
Les hauts murs d'or harmonieux d'un sanctuaire.

Il chante, assis au bord du ciel splendide, Orphée!
Le roc marche, et trébuche; et chaque pierre fée
Se sent un poids nouveau qui vers l'azur délire!

D'un Temple à demi nu le soir baigne l'essor,
Et soi-même il s'assemble et s'ordonne dans l'or
À l'âme immense du grand hymne sur la lyre!

Orpheus

In the mind's eye, under the myrtles, I create
Orpheus, Man of Wonders!...Fire falls from the pure
    circuses:
It transforms the bald peak into a trophy of majesty
Whence exhales resonant the act of a god.

Should the god sing, he rends the all-powerful site;
The sun witnesses the horror of stones moving:
An unimaginable wail calls forth dazzling
The high gold harmonious walls of a sanctuary.

Singing, Orpheus sits on the sky's resplendent rim!
A rock walks, and staggers: and every stone bewitched
Feels a new pull within it raving sky-wards!

Evening bathes a half-naked temple as it soars
And spontaneously assembles, taking shape in the gold,
Obeying the giant soul of the great hymn on the lyre!

Naissance de Vénus

De sa profonde mère, encor froide et fumante,
Voici qu'au seuil battu de tempêtes, la chair
Amèrement vomie au soleil par la mer,
Se délivre des diamants de la tourmente.

Son sourire se forme, et suit sur ses bras blancs
Qu'éplore l'orient d'une épaule meurtrie,
De l'humide Thétis la pure pierrerie,
Et sa tresse se fraye un frisson sur ses flancs.

Le frais gravier, qu'arrose et fuit sa course agile,
Croule, creuse rumeur de soif, et le facile
Sable a bu les baisers de ses bonds puérils;

Mais de mille regards ou perfides ou vagues,
Son œil mobile mêle aux éclairs de périls
L'eau riante, et la danse infidèle des vagues.

Birth of Venus

Out of her mother's depths, still cold and steaming,
Look, on the belabored sill of storms, the flesh
Bitterly vomited up by the sea to the sun,
Delivers itself from the diamonds of turmoil.

Her smile comes to being, and along her snowy arms,
(Be-gloomed by the orient of a shoulder's bruise)
Follows the pure jewels of watery Thetis,
And her tress blazes a shiver along her flanks.

The cool shingle, sprinkled by her flying feet,
Crumbles, noising a hollow thirst, and the facile
Sand has drained the kisses of her childish leaps.

But with a thousand glances, traitorous or vague,
Her quick eye is a mingling of perilous lightnings,
Water's laughter, and the fickle dancing of the waves.

Féerie

La lune mince verse une lueur sacrée,
Toute une jupe d'un tissu d'argent léger,
Sur les bases de marbre où vient l'Ombre songer
Que suit d'un char de perle une gaze nacrée.

Pour les cygnes soyeux qui frôlent les roseaux
De carènes de plume à demi lumineuse,
Elle effeuille infinie une rose neigeuse
Dont les pétales font des cercles sur les eaux...

Est-ce vivre?...Ô désert de volupté pâmée
Où meurt le battement faible de l'eau lamée,
Usant le seuil secret des échos de cristal...

La chair confuse des molles roses commence
À frémir, si d'un cri le diamant fatal
Fêle d'un fil de jour toute la fable immense.

Faery

The slim moon sheds a consecrated gleam,
A whole wide skirt of light silvery tissue
Over the marble floors where the Shadow comes brooding,
The sheeny gauze of a chariot of pearl in her train.

For the silky swans as they brush by the reeds
With their half-luminous and feathery keels,
She is disleafing an infinite snowy rose
Whose petals send out circles on the waters....

Is this to live?...Oh desert of swooned bliss
Where the frail beat of the silvered water dies,
Wearing at the secret sill of the crystal echoes....

Abashed, the flesh of the soft roses begins
To shudder, should the fatal diamond of a cry
Crack with a thread of daylight the whole immense fable.

Même Féerie

La lune mince verse une lueur sacrée,
Comme une jupe d'un tissu d'argent léger,
Sur les masses de marbre où marche et croit songer
Quelque vierge de perle et de gaze nacrée.

Pour les cygnes soyeux qui frôlent les roseaux
De carènes de plume à demi lumineuse,
Sa main cueille et dispense une rose neigeuse
Dont les pétales font des cercles sur les eaux.

Délicieux désert, solitude pâmée,
Quand le remous de l'eau par la lune lamée
Compte éternellement ses échos de cristal,

Quel cœur pourrait souffrir l'inexorable charme
De la nuit éclatante au firmament fatal,
Sans tirer de soi-même un cri pur comme une arme?

Same Faery

The slim moon sheds a consecrated gleam,
It is like a skirt of lightly silvered tissue,
On the blocks of marble where walks, thinking she dreams,
Some virgin made of pearl and sheeny gauze.

For the silky swans as they brush by the reeds
With their half-luminous and feathery keels,
Her fingers cull and shed a snowy rose
Whose petals send out circles on the waters.

Desert delectable, swooned-away solitude,
When the eddying water silvered by the moon
Eternally counts up its crystalline echoes,

What heart could endure the inexorable charm
Of this dazzling night and its sky of doom,
Without unsheathing a cry naked as a blade?

Baignée

Un fruit de chair se baigne en quelque jeune vasque,
(Azur dans les jardins tremblants) mais hors de l'eau,
Isolant la torsade aux puissances de casque,
Luit le chef d'or que tranche à la nuque un tombeau.

Éclose la beauté par la rose et l'épingle !
Du miroir même issue où trempent ses bijoux,
Bizarres feux brisés dont le bouquet dur cingle
L'oreille abandonnée aux mots nus des flots doux.

Un bras vague inondé dans le néant limpide
Pour une ombre de fleur à cueillir vainement
S'effile, ondule, dort par le délice vide,

Si l'autre, courbé pur sous le beau firmament,
Parmi la chevelure immense qu'il humecte,
Capture dans l'or simple un vol ivre d'insecte.

Immersed

A fruit of flesh is bathing in some young fountain-pool,
(Sky blue in shimmering gardens) but above the water,
Isolating the twisted braids strong as a helmet,
Shines the gold head cut off at the nape by a tomb.

Beauty brought to birth by the rose and hairpin !
Issuing from the very mirror where she steeps her jewels,
Bizarre broken fires whose hard cluster stings
The ear leant to the naked speech of the soft ripples.

A vague arm submerged in that limpid non-being
Uselessly to cull the reflection of a flower
Grows thin, undulates, dozes in the delicious void,

While the other, purely curved under the clear heaven,
Amid the immense coiffure it be-sprinkles,
Arrests a crazy insect's flight in the pure gold.

Au bois dormant

La princesse, dans un palais de rose pure,
Sous les murmures, sous la mobile ombre dort,
Et de corail ébauche une parole obscure
Quand les oiseaux perdus mordent ses bagues d'or.

Elle n'écoute ni les gouttes, dans leurs chutes,
Tinter d'un siècle vide au lointain le trésor,
Ni, sur la forêt vague, un vent fondu de flûtes
Déchirer la rumeur d'une phrase de cor.

Laisse, longue, l'écho rendormir la diane,
Ô toujours plus égale à la molle liane
Qui se balance et bat tes yeux ensevelis.

Si proche de ta joue et si lente la rose
Ne va pas dissiper ce délice de plis
Secrètement sensible au rayon qui s'y pose.

Sleeping Beauty

The princess, in a palace of pure rose,
Under the murmurs, under the moving shadow sleeps,
And half-forms in coral some vague word
Whenever the strayed birds peck at her gold rings.

She listens neither to the drops in their falling flights
Ringing faintly on the treasures of an empty age,
Nor, over the dim forest, to the melted wind of flutes
Rending through the rumor of the horn's phrase.

Let, long, let the echo lull the reveille,
O you who grow ever more like the pliant liana
That sways and beats over your buried eyes.

So gradual and so close by your cheek, the rose
Will not dispel that bliss of folded petals
Secretly sensitive to the ray resting there.

César

César, calme César, le pied sur toute chose,
Les poings durs dans la barbe, et l'œil sombre peuplé
D'aigles et des combats du couchant contemplé,
Ton cœur s'enfle, et se sent toute-puissante Cause.

Le lac en vain palpite et lèche son lit rose;
En vain d'or précieux brille le jeune blé;
Tu durcis dans les nœuds de ton corps rassemblé
L'ordre, qui doit enfin fendre ta bouche close.

L'ample monde, au delà de l'immense horizon,
L'Empire attend l'éclair, le décret, le tison
Qui changeront le soir en furieuse aurore.

Heureux là-bas sur l'onde, et bercé du hasard,
Un pêcheur indolent qui flotte et chante, ignore
Quelle foudre s'amasse au centre de César.

Caesar

Caesar, calm Caesar, all things beneath your foot,
Hard fists in your beard, your dark eye peopled
By the eagles and battles in the sunset's gaze,
Your heart swells and feels itself all-efficient Cause.

In vain the lake palpitates, licking its rosy bed;
In vain the young corn twinkles with precious gold;
You are toughening in the knots of your concentrated body
The command that will finally break your sealed lips.

The wide world beyond the immense horizon,
The Empire awaits the flash, the decree, the fuse
Transforming the evening into a furious dawn.

Happy there below, on the wave chance-rocked,
An indolent fisherman sings and floats, oblivious
Of what lightning accumulates in Caesar's midst.

Le Bois amical

Nous avons pensé des choses pures
Côte à côte, le long des chemins,
Nous nous sommes tenus par les mains
Sans dire...parmi les fleurs obscures;

Nous marchions comme des fiancés
Seuls, dans la nuit verte des prairies;
Nous partagions ce fruit de féeries
La lune amicale aux insensés

Et puis, nous sommes morts sur la mousse,
Trés loin, tout seuls parmi l'ombre douce
De ce bois intime et murmurant;

Et là-haut, dans la lumière immense,
Nous nous sommes trouvés en pleurant
Ô mon cher compagnon de silence !

The Friendly Wood

We were thinking of purest things
Side by side, along the paths,
We held each other by the hand
Unsaying...among the dim flowers;

We walked like affianced ones
Alone, in the green night of meadows;
We were sharing that faery fruit
The moon, kindly to the mad.

And then, we died on the moss,
Far off, all alone in the mild shades
Of the intimate and murmurous wood;

And up there in the immense light,
With tears we two found each other,
O my dear companion of silence!

Les Vaines Danseuses

Celles qui sont des fleurs légères sont venues,
Figurines d'or et beautés toutes menues
Où s'irise une faible lune...Les voici
Mélodieuses fuir dans le bois éclairci.
De mauves et d'iris et de nocturnes roses
Sont les grâces de nuit sous leurs danses écloses.
Que de parfums voilés dispensent leurs doigts d'or !
Mais l'azur doux s'effeuille en ce bocage mort
Et de l'eau mince luit à peine, reposée
Comme un pâle trésor d'une antique rosée
D'où le silence en fleur monte...Encor les voici
Mélodieuses fuir dans le bois éclairci.
Aux calices aimés leurs mains sont gracieuses;
Un peu de lune dort sur leurs lèvres pieuses
Et leurs bras merveilleux aux gestes endormis
Aiment à dénouer sous les myrtes amis
Leurs liens fauves et leurs caresses...Mais certaines,
Moins captives du rythme et des harpes lointaines,
S'en vont d'un pas subtil au lac enseveli
Boire des lys l'eau frêle où dort le pur oubli.

The Vain Dancers

They who are as light as flowers came,
Golden figurines and beauties in miniature
Irised by a pallid moon.... See how they
Glide away like tunes into the clear wood.
Of mallow, and iris, and nocturnal roses
Are the night charms that blossom beneath their dances.
How many veiled perfumes are shed by their gold fingers !
But the soft azure disleafs in this dead grove
And a thin water scarcely gleams, laid there
Like a pale treasury of ancient dew
Whence silence rises like a flower.... See them anew
Glide away like tunes into the clear wood.
To the loved flower-cups their hands are gracious;
A ghost of moon slumbers on their devout lips
And their marvelous arms with gestures sleep-lulled
Love to unwind under the friendly myrtles
Their wild enlacings and their caresses....But one or two,
Less captive to the rhythm and the remote harps,
Make off on subtle step towards the buried lake
To drink the lilies' frail draught where pure oblivion sleeps.

Un feu distinct...

Un feu distinct m'habite, et je vois froidement
La violente vie illuminée entière...
Je ne puis plus aimer seulement qu'en dormant
Ses actes gracieux mélangés de lumière.

Mes jours viennent la nuit me rendre des regards,
Après le premier temps de sommeil malheureux;
Quand le malheur lui-même est dans le noir épars
Ils reviennent me vivre et me donner des yeux.

Que si leur joie éclate, un écho qui m'éveille
N'a rejeté qu'un mort sur ma rive de chair,
Et mon rire étranger suspend à mon oreille,

Comme à la vide conque un murmure de mer,
Le doute, — sur le bord d'une extrême merveille,
Si je suis, si je fus, si je dors ou je veille?

A Distinct Fire...

A distinct fire informs me, and coldly I can see
Life in her violence lit up entire....
I can no longer love only when I am sleeping
The grace of her actions mingling with radiance.

At night my days come to give back certain looks,
After the first era of miserable sleep;
When unhappiness itself is diffused in the dark
They come back to live me, and to give me eyes.

But if their joy breaks out, an echo awakening me
Throws up a mere cadaver on my shore of flesh,
And my alien laugh leaves hanging in my ear,

Like a murmuring sea in the empty shell,
A doubt—on the edge of uttermost marvel—
Whether I am, or was, whether I sleep or wake?

Narcisse parle

Narcissae placandis manibus.

Ô frères ! tristes lys, je languis de beauté
Pour m'être désiré dans votre nudité,
Et vers vous, Nymphe, Nymphe, ô Nymphe des fontaines,
Je viens au pur silence offrir mes larmes vaines.

Un grand calme m'écoute, où j'écoute l'espoir.
La voix des sources change et me parle du soir;
J'entends l'herbe d'argent grandir dans l'ombre sainte,
Et la lune perfide élève son miroir
Jusque dans les secrets de la fontaine éteinte.

Et moi ! De tout mon cœur dans ces roseaux jeté,
Je languis, ô saphir, par ma triste beauté !
Je ne sais plus aimer que l'eau magicienne
Où j'oubliai le rire et la rose ancienne.

Que je déplore ton éclat fatal et pur,
Si mollement de moi fontaine environnée,
Où puisèrent mes yeux dans un mortel azur
Mon image de fleurs humides couronnée !

Hélas ! L'image est vaine et les pleurs éternels !
À travers les bois bleus et les bras fraternels,
Une tendre lueur d'heure ambiguë existe,
Et d'un reste du jour me forme un fiancé
Nu, sur la place pâle où m'attire l'eau triste...
Délicieux démon, désirable et glacé !

Narcissus Speaks

To placate the shades of Narcissa.

O brothers, mournful lilies, I am dying of beauty
For having desired myself in your nakedness,
And, Nymph, it is to you, O Nymph of the fountains,
I come offering vain tears to this utter silence.

A great calm listens to me, where I listen to hope.
The voice of the springs changes, and speaks to me of
    evening;
I hear the silvery grass growing in the holy shade,
And the traitorous moon lifts up her mirror
Even into the secrets of the exhausted fountain.

And I! Flinging me down bodily in these reeds,
I am dying, O sapphire, of my own sad beauty!
I can love nothing now but the bewitching water
Where I forgot laughter and the rose of former times.

How I rue your pure and fatal glitter,
Fountain so softly surrounded by me,
Where my eyes drank in, from a mortal azure,
My own image crowned with moistened flowers!

Ah, that image is vain, and tears are eternal!
Through the blue of the woods and their fraternal arms
A tender gleam of time ambiguous exists,
Where from an ember of day is fashioned a betrothed
Naked, on the pale space where the water draws me....
Delicious demon, desirable and icy!

29

Voici dans l'eau ma chair de lune et de rosée,
Ô forme obéissante à mes yeux opposée !
Voici mes bras d'argent dont les gestes sont purs !...
Mes lentes mains dans l'or adorable se lassent
D'appeler ce captif que les feuilles enlacent,
Et je crie aux échos les noms des dieux obscurs !...

Adieu, reflet perdu sur l'onde calme et close,
Narcisse...ce nom même est un tendre parfum
Au cœur suave. Effeuille aux mânes du défunt
Sur ce vide tombeau la funérale rose.

Sois, ma lèvre, la rose effeuillant le baiser
Qui fasse un spectre cher lentement s'apaiser,
Car la nuit parle à demi-voix, proche et lointaine,
Aux calices pleins d'ombre et de sommeils légers.
Mais la lune s'amuse aux myrtes allongés.

Je t'adore, sous ces myrtes, ô l'incertaine
Chair pour la solitude éclose tristement
Qui se mire dans le miroir au bois dormant.
Je me délie en vain de ta présence douce,
L'heure menteuse est molle aux membres sur la mousse
Et d'un sombre délice enfle le vent profond.

Adieu, Narcisse...Meurs ! Voici le crépuscule.
Au soupir de mon cœur mon apparence ondule,
La flûte, par l'azur enseveli module
Des regrets de troupeaux sonores qui s'en vont.
Mais sur le froid mortel où l'étoile s'allume,
Avant qu'un lent tombeau ne se forme de brume,
Tiens ce baiser qui brise un calme d'eau fatal !

Here in the water is my body of moon and dew,
Form compliant still opposed to my gaze !
Here are my silvery arms of purest gestures. . . .
My slow hands weary in the adorable gilding
Of luring that captive bound among the leaves,
And I shout the names of unknown gods to the echoes !. . .

Farewell, lost image on the enclosed, calm pool,
Narcissus. . .the very name is a tender perfume
To the soothed heart. To the shades of the departed,
Shed on this empty tomb the funereal rose.

Be my lip the rose shedding a kiss's petals
Bringing a gradual peace to a shade beloved,
For night speaks in a whisper, far and near,
To the flower-cups filled with shadows and light slumbers.
But the moon trifles among the lengthening myrtles.

I worship you, under those myrtles, oh uncertain
Flesh, sadly offering your flower to solitude,
Wondering at yourself in the sleeping forest's mirror.
In vain I unbind myself from your sweet presence,
The deceitful hour is kind to limbs stretched on the moss,
It fills the deep wind with a solemn bliss.

Farewell, Narcissus. . . .Die ! Twilight is here,
At the heart's sighing my image undulates,
The flute, against the entombed azure, warbles
Longings of the sounding herds as they go their way.
But on the mortal chill where a star is lit,
Before the mist forms a gradual tomb,
Accept this kiss breaking the water's fatal calm !

L'espoir seul peut suffire à rompre ce cristal.
La ride me ravisse au souffle qui m'exile
Et que mon souffle anime une flûte gracile
Dont le joueur léger me serait indulgent !...

Évanouissez-vous, divinité troublée !
Et, toi, verse à la lune, humble flûte isolée,
Une diversité de nos larmes d'argent.

Hope alone can avail to cleave this crystal.
Let the ripple ravish me on the breath that banishes
And may my breath inspire some slender flute-song
Whose carefree player thinks of me kindly !. . .

Faint away, vanish, troubled divinity !
And pour out to the moon, humble and lonely flute,
Our silvery tears in your diversity.

Épisode

Un soir favorisé de colombes sublimes,
La pucelle doucement se peigne au soleil.
Aux nénuphars de l'onde elle donne un orteil
Ultime, et pour tiédir ses froides mains errantes
Parfois trempe au couchant leurs roses transparentes.
Tantôt, si d'une ondée innocente, sa peau
Frissonne, c'est le dire absurde d'un pipeau,
Flûte dont le coupable aux dents de pierrerie
Tire un futile vent d'ombre et de rêverie
Par l'occulte baiser qu'il risque sous les fleurs.
Mais presque indifférente aux feintes de ces pleurs,
Ni se divinisant par aucune parole
De rose, elle démêle une lourde auréole;
Et tirant de sa nuque un plaisir qui la tord,
Ses poings délicieux pressent la touffe d'or
Dont la lumière coule entre ses doigts limpides !
...Une feuille meurt sur ses épaules humides,
Une goutte tombe de la flûte sur l'eau,
Et le pied pur s'épeure comme un bel oiseau
Ivre d'ombre...

Episode

One evening, honored by sublime doves,
Softly the maid combs her hair in the sun.
To the waterlilies she concedes a last touch
Of her toe, and to warm her cold erratic hands
From time to time, dips their clear pink in the sunset.
Or again, should her skin shiver at an innocent
Ripple, it's only the silly utterance of a pipe,
Flute whose guilty player of the jeweled teeth
Draws a futile breath of shadow and reverie,
By the occult kiss he risks under the flowers.
But untouched almost by this pretense of tears,
And not deigning to assume the goddess by
One rosebud word, she is unwinding a heavy aureole;
And drawing from her nape a writhing pleasure,
Her sweet gripped fists squeeze the golden mass
Whose radiance pours through her limpid fingers!
...A leaf is dying on her moist shoulders,
A drop falls from the flute into the water,
And her pure foot takes fright like a lovely bird
Crazed by the dark...

Vue

Si la plage penche, si
L'ombre sur l'œil s'use et pleure
Si l'azur est larme, ainsi
Au sel des dents pure affleure

La vierge fumée ou l'air
Que berce en soi puis expire
Vers l'eau debout d'une mer
Assoupie en son empire

Celle qui sans les ouïr
Si la lèvre au vent remue
Se joue à évanouir
Mille mots vains où se mue

Sous l'humide éclair de dents
Le très doux feu du dedans.

View

If the beach tilts, and if
Shadow wears on the eye and weeps
If the sky is teardrop, so,
Pure and sheer on the salt of the teeth

Is the virgin breath which she
Cradles in herself then exhales
Into the direct wind of a sea
Grown drowsy in its empire

She who without hearing them
When the lip stirs in the wind
Plays at dispersing a thousand
Vain words wherein mutates

Under the moist flash of the teeth
The tenderest fire there within.

Valvins

Si tu veux dénouer la forêt qui t'aère
Heureuse, tu te fonds aux feuilles, si tu es
Dans la fluide yole à jamais littéraire,
Traînant quelques soleils ardemment situés

Aux blancheurs de son flanc que la Seine caresse
Émue, ou pressentant l'après-midi chanté,
Selon que le grand bois trempe une longue tresse,
Et mélange ta voile au meilleur de l'été.

Mais toujours près de toi que le silence livre
Aux cris multipliés de tout le brut azur,
L'ombre de quelque page éparse d'aucun livre

Tremble, reflet de voile vagabonde sur
La poudreuse peau de la rivière verte
Parmi le long regard de la Seine entr'ouverte.

Valvins

Should you seek to untangle the forest that cools you
Blissful, you melt into the leaves, suppose you are
In the fluid and for all time literary yawl
Trailing numbers of suns, burningly poised

On the whitenesses of its flanks caressed by
The emotive Seine, or adumbrating the sung afternoon,
As the giant wood immerses a long tress
And blends your sail with the essence of summer.

But ever close to you, surrendered by the silence
To the miscellaneous cries of all the raw azure,
The ghost of a scattered page of a non-existent

Book quivers suggesting an errant sail
Upon the powdery skin of the virid river
Amid the long gaze of the half-opened Seine.

Été

À Francis Vielé-Griffin

Été, roche d'air pur, et toi, ardente ruche,
Ô mer ! Éparpillée en mille mouches sur
Les touffes d'une chair fraîche comme une cruche,
Et jusque dans la bouche où bourdonne l'azur ;

Et toi, maison brûlante, Espace, cher Espace
Tranquille, où l'arbre fume et perd quelques oiseaux,
Où crève infiniment la rumeur de la masse
De la mer, de la marche et des troupes des eaux,

Tonnes d'odeurs, grands ronds par les races heureuses
Sur le golfe qui mange et qui monte au soleil,
Nids purs, écluses d'herbe, ombres des vagues creuses,
Bercez l'enfant ravie en un poreux sommeil !

Dont les jambes (mais l'une est fraîche et se dénoue
De la plus rose), les épaules, le sein dur,
Le bras qui se mélange à l'écumeuse joue
Brillent abandonnés autour du vase obscur

Où filtrent les grands bruits pleins de bêtes puisées
Dans les cages de feuille et les mailles de mer
Par les moulins marins et les huttes rosées
Du jour...Toute la peau dore les treilles d'air.

Summer

To Francis Vielé-Griffin

Summer, cliff of pure air and you, burning hive,
O sea! Scattered in a thousand beauty spots
Over the tufts of a flesh cool as a pitcher,
And on, into the mouth where the blue sky booms;

And you, fiery house of Space, dear, tranquil
Space, where a tree smokes and sheds a few birds,
Where continually breaks the murmur of the sea's
Mass, the marchings and troopings of the waters,

Casks of odors, great wheelings by the cheerful races
Above the devouring gulf that rises sun-wards,
Pure nests, sluices of grass, shadows of hollow waves,
Rock the girl's delight in a porous slumber!

Her whose legs (one of them cool and releasing itself
From the rosier one), whose shoulders, whose firm breasts,
Whose arm that melts mingling with the foamy cheek,
All gleam in abandonment about the dim vase

Where filter the great rumors thronged with creatures
Imbibed in the leafy cages and meshes of the sea
By the marine mills and the roseate cabins
Of the light....All her skin gilds the trellises of air.

41

Profusion du soir

Poème abandonné...

Du Soleil soutenant la puissante paresse
Qui plane et s'abandonne à l'œil contemplateur,
Regard!...Je bois le vin céleste, et je caresse
Le grain mystérieux de l'extrême hauteur.

Je porte au sein brûlant ma lucide tendresse,
Je joue avec les feux de l'antique inventeur;
Mais le dieu par degrés qui se désintéresse
Dans la pourpre de l'air s'altère avec lenteur.

Laissant dans le champ pur battre toute l'idée,
Les travaux du couchant dans la sphère vidée
Connaissent sans oiseaux leur entière grandeur.

L'Ange frais de l'œil nu pressent dans sa pudeur,
Haute nativité d'étoile élucidée,
Un diamant agir qui berce la splendeur...

*

Ô soir, tu viens épandre un délice tranquille,
Horizon des sommeils, stupeur des cœurs pieux,
Persuasive approche, insidieux reptile,
Et rose que respire un mortel immobile
Dont l'œil doré s'engage aux promesses des cieux.

*

Abundance of Evening

Unfinished Poem...

Withstanding the Sun's all-powerful laziness
Soaring and self-surrendered to the thinking eye,
Gaze !...I am drinking heaven's wine, caressing
The mysterious texture of the uttermost height.

Conveying my lucid tenderness to the heart of fire,
I dally with the flames of the prime inventor;
But gradually the god, growing disinterested,
Begins to waste slowly in the purple of the air.

Leaving the one thought free play in the pure field,
The labors of the sunset in the emptied sphere
Birdless now attain to their full grandeur.

The cool Angel of the naked eye senses in its chastity
—High nativity of an elucidated star—
The action of a diamond piercing the splendor.

*

Ah evening, you come shedding a delectable calm,
Sky-line of slumbers, astounding the devout,
Onset of persuasion, insidious reptile,
Rose respired by a motionless mortal
Whose golden eye enters on the heavens' promises.

*

Sur tes ardents autels son regard favorable
Brûle, l'âme distraite, un passé précieux.
Il adore dans l'or qui se rend adorable
Bâtir d'une vapeur un temple mémorable,
Suspendre au sombre éther son risque et son récif,
Et vole, ivre des feux d'un triomphe passif,
Sur l'abîme aux ponts d'or rejoindre la Fortune;
— Tandis qu'aux bords lointains du Théâtre pensif,
Sous un masque léger glisse la mince lune...

*

...Ce vin bu, l'homme bâille, et brise le flacon.
Aux merveilles du vide il garde une rancune;
Mais le charme du soir fume sur le balcon
Une confusion de femme et de flocon...

*

— Ô Conseil !...Station solennelle !...Balance
D'un doigt doré pesant les motifs du silence !
Ô sagesse sensible entre les dieux ardents !
— De l'espace trop beau, préserve-moi, balustre !
Là, m'appelle la mer !...Là, se penche l'illustre
Vénus Vertigineuse avec ses bras fondants !

*

Mon œil, quoiqu'il s'attache au sort souple des ondes,
Et boive comme en songe à l'éternel verseau,
Garde une chambre fixe et capable des mondes;
Et ma cupidité des surprises profondes
Voit à peine au travers du transparent berceau
Cette femme d'écume et d'algue et d'or que roule
Sur le sable et le sel la meule de la houle.

*

44

On your burning altars his propitious gaze
Absentmindedly consumes a precious past.
He adores, in that pure ore as it grows adorable,
To build a memorable temple out of vapors,
To hang his risk and reef in the dark ether,
And wild with those passively triumphal fires, he darts
Across the golden-bridged abyss to overtake Chance;
—Meanwhile in the far wings of the pensive Theater
Under a light mask the thin moon glides on....

*

...This wine drunk, man yawns, and smashes the flagon,
Nursing a grudge against the marvels of the void;
But over the balcony the charm of evening steams
A confused flurry of cloud-flake and woman....

*

—Ah, Counsel!...Solemn deliberation!...Balances,
Weighing the motives of silence with a gold pointer,
Wisdom made visible between the gods on fire.
—From beauty's excess in space save me, baluster!
That way pulls the sea!...And there leans dazzling
Venus the Vertiginous with her melting arms!

*

My eye, though it clings to the waves' supple destinies,
And as if dreaming drinks at the eternal Water-carrier,
Still keeps free a fixed room, capacious of worlds,
And my avidity for surprises in depth
No more than glimpses through the rocking transparency
That woman's form of foam and gold and weed rolled
On the sand and salt by the pounding of the surf.

*

Pourtant je place aux cieux les ébats d'un esprit;
Je vois dans leurs vapeurs des terres inconnues,
Des déesses de fleurs feindre d'être des nues,
Des puissances d'orage errer à demi nues,
Et sur les roches d'air du soir qui s'assombrit,
Telle divinité s'accoude. Un ange nage.
Il restaure l'espace à chaque tour de rein.
Moi, qui jette ici-bas l'ombre d'un personnage,
Toutefois délié dans le plein souverain,
Je me sens qui me trempe, et pur qui me dédaigne !
Vivant au sein futur le souvenir marin,
Tout le corps de mon choix dans mes regards se baigne !

*

Une crête écumeuse, énorme et colorée
Barre, puissamment pure, et plisse le parvis.
Roule jusqu'à mon cœur la distance dorée,
Vague !... Croulants soleils aux horizons ravis,
Tu n'iras pas plus loin que la ligne ignorée
Qui divise les dieux des ombres où je vis.

*

Une volute lente et longue d'une lieue
Semant les charmes lourds de sa blanche torpeur
Où se joue une joie, une soif d'être bleue,
Tire le noir navire épuisé de vapeur...

*

Mais pesants et neigeux les monts du crépuscule,
Les nuages trop pleins et leurs seins copieux,
Toute la majesté de l'Olympe recule,

And yet I situate a mind at play in the heavens;
In its vapors I see unknown territories,
Goddesses made of flowers masquerading as clouds,
Storm potentates wandering half naked,
And on the airy cliffs of evening growing gloomier
Some god or other leans an elbow. A swimming angel
Renews the shape of space at every sidestroke.
And I, who cast the shadow of a person down here,
Nevertheless released into the sovereign plenum,
I can feel myself immersed, pure in self-disdain!
Living the marine memory in the heart of the future,
The elect form of my choice basks complete in my gaze!

*

A ridge of foam, colossal and filled with color,
Powerfully pure, walls in and creases the foreshore.
Roll the gold distance to where my heart beats,
Breaker!...Crumbling suns raped from the horizon,
You can advance no further than the viewless barrier
Dividing the gods from the shades where I live.

*

A languorous volute a full league in length,
Strewing the heavy charms of its snowy torpor
Where a joy flickers, a longing to be blue,
Pulls at the black ship exhausted of its vapor....

*

But ponderous, snowclad, the mountains of dusk,
The clouds copious-bosomed and replete,
All the royalty of Olympus is receding,

47

Car voici le signal, voici l'or des adieux,
Et l'espace a humé la barque minuscule...

*

Lourds frontons du sommeil toujours inachevés,
Rideaux bizarrement d'un rubis relevés
Pour le mauvais regard d'une sombre planète,
Les temps sont accomplis, les désirs se sont tus,
Et dans la bouche d'or, bâillements combattus,
S'écartèlent les mots que charmait le poète...
Les temps sont accomplis, les désirs se sont tus.

*

Adieu, Adieu!...Vers vous, ô mes belles images,
Mes bras tendent toujours l'insatiable port!
Venez, effarouchés, hérissant vos plumages,
Voiliers aventureux que talonne la mort!
Hâtez-vous, hâtez-vous!...La nuit presse!...Tantale
Va périr! Et la joie éphémère des cieux!
Une rose naguère aux ténèbres fatale,
Une toute dernière rose occidentale
Pâlit affreusement sur le soir spacieux...
Je ne vois plus frémir au mât du belvédère
Ivre de brise un sylphe aux couleurs de drapeau,
Et ce grand port n'est qu'un noir débarcadère
Couru du vent glacé que sent venir ma peau!

Fermez-vous! Fermez-vous! Fenêtres offensées!
Grands yeux qui redoutez la véritable nuit!
Et toi, de ces hauteurs d'astres ensemencées,
Accepte, fécondé de mystère et d'ennui,
Une maternité muette de pensées...

48

For now comes the signal, the farewell glitter,
And the tiny bark has been snuffed up by space....

*

    Heavy pediments of sleep, forever unfinished,
Curtains weirdly pinned back with a ruby
To meet the malign gaze of a gloomy planet,
The time is now accomplished, desires grow mute,
And in the golden mouth, struggling with yawns,
The words the poet charmed are broken on the wheel....
    The time is now accomplished, desires grow mute.

*

Goodbye, goodbye !...My arms, oh glorious images,
Still stretch out to you their insatiable harbor !
Flustered and bristling your plumage, come,
Sail-winged adventurers with death on your heels,
Hurry, hurry !...Night speeds....Tantalus
Is perishing ! And the sky's ephemeral ecstasies !
A rose until lately lethal to the glooms,
An altogether final occidental rose
Grows atrociously pale on the width of evening....
    On the viewing-tower's mast I can no longer
See the breeze-crazed sylph, shivering its flag colors,
And this great harbor is now a black platform
Swept by an icy wind my skin can feel approach !

    Shut, shut your injured senses, windows,
Huge eyes, fearful of the genuine night !
    And you, out of those heights scattered with star seed,
Accept, impregnated with mystery and boredom,
A mute maternal labor of meditations....

Anne

À André Lebey

Anne qui se mélange au drap pâle et délaisse
Des cheveux endormis sur ses yeux mal ouverts
Mire ses bras lointains tournés avec mollesse
Sur la peau sans couleur du ventre découvert.

Elle vide, elle enfle d'ombre sa gorge lente,
Et comme un souvenir pressant ses propres chairs,
Une bouche brisée et pleine d'eau brûlante
Roule le goût immense et le reflet des mers.

Enfin désemparée et libre d'être fraîche,
La dormeuse déserte aux touffes de couleur
Flotte sur son lit blême, et d'une lèvre sèche,
Tette dans la ténèbre un souffle amer de fleur.

Et sur le linge où l'aube insensible se plisse,
Tombe, d'un bras de glace effleuré de carmin,
Toute une main défaite et perdant le délice
À travers ses doigts nus dénoués de l'humain.

Au hasard ! À jamais, dans le sommeil sans hommes
Pur des tristes éclairs de leurs embrassements,
Elle laisse rouler les grappes et les pommes
Puissantes, qui pendaient aux treilles d'ossements,

Qui riaient, dans leur ambre appelant les vendanges,
Et dont le nombre d'or de riches mouvements
Invoquait la vigueur et les gestes étranges
Que pour tuer l'amour inventent les amants...

*

Anne

To André Lebey

Anne who blends with the pale sheet, leaving forlorn
The hair drowsing over her just opened eyes,
Gazes remotely at her arms weakly folded
On the colorless surface of the uncovered belly.

Slow her chest heaves emptying and filling with shadow
And, like a memory squeezing her very flesh,
A shattered mouth filled with watery fire
Revolves the immense savor and afterthought of seas.

Abandoned now and freed at last to coolness,
The sleeper unmanned, blotched with patches of color,
Adrift on her ghostly bed, with a dry lip
Sucks in her dark at a flower's bitter breath.

And on the linen where dawn stealthily creases,
An arm of ice grazed with carmine lets fall
The hand all undone, losing its hold on delight
Through the bare fingers absolved from the human.

At random, forever in that sleep of no men,
Clear of the sullen thunderbolts of their huggings,
Passive she lets roll the clusters, the powerful
Fruits hanging on the trellises of bone,

Fruits that laughed, their amber clamoring for vintage,
And whose wealth of movements in their golden numbers,
Summoned up the force, and the weird gestures
That lovers invent so as to kill off love.

*

Sur toi, quand le regard de leurs âmes s'égare,
Leur cœur bouleversé change comme leurs voix,
Car les tendres apprêts de leur festin barbare
Hâtent les chiens ardents qui tremblent dans ces rois...

À peine effleurent-ils de doigts errants ta vie,
Tout leur sang les accable aussi lourd que la mer,
Et quelque violence aux abîmes ravie
Jette ces blancs nageurs sur tes roches de chair...

Récifs délicieux, Île toute prochaine,
Terre tendre, promise aux démons apaisés,
L'amour t'aborde, armé des regards de la haine,
Pour combattre dans l'ombre une hydre de baisers !

*

Ah, plus nue et qu'imprègne une prochaine aurore,
Si l'or triste interroge un tiède contour,
Rentre au plus pur de l'ombre où le Même s'ignore,
Et te fais un vain marbre ébauché par le jour !

Laisse au pâle rayon ta lèvre violée
Mordre dans un sourire un long germe de pleur,
Masque d'âme au sommeil à jamais immolée
Sur qui la paix soudaine a surpris la douleur !

Plus jamais redorant tes ombres satinées,
La vieille aux doigts de feu qui fendent les volets
Ne viendra t'arracher aux grasses matinées
Et rendre au doux soleil tes joyeux bracelets...

Mais suave, de l'arbre extérieur, la palme
Vaporeuse remue au delà du remords,
Et dans le feu, parmi trois feuilles, l'oiseau calme
Commence le chant seul qui réprime les morts.

When, on you, their souls' gaze goes roving,
Their hearts turn over, altering with their voices,
For the tender foretaste of their barbaric orgies
Harries the eager dogs that quiver in those kings....

As soon as their groping fingers graze your life,
All their blood whelms them like a heavy sea,
And a violence whipped up out of the depths
Flings those white swimmers on your rocks of flesh....

Delectable reefs, Island all approachable,
Promised land of tenderness for the demons appeased,
Love boards you armed with looks of hatred
To wrestle in the dark with a hydra of kisses!

*

Ah, ever more naked and pregnant with a near dawn,
Should the ominous gold grope at a warm contour,
Back with you into pure night where the Same is unknown,
Turn to a marble void in day's dim outline!

In the pallid sun-gleam let your ravaged lip
Bite smilingly on the long stalk of a tear,
Mask of a soul consigned forever to sleep
Where a sudden peace has taken pain unaware.

Never again regilding your satiny shadows
Will the she-ancient's fiery fingers pierce the shutters,
Come to drag you from a long, lazy morning,
Reviving your merry bracelets in the soft sun....

But suavely the tree out there waves its palm
Vaporous from the other shore of remorse,
And in the flame, between three leaves, the placid bird
Begins the one song whereby the dead are quelled.

Air de Sémiramis

À Camille Mauclair

Dès l'aube, chers rayons, mon front songe à vous ceindre !
À peine il se redresse, il voit d'un œil qui dort
Sur le marbre absolu, le temps pâle se peindre,
L'heure sur moi descendre et croître jusqu'à l'or...

...«Existe !... Sois enfin toi-même ! dit l'Aurore,
Ô grande âme, il est temps que tu formes un corps !
Hâte-toi de choisir un jour digne d'éclore,
Parmi tant d'autres feux, tes immortels trésors !

Déjà, contre la nuit lutte l'âpre trompette !
Une lèvre vivante attaque l'air glacé;
L'or pur, de tour en tour, éclate et se répète,
Rappelant tout l'espace aux splendeurs du passé !

Remonte aux vrais regards ! Tire-toi de tes ombres,
Et comme du nageur, dans le plein de la mer,
Le talon tout-puissant l'expulse des eaux sombres,
Toi, frappe au fond de l'être ! Interpelle ta chair,

Traverse sans retard ses invincibles trames,
Épuise l'infini de l'effort impuissant,
Et débarrasse-toi d'un désordre de drames
Qu'engendrent sur ton lit les monstres de ton sang !

J'accours de l'Orient suffire à ton caprice !
Et je te viens offrir mes plus purs aliments;
Que d'espace et de vent ta flamme se nourrisse !
Viens te joindre à l'éclat de mes pressentiments !»

*

54

Aria for Semiramis

To Camille Mauclair

At dawn, beloved rays, my brow dreams your diadem!
No sooner raised than it watches with eyes still asleep
Pale time limning itself on the imperious marble,
The hour alighting on me and ripening to gold....

...*"Exist!"* the Dawn whispers, *"Be finally yourself!*
Now is the time, great soul, to fashion you a body.
Make haste, choose a day worthy to disclose
Among so many fires, your own immortal glories!

Already the harsh trumpet battles with the dark,
A living lip attacks the icy air;
From tower to tower re-echoing pure gold breaks
Recalling all space to the splendors that were!

Arise to real seeing! Drag yourself from your shades,
And like the swimmer whose heel, in the full sea,
All-powerful pushes him out of the dark waters,
Press at your being's depths! Interrogate your flesh,

Traverse relentless its unconquerable wiles,
Exhaust the infinity of its striving weakness,
And rid yourself of the dramas, the chaos
Which the monsters of your blood begot in your sleep....

I've run from the East to satisfy your caprice!
And I come to you offering my purest sustenance;
Let your flame feed on the winds of space,
Add yourself to the splendor that I announce!"

*

— Je réponds!...Je surgis de ma profonde absence!
Mon cœur m'arrache aux morts que frôlait mon sommeil,
Et vers mon but, grand aigle éclatant de puissance,
Il m'emporte!...Je vole au-devant du soleil!

Je ne prends qu'une rose et fuis...La belle flèche
Au flanc!...Ma tête enfante une foule de pas...
Ils courent vers ma tour favorite, où la fraîche
Altitude m'appelle, et je lui tends les bras!

Monte, ô Sémiramis, maîtresse d'une spire
Qui d'un cœur sans amour s'élance au seul honneur!
Ton œil impérial a soif du grand empire
À qui ton sceptre dur fait sentir le bonheur...

Ose l'abîme!...Passe un dernier pont de roses!
Je t'approche, péril! Orgueil plus irrité!
Ces fourmis sont à moi! Ces villes sont mes choses,
Ces chemins sont les traits de mon autorité!

C'est une vaste peau de fauve que mon royaume!
J'ai tué le lion qui portait cette peau;
Mais encor le fumet du féroce fantôme
Flotte chargé de mort, et garde mon troupeau!

Enfin, j'offre au soleil le secret de mes charmes!
Jamais il n'a doré de seuil si gracieux!
De ma fragilité je goûte les alarmes
Entre le double appel de la terre et des cieux.

Repas de ma puissance, intelligible orgie,
Quel parvis vaporeux de toits et de forêts
Place aux pieds de la pure et divine vigie,
Ce calme éloignement d'événements secrets!

—I respond. . .I rise out of my depths of absence.
My heart drags me from the dead who fringed my sleep,
And like a great eagle dazzling with power carries me
Towards my goal !. . .I fly faster than the sun !

I snatch only a rose and am gone. . . .That lovely spur
At my side !. . .My brain begets a throng of paces
Running towards my favorite tower where cool
The altitude calls me, I stretch my arms to it.

Climb, oh Semiramis, mistress of a spire
That leaps from a heart pure of love to pure glory !
Your imperial eye thirsts for the great empire
On which your ruthless sceptre imposed happiness. . . .

Dare the abyss !. . .Cross a final bridge of roses.
Peril, I am approaching ! Pride, grow to fury !
Those ants are all mine ! Those cities my chattels,
Those roads are the penstrokes of my authority !

The vast skin of a wild beast is my kingdom.
It was I killed the lion who wore that skin !
But still the stench of that ferocious phantom
Floats, charged with death, to fence my flocks in !

At last I offer the sun my secret charms.
Never has it gilded so gracious a threshold !
Of my own fragility I savor the alarms
Between the double call of earth and sky !

Intelligible orgy, feast of my own might,
What vaporous precinct of roofs and forests
Lays at a pure and divine sentinel's feet
This becalmed remoteness of hidden events !

L'âme enfin sur ce faîte a trouvé ses demeures !
Ô de quelle grandeur, elle tient sa grandeur
Quand mon cœur soulevé d'ailes intérieures
Ouvre au ciel en moi-même une autre profondeur !

Anxieuse d'azur, de gloire consumée,
Poitrine, gouffre d'ombre aux narines de chair,
Aspire cet encens d'âmes et de fumée
Qui monte d'une ville analogue à la mer !

Soleil, soleil, regarde en toi rire mes ruches !
L'intense et sans repos Babylone bruit,
Toute rumeurs de chars, clairons, chaînes de cruches
Et plaintes de la pierre au mortel qui construit.

Qu'ils flattent mon désir de temples implacables,
Les sons aigus de scie et les cris des ciseaux,
Et ces gémissements de marbres et de câbles
Qui peuplent l'air vivant de structure et d'oiseaux !

Je vois mon temple neuf naître parmi les mondes,
Et mon vœu prendre place au séjour des destins;
Il semble de soi-même au ciel monter par ondes
Sous le bouillonnement des actes indistincts.

Peuple stupide, à qui ma puissance m'enchaîne,
Hélas ! mon orgueil même a besoin de tes bras !
Et que ferait mon cœur s'il n'aimait cette haine
Dont l'innombrable tête est si douce à mes pas?

Plate, elle me murmure une musique telle
Que le calme de l'onde en fait de sa fureur,
Quand elle se rapaise aux pieds d'une mortelle
Mais qu'elle se réserve un retour de terreur.

At last on this height the soul has found its place!
Ah, from what grandeur does it draw its grandeur,
When my heart lifting on interior wings
Opens my own to equal the sky's depth!

Breast panting for blue air, consumed with glory,
Abyss of darkness with nostrils of flesh,
Breathe in this incense of smoke and living beings
Rising from a city that images the sea!

Sun, see how my hives laugh in your blaze!
Babylon the restless noises its intensity,
All a-din with chariots, clarions, pitchers on pulleys,
And outcries of stone to the mortal who builds.

Let them flatter my lust with implacable temples,
The shrill moan of saws and shriek of chisels,
The grinding sighs of marbles and cables
That people the living air with birds and architecture!

I see my new temple take birth among the worlds,
And my vow find its dwelling among the destinies;
It seems of itself to rise skywards in waves
Beneath the ferment of confused activities.

Crass populace, to whom my power fetters me,
Alas, my very pride needs the strength of your arms!
And what could my heart do without loving this hatred
Whose innumerable head is so soft to my steps?

Flatly it murmurs to me a music of a kind
Like the calm that a wave makes of its own fury,
Growing pacified at the feet of a mortal,
Though it hold in reserve a fresh bout of terror.

En vain j'entends monter contre ma face auguste
Ce murmure de crainte et de férocité:
À l'image des dieux la grande âme est injuste
Tant elle s'appareille à la nécessité !

Des douceurs de l'amour quoique parfois touchée,
Pourtant nulle tendresse et nuls renoncements
Ne me laissent captive et victime couchée
Dans les puissants liens du sommeil des amants !

Baisers, baves d'amour, basses béatitudes,
Ô mouvements marins des amants confondus,
Mon cœur m'a conseillé de telles solitudes,
Et j'ai placé si haut mes jardins suspendus

Que mes suprêmes fleurs n'attendent que la foudre
Et qu'en dépit des pleurs des amants les plus beaux,
À mes roses, la main qui touche tombe en poudre:
Mes plus doux souvenirs bâtissent des tombeaux !

Qu'ils sont doux à mon cœur les temples qu'il enfante
Quand tiré lentement du songe de mes seins,
Je vois un monument de masse triomphante
Joindre dans mes regards l'ombre de mes desseins !

Battez, cymbales d'or, mamelles cadencées,
Et roses palpitant sur ma pure paroi !
Que je m'évanouisse en mes vastes pensées,
Sage Sémiramis, enchanteresse et roi !

Mounting in the face of my majesty it makes no odds,
This murmur I hear, of fear and ferocity,
The great soul's injustice equals that of gods,
So closely is it matched with necessity !

Though the solace of love has sometimes touched me,
Yet no self-abandonment, no tenderness
Can leave me captive or couch me a victim
In the powerful bonds of lovers' sleep !

Kisses, slaver of love, base beatitudes,
Oh drowning struggles of lovers interlaced,
My heart has counseled me to such solitudes,
And my hanging gardens are so loftily placed

That my topmost flowers await only lightning flashes
And for all the tears of the handsomest lovers,
The hand that touches my roses drops to ashes;
My tenderest memories are tomb-builders !

How sooth to my heart are the temples it creates
When, slowly drawn from the dream of my breasts,
I watch a monument whose triumphant mass
Overtakes in my eyes the shadow of my designs.

Clash, gold cymbals, nippled breasts in cadence,
And roses on my pure barrier palpitating,
Let me swoon away in my own thoughts' vastness,
Wise Semiramis, enchantress, and king !

L'Amateur de poèmes

SI je regarde tout à coup ma véritable pensée, je ne me console pas de devoir subir cette parole intérieure sans personne et sans origine; ces figures éphémères; et cette infinité d'entreprises interrompues par leur propre facilité, qui se transforment l'une dans l'autre, sans que rien ne change avec elles. Incohérente sans le paraître, nulle instantanément comme elle est spontanée, la pensée, par sa nature, manque de style.

MAIS je n'ai pas tous les jours la puissance de proposer à mon attention quelques êtres nécessaires, ni de feindre les obstacles spirituels qui formeraient une apparence de commencement, de plénitude et de fin, au lieu de mon insupportable fuite.

UN poème est une durée, pendant laquelle, lecteur, je respire une loi qui fut préparée; je donne mon souffle et les machines de ma voix; ou seulement leur pouvoir, qui se concilie avec le silence.

JE m'abandonne à l'adorable allure: lire, vivre où mènent les mots. Leur apparition est écrite. Leurs sonorités concertées. Leur ébranlement se compose, d'après une méditation antérieure, et ils se précipiteront en groupes magnifiques ou purs, dans la résonance. Même mes étonnements sont assurés: ils sont cachés d'avance, et font partie du nombre.

MU par l'écriture fatale, et si le mètre toujours futur enchaîne sans retour ma mémoire, je ressens chaque parole

The Lover of Poems

IF I take a sudden look at my thought as it is, I can feel no comfort in having to endure that interior speech, impersonal, without source; those transitory shapes; and that endless series of speculations broken off by their own facility, transforming one into the next, without changing anything in their course. Incoherent without seeming to be so, instantly nullified in proportion to its own spontaneity, thought, by its very nature, is lacking in style.

BUT I do not possess every day the ability to fix my concentration on certain needful entities, nor to simulate those mental limits that would create an impression of beginning, fullness and ending, in place of my intolerable flux.

A POEM is a continuity during which, reader, I breathe in accordance with a pre-established law; what I contribute is my breathing and the mechanics of my voice; or simply their potential, which can be reconciled with silence.

I SURRENDER to the divine rhythm: reading, living where the words may lead. As they appear, they are written down. Their sonorities are harmonized. Their disturbance re-forms itself, along premeditated lines, until they spring, splendidly and chastely grouped, into resonance. Even what surprises me is guaranteed; it is concealed in advance, and is a constituent part of Number.

STIRRED to the fatal act of writing—and provided the ever-to-be measure irretrievably fixes my memory—I feel the

dans toute sa force, pour l'avoir indéfiniment attendue. Cette mesure qui me transporte et que je colore, me garde du vrai et du faux. Ni le doute ne me divise, ni la raison ne me travaille. Nul hasard, mais une chance extraordinaire se fortifie. Je trouve sans effort le langage de ce bonheur; et je pense par artifice, une pensée toute certaine, merveilleuse-ment prévoyante, — aux lacunes calculées, sans ténèbres involontaires, dont le mouvement me commande et la quantité me comble: une pensée singulièrement achevée.

whole force of each single word, thanks to my prolonged waiting upon it. This uplifting rhythm, which I fill with color, keeps me free of false and true. I am divided by no doubt, tormented by no reasoning. Nothing random, but an extraordinary stroke of luck asserts and confirms itself. Without struggle, I can find the language for this felicity; and by way of artifice I can think a thought that is all certainty, miraculously provident—whose leaps are calculated, with no unwilled obscurities, and whose movement controls, whose wholeness fulfils me: a singularly perfected thought.

LA JEUNE PARQUE

THE YOUNG FATE

À André Gide
Depuis bien des années j'avais laissé l'art des vers:
essayant de m'y astreindre encore, j'ai fait cet exercice
que je te dédie.
1917

To André Gide
For many years I had given up the art of verse: in attempting to
submit myself to it once more, I composed this exercise
which I dedicate to you.
1917

La Jeune Parque

Le Ciel a-t-il formé cet amas de merveilles
Pour la demeure d'un serpent?
Pierre Corneille

Qui pleure là, sinon le vent simple, à cette heure
Seule, avec diamants extrêmes?...Mais qui pleure,
Si proche de moi-même au moment de pleurer?

Cette main, sur mes traits qu'elle rêve effleurer,
Distraitement docile à quelque fin profonde,
Attend de ma faiblesse une larme qui fonde,
Et que de mes destins lentement divisé,
Le plus pur en silence éclaire un cœur brisé.
La houle me murmure une ombre de reproche,
Ou retire ici-bas, dans ses gorges de roche,
Comme chose déçue et bue amèrement,
Une rumeur de plainte et de resserrement...
Que fais-tu, hérissée, et cette main glacée,
Et quel frémissement d'une feuille effacée
Persiste parmi vous, îles de mon sein nu?...
Je scintille, liée à ce ciel inconnu...
L'immense grappe brille à ma soif de désastres.

Tout-puissants étrangers, inévitables astres
Qui daignez faire luire au lointain temporel
Je ne sais quoi de pur et de surnaturel;
Vous qui dans les mortels plongez jusques aux larmes
Ces souverains éclats, ces invincibles armes,
Et les élancements de votre éternité,
Je suis seule avec vous, tremblante, ayant quitté

The Young Fate

Did Heaven form this mass of marvels
To be a serpent's dwelling-place?
Pierre Corneille

Who is that weeping, if not simply the wind,
At this sole hour, with ultimate diamonds?...But who
Weeps, so close to myself on the brink of tears?

This hand of mine, dreaming it strokes my features,
Absently submissive to some deep-hidden end,
Waits for a tear to melt out of my weakness
And, gradually dividing from my other destinies,
For the purest to enlighten a broken heart in silence.
The surf murmurs to me the shadow of a reproach,
Or withdraws below, in its rocky gorges,
Like a disappointed thing, drunk back in bitterness,
A rumor of lamentation and self-constraint....
What seek you, bristling, erect? And this hand of ice,
And what shivering of an effaced leaf is it
Persists amid you, isles of my naked breast?...
I am glittering and bound to this unknown heaven....
The giant cluster gleams on my thirst for disasters.

Omnipotent, alien, inescapable stars
Who deign to let shine in the distances of time
Something I cannot conceive—supernatural, pure;
You who plunge into mortals to the depth of tears
Those sovereign rays, weapons invincible,
The shooting glances of your eternity,
I am alone with you, shivering, having left

Ma couche; et sur l'écueil mordu par la merveille,
J'interroge mon cœur quelle douleur l'éveille,
Quel crime par moi-même ou sur moi consommé?...
...Ou si le mal me suit d'un songe refermé,
Quand (au velours du souffle envolé l'or des lampes)
J'ai de mes bras épais environné mes tempes,
Et longtemps de mon âme attendu les éclairs?
Toute? Mais toute à moi, maîtresse de mes chairs,
Durcissant d'un frisson leur étrange étendue,
Et dans mes doux liens, à mon sang suspendue,
Je me voyais me voir, sinueuse, et dorais
De regards en regards, mes profondes forêts.

J'y suivais un serpent qui venait de me mordre.

Quel repli de désirs, sa traîne!...Quel désordre
De trésors s'arrachant à mon avidité,
Et quelle sombre soif de la limpidité!

Ô ruse!...À la lueur de la douleur laissée
Je me sentis connue encor plus que blessée...
Au plus traître de l'âme, une pointe me naît;
Le poison, mon poison, m'éclaire et se connaît:
Il colore une vierge à soi-même enlacée,
Jalouse...Mais de qui, jalouse et menacée?
Et quel silence parle à mon seul possesseur?

Dieux! Dans ma lourde plaie une secrète sœur
Brûle, qui se préfère à l'extrême attentive.

My couch; and over the reef gnawn away by marvel
I ask my heart what pain keeps it awake,
What crime committed against me or by myself?...
...Or whether the pain dogs me from a dream sealed up
When (the lamps' gold swept out by a velvet breath)
With my dense arms pressed about my temples
I waited long and long for my soul's lightnings?
All me? Yes, me entire, mistress of my flesh,
Stiffening with a shiver all its strange extent,
And in my own tender bonds, hung on my blood,
I saw me seeing myself, sinuous, and
From gaze to gaze gilded my innermost forests.

I was tracking a snake there that had just stung me.

What a coil of lusts, his trail!...What a riot
Of riches wrenched away from my longing,
And ah, that obscure thirst for limpidity!

O trickery!...Left illumined by the pain
I felt I was found out even more than stricken....
In my soul's most treacherous place a sting is born;
That poison of mine enlightens me, knows its skill:
It pictures a virgin wound upon herself,
Jealous....But of whom, and by whom menaced?
And what silence is it speaks to my sole possessor?

Gods! In my loaded wound a secret sister burns
Who loves herself more than her watchful opposite.

«Va! je n'ai plus besoin de ta race naïve,
Cher Serpent...Je m'enlace, être vertigineux!
Cesse de me prêter ce mélange de nœuds
Ni ta fidélité qui me fuit et devine...
Mon âme y peut suffire, ornement de ruine!
Elle sait, sur mon ombre égarant ses tourments,
De mon sein, dans les nuits, mordre les rocs charmants;
Elle y suce longtemps le lait des rêveries...
Laisse donc défaillir ce bras de pierreries
Qui menace d'amour mon sort spirituel...
Tu ne peux rien sur moi qui ne soit moins cruel,
Moins désirable...Apaise alors, calme ces ondes,
Rappelle ces remous, ces promesses immondes...
Ma surprise s'abrège, et mes yeux sont ouverts.
Je n'attendais pas moins de mes riches déserts
Qu'un tel enfantement de fureur et de tresse:
Leurs fonds passionnés brillent de sécheresse
Si loin que je m'avance et m'altère pour voir
De mes enfers pensifs les confins sans espoir...
Je sais...Ma lassitude est parfois un théâtre.
L'esprit n'est pas si pur que jamais idolâtre
Sa fougue solitaire aux élans de flambeau
Ne fasse fuir les murs de son morne tombeau.
Tout peut naître ici-bas d'une attente infinie.
L'ombre même le cède à certaine agonie,
L'âme avare s'entr'ouvre, et du monstre s'émeut
Qui se tord sur le pas d'une porte de feu...
Mais, pour capricieux et prompt que tu paraisses,
Reptile, ô vifs détours tout courus de caresses,
Si proche impatience et si lourde langueur,
Qu'es-tu, près de ma nuit d'éternelle longueur?
Tu regardais dormir ma belle négligence...

"Go, I no longer need your simple kind,
Dear Snake....I coil, vertiginous being, on myself!
Lend me no longer your enwound confusion
And your fidelity that eludes and knows me....
My soul, a ruin's ornament, will suffice instead!
She, her torments straying over my shadow,
Can bite the witching rocks, my breasts, by night;
There she sucks for long at the milk of reverie....
So let it yield and loosen, that arm bejeweled
Menacing my spiritual lot with love....
You have no power over me that would not be less cruel,
Less desirable....So appease, calm these waves,
Withdraw those eddyings, those foul promises....
My amazement is cut short, my eyes are opened.
I expected no less from my rich deserts
Than such a pregnancy of fire and tresses;
Their passionate distances glitter with barrenness
The further I press, dry with the thirst to see
The hopeless confines of my thought's infernos....
I know...Sometimes my weariness is a theater.
The mind is not so pure that, never idolatrous,
Its solitary ardor flaming out like a torch
Cannot dismiss the walls of its gloomy tomb.
To infinite waiting, here below, all may come.
Darkness itself yields to unfailing agony,
The grasping soul half opens, alarmed at the monster
Writhing on the threshold of a doorway of fire....
But capricious and alert though you appear,
Reptile, oh sudden coils all rippling with caresses,
Intolerance so instant, so loaded with languor,
What are you compared with my night eternally long?
You were admiring my fine, careless slumber....

Mais avec mes périls, je suis d'intelligence,
Plus versatile, ô Thyrse, et plus perfide qu'eux.
Fuis-moi ! du noir retour reprends le fil visqueux !
Va chercher des yeux clos pour tes danses massives.
Coule vers d'autres lits tes robes successives,
Couve sur d'autres cœurs les germes de leur mal,
Et que dans les anneaux de ton rêve animal
Halète jusqu'au jour l'innocence anxieuse !...
Moi, je veille. Je sors, pâle et prodigieuse,
Toute humide des pleurs que je n'ai point versés,
D'une absence aux contours de mortelle bercés
Par soi seule...Et brisant une tombe sereine,
Je m'accoude inquiète et pourtant souveraine,
Tant de mes visions parmi la nuit et l'œil,
Les moindres mouvements consultent mon orgueil. »

Mais je tremblais de perdre une douleur divine !
Je baisais sur ma main cette morsure fine,
Et je ne savais plus de mon antique corps
Insensible, qu'un feu qui brûlait sur mes bords :

Adieu, pensai-je, MOI, mortelle sœur, mensonge...

Harmonieuse MOI, différente d'un songe,
Femme flexible et ferme aux silences suivis
D'actes purs !...Front limpide, et par ondes ravis,
Si loin que le vent vague et velu les achève,
Longs brins légers qu'au large un vol mêle et soulève,
Dites !...J'étais l'égale et l'épouse du jour,
Seul support souriant que je formais d'amour
À la toute-puissante altitude adorée...

But I, oh Thyrsus, am in league with my own perils,
More resourceful, and more cunning I than they.
Begone! Resume the viscous track of your dark retreat!
Go and find closed eyes for your ponderous dances,
Towards other beds slide your shedding robes,
Hatch on other hearts the seeds of their suffering,
And within the circlings of your animal dream
Let troubled innocence sleep panting till dawn!
I am awake. Pale, a thing of wonder,
Moist with the tears I have not shed, I emerge
From an absence lulled by itself alone, shaped
Like a mortal woman....And breaking a tomb serene,
I lean on my arm, uneasy and yet supreme,
So much do the slightest stirrings of my visions
Between night and the eye defer to my pride."

But I shuddered at the loss of a divine sorrow!
On my hand I would kiss that tiny sting,
And I knew no more of my former insensible
Body, than a fire that burned along its rims:

Farewell, thought I, mortal ME, sister, falsehood....

Thing of harmony, ME, unlike a dream,
Firm, flexible, feminine, whose silences lead
To pure acts! Limpid brow, and swept in waves
As far as the vague tressed wind carries them,
Long light strands mingled and lifted in the breeze,
Tell me!...I was the equal and spouse of light,
Sole smiling pillar of love that I formed
For the adored omnipotence of the height....

Quel éclat sur mes cils aveuglément dorée,
Ô paupières qu'opprime une nuit de trésor,
Je priais à tâtons dans vos ténèbres d'or !
Poreuse à l'éternel qui me semblait m'enclore,
Je m'offrais dans mon fruit de velours qu'il dévore;
Rien ne me murmurait qu'un désir de mourir
Dans cette blonde pulpe au soleil pût mûrir :
Mon amère saveur ne m'était point venue.
Je ne sacrifiais que mon épaule nue
À la lumière; et sur cette gorge de miel,
Dont la tendre naissance accomplissait le ciel,
Se venait assoupir la figure du monde.
Puis dans le dieu brillant, captive vagabonde,
Je m'ébranlais brûlante et foulais le sol plein,
Liant et déliant mes ombres sous le lin.
Heureuse ! À la hauteur de tant de gerbes belles,
Qui laissait à ma robe obéir les ombelles,
Dans les abaissements de leur frêle fierté;
Et si, contre le fil de cette liberté,
Si la robe s'arrache à la rebelle ronce,
L'arc de mon brusque corps s'accuse et me prononce,
Nu sous le voile enflé de vivantes couleurs
Que dispute ma race aux longs liens de fleurs !

Je regrette à demi cette vaine puissance...
Une avec le désir, je fus l'obéissance
Imminente, attachée à ces genoux polis;
De mouvements si prompts mes vœux étaient remplis
Que je sentais ma cause à peine plus agile !
Vers mes sens lumineux nageait ma blonde argile,
Et dans l'ardente paix des songes naturels,
Tous ces pas infinis me semblaient éternels.

Ah, the dazzle on my brows blindingly gilded,
Eyelids overborne by a night of riches,
Gropingly I was praying in your golden glooms!
Porous to the eternal that seemed to enwrap me,
I offered my velvet fruit which it devours;
No hint was whispered that a death-longing
Might ripen in this blond, sunlit flesh:
My bitter savor was still unknown to me.
All I sacrificed was my naked shoulder
To the light; and on this bosom of honey
Whose tender nativity was heaven's fulfilment
There came to lull itself the shape of the world.
Then in the god's splendor, a straying prisoner,
Burningly I moved, pressed the solid ground,
Binding, unbinding my shadows beneath the linen.
Happy! Of a height with all those lovely sheaves,
I who let their umbels obey my dress,
With the abasings of their fragile pride;
And if, against the current of this freedom,
If the dress is dragged by the rebel brambles,
The arc of my sudden body reveals me pronounced
Naked in the veil swelling with living colors
In which my kind vies with the long trammels of flowers!

I half regret that vain potency. . . .
At one with desire, I was the imminent
Obedience implicit in these smooth knees;
My wishes answered by such instant movements,
I felt my cause itself scarcely more agile!
My blond clay swam up to my lucid senses,
And in the burning calm of natural dreams
All those continual steps seemed to me eternal.

Si ce n'est, ô Splendeur, qu'à mes pieds l'ennemie,
Mon ombre! la mobile et la souple momie,
De mon absence peinte effleurait sans effort
La terre où je fuyais cette légère mort.
Entre la rose et moi, je la vois qui s'abrite;
Sur la poudre qui danse, elle glisse et n'irrite
Nul feuillage, mais passe, et se brise partout...
Glisse! Barque funèbre...

       Et moi vive, debout,
Dure, et de mon néant secrètement armée,
Mais, comme par l'amour une joue enflammée,
Et la narine jointe au vent de l'oranger,
Je ne rends plus au jour qu'un regard étranger...
Oh! combien peut grandir dans ma nuit curieuse
De mon cœur séparé la part mystérieuse,
Et de sombres essais s'approfondir mon art!...
Loin des purs environs, je suis captive, et par
L'évanouissement d'arômes abattue,
Je sens sous les rayons, frissonner ma statue,
Des caprices de l'or, son marbre parcouru.
Mais je sais ce que voit mon regard disparu;
Mon œil noir est le seuil d'infernales demeures!
Je pense, abandonnant à la brise les heures
Et l'âme sans retour des arbustes amers,
Je pense, sur le bord doré de l'univers,
À ce goût de périr qui prend la Pythonisse
En qui mugit l'espoir que le monde finisse.
Je renouvelle en moi mes énigmes, mes dieux,
Mes pas interrompus de paroles aux cieux,
Mes pauses, sur le pied portant la rêverie,

If only, oh Splendor, it were not for the enemy
My shadow at my feet, mobile, supple mummy
Effortlessly skimming, portrait of my absence,
The earth where I was fleeing that weightless death.
Between the rose and me I see it lurking;
Over the dancing dust it glides, never stirring
The leafage, passes and breaks on anything....
Glide, funereal bark !...

           And I alive, erect,
Stubborn, and secretly armed with my inner void,
But one cheek on fire as though with love,
My nostril married to the wind from the orange grove,
I can give the light no more than a stranger's look....
Ah ! how much may it grow in my questing night,
That secret half of my divided heart,
And my skill grow deeper from obscure probings !...
Far from pure atmospheres, I am a captive,
And overcome by the fainting away of perfumes
I can feel my statue quiver beneath the rays,
Its marble coursed by the caprices of gold.
But I know what my vanished look can see;
My darkened eye is the door to infernal abodes !
I muse, letting hours waste in the wind
With the evanescent breath of the bitter shrubs,
On the golden edge of the universe, I muse
On that taste for death that takes the Pythoness
In whom a hope howls that the world may cease.
In myself I renew my gods, my enigmas,
My pacings interrupted by words to the heavens,
My pauses, on a step bearing a reverie

Qui suit au miroir d'aile un oiseau qui varie,
Cent fois sur le soleil joue avec le néant,
Et brûle, au sombre but de mon marbre béant.

O dangereusement de son regard la proie !

Car l'œil spirituel sur ses plages de soie
Avait déjà vu luire et pâlir trop de jours
Dont je m'étais prédit les couleurs et le cours.
L'ennui, le clair ennui de mirer leur nuance,
Me donnait sur ma vie une funeste avance:
L'aube me dévoilait tout le jour ennemi.
J'étais à demi morte; et peut-être, à demi
Immortelle, rêvant que le futur lui-même
Ne fût qu'un diamant fermant le diadème
Où s'échange le froid des malheurs qui naîtront
Parmi tant d'autres feux absolus de mon front.

Osera-t-il, le Temps, de mes diverses tombes,
Ressusciter un soir favori des colombes,
Un soir qui traîne au fil d'un lambeau voyageur
De ma docile enfance un reflet de rougeur,
Et trempe à l'émeraude un long rose de honte?

Souvenir, ô bûcher, dont le vent d'or m'affronte,
Souffle au masque la pourpre imprégnant le refus
D'être en moi-même en flamme une autre que je fus...
Viens, mon sang, viens rougir la pâle circonstance
Qu'ennoblissait l'azur de la sainte distance,
Et l'insensible iris du temps que j'adorai !

That follows in a wing's mirror a varying bird,
Wagers a hundred times void against sun,
And burns, at the dark goal of my gaping marble.

Oh, dangerously a prey to the gazing self!

For already the mind's eye on its silken strands
Had watched shine and fade too many days
Whose colors and whose course I had foreseen.
The clear-eyed tedium of seeing through their changes
Gave me a sinister start over my life:
Dawn unveiled to me the whole hostile day.
Half of me was dead; and the other perhaps
Immortal, dreaming that the future itself
Was only a diamond completing the diadem
Where sorrows-to-be exchange their icy gleams
Among all the other supreme fires of my brow.

Will Time dare, out of my diverse tombs,
To resurrect some sunset favored by doves,
An evening that trails after a rag of cloud
Some flushed reflection of my docile childhood,
Dipping a long flush of shame in the emerald?

Memory, bonfire whose gold wind assaults me,
Blow and empurple my mask with the refusal
To be, in myself aflame, another than I was....
Come, blood, redden the circumstantial pallor
Made noble once by the blue of holy distance,
And the infinite slow iris of the time I loved!

Viens! consumer sur moi ce don décoloré;
Viens! que je reconnaisse et que je les haïsse,
Cette ombrageuse enfant, ce silence complice,
Ce trouble transparent qui baigne dans les bois...
Et de mon sein glacé rejaillisse la voix
Que j'ignorais si rauque et d'amour si voilée...
Le col charmant cherchant la chasseresse ailée.

Mon cœur fut-il si près d'un cœur qui va faiblir?

Fut-ce bien moi, grands cils, qui crus m'ensevelir
Dans l'arrière douceur riant à vos menaces...
Ô pampres sur ma joue errant en fils tenaces,
Ou toi...de cils tissue et de fluides fûts,
Tendre lueur d'un soir brisé de bras confus?

QUE DANS LE CIEL PLACÉS, MES YEUX TRACENT
    MON TEMPLE!
ET QUE SUR MOI REPOSE UN AUTEL SANS EXEMPLE!
Criaient de tout mon corps la pierre et la pâleur...
La terre ne m'est plus qu'un bandeau de couleur
Qui coule et se refuse au front blanc de vertige...
Tout l'univers chancelle et tremble sur ma tige,
La pensive couronne échappe à mes esprits,
La Mort veut respirer cette rose sans prix
Dont la douceur importe à sa fin ténébreuse!

Que si ma tendre odeur grise ta tête creuse,
Ô Mort, respire enfin cette esclave de roi:
Appelle-moi, délie!...Et désespère-moi,
De moi-même si lasse, image condamnée!

Come burn on me that dower of drained color,
Come! Let me recognize so that I may hate
That moody child, that conniving silence,
That troubled clarity that bathes in woods....
And from my icy breast let there break the voice
I did not know was so hoarse, so veiled with love....
The charming neck seeking the winged huntress.

Was my heart so close by a heart ready to weaken?

Was it truly I, great lashes, who thought to bury me
In the after-sweetness that laughed at your threats....
O vine-stalks grazing my cheek with clutching tendrils,
Or you...woven of lashes and fluid columns,
Tender evening gleam broken by mingling arms?

LET MY EYES, FIXED IN HEAVEN, TRACE MY
    TEMPLE,
AND LET REPOSE ON ME AN ALTAR UNEXAMPLED!
This was the cry of all my body's stony pallor....
Earth is no more to me now than a fillet of color
That slips and falls from my white dizzy brow....
The whole universe quivers and gives on my stem,
The crown of thought is falling from my senses,
Death seeks to inhale this priceless rose
Whose sweetness matters to its dark purpose!

But if my tender perfume turns your hollow head,
Oh Death, breathe in at once this royal slave:
Summon me, release!...And drive me to despair,
So self-weary am I, a sentenced image!

Écoute...N'attends plus...La renaissante année
À tout mon sang prédit de secrets mouvements:
Le gel cède à regret ses derniers diamants...
Demain, sur un soupir des Bontés constellées,
Le printemps vient briser les fontaines scellées:
L'étonnant printemps rit, viole...On ne sait d'où
Venu? Mais la candeur ruisselle à mots si doux
Qu'une tendresse prend la terre à ses entrailles...
Les arbres regonflés et recouverts d'écailles
Chargés de tant de bras et de trop d'horizons,
Meuvent sur le soleil leurs tonnantes toisons,
Montent dans l'air amer avec toutes leurs ailes
De feuilles par milliers qu'ils se sentent nouvelles...
N'entends-tu pas frémir ces noms aériens,
Ô Sourde!...Et dans l'espace accablé de liens,
Vibrant de bois vivace infléchi par la cime,
Pour et contre les dieux ramer l'arbre unanime,
La flottante forêt de qui les rudes troncs
Portent pieusement à leurs fantasques fronts,
Aux déchirants départs des archipels superbes,
Un fleuve tendre, ô Mort, et caché sous les herbes?

Quelle résisterait, mortelle, à ces remons?
Quelle mortelle?

            Moi si pure, mes genoux
Pressentent les terreurs de genoux sans défense...
L'air me brise. L'oiseau perce de cris d'enfance
Inouïs...l'ombre même où se serre mon cœur,
Et, roses! mon soupir vous soulève, vainqueur
Hélas! des bras si doux qui ferment la corbeille...

You hear.... Wait no longer.... The newborn year
To all my blood foretells secret impulses:
Rueful the frost relinquishes its last diamonds....
Tomorrow, at a sigh of the constellated Bounties,
Spring comes to break the sealed-up fountains:
Astounding spring, laughing, raping.... Where
Can it come from? Its frankness brims with speech
So soft, earth's entrails are seized with tenderness....
The trees re-swelling and clothed in new scales,
Loaded with all those arms and endless horizons,
Brandish against the sun their resounding fleeces,
Rise into the sharp air with all their wings
Of leaves in myriads they feel new-grown....
Do you not hear those airy names trembling,
Deaf One...And in space loaded with chains,
Vibrant with living timber twisted by its summit,
The unanimous tree rowing with and against the gods,
The undulating forest whose rough trunks
Bear devoutly up to their antic brows,
At the rending departures of those proud archipelagoes,
A tender river, O Death, hidden beneath the grass?

Who could resist, mortal, such turmoils as these,
Who among mortals?

                    Pure as I am, my knees
Can feel the terrors of knees without defense....
I am broken by air. With unspeakable infant cries
The bird pierces...the very shadow where my heart shrinks,
And roses! the sigh I heave lifts you, vanquishing
Alas, the arms so soft folded about your cradle....

Oh ! parmi mes cheveux pèse d'un poids d'abeille,
Plongeant toujours plus ivre au baiser plus aigu,
Le point délicieux de mon jour ambigu...
Lumière !...Ou toi, la Mort ! Mais le plus prompt me
    prenne !...
Mon cœur bat ! mon cœur bat ! Mon sein brûle et
    m'entraîne !
Ah ! qu'il s'enfle, se gonfle et se tende, ce dur
Très doux témoin captif de mes réseaux d'azur...
Dur en moi...mais si doux à la bouche infinie !...

Chers fantômes naissants dont la soif m'est unie,
Désirs ! Visages clairs !...Et vous, beaux fruits d'amour,
Les dieux m'ont-ils formé ce maternel contour
Et ces bords sinueux, ces plis et ces calices,
Pour que la vie embrasse un autel de délices,
Où mêlant l'âme étrange aux éternels retours,
La semence, le lait, le sang coulent toujours?
Non ! L'horreur m'illumine, exécrable harmonie !
Chaque baiser présage une neuve agonie...
Je vois, je vois flotter, fuyant l'honneur des chairs
Des mânes impuissants les millions amers...
Non, souffles ! Non, regards, tendresses...mes convives,
Peuple altéré de moi suppliant que tu vives,
Non, vous ne tiendrez pas de moi la vie !...Allez,
Spectres, soupirs la nuit vainement exhalés,
Allez joindre des morts les impalpables nombres !
Je n'accorderai pas la lumière à des ombres,
Je garde loin de vous, l'esprit sinistre et clair...
Non ! Vous ne tiendrez pas de mes lèvres l'éclair !...
Et puis...mon cœur aussi vous refuse sa foudre.
J'ai pitié de nous tous, ô tourbillons de poudre !

Ah, through my hair weighs with a bee's weight,
Plunging ever wilder to the sharpest kiss,
The delectable glint of my ambiguous dawn....
Light!...Or else, Death! But let the quicker seize me!...
My heart beats! It beats! My burning breast impels me!
Ah, let it swell, dilate and stretch, that hard
Too soft witness prisoned in my nets of azure....
Hard in me...yet so soft to infinity's mouth!

Dear dawning phantoms whose thirst is one with me,
Desires! Bright faces!...And you, love's lovely fruits,
Have the gods shaped me this maternal contour
And these sinuous verges, folds and hollows,
So that life might hug an altar of delight
Where, mingling the alien soul's continual changes,
Fertility, milk and blood forever flow?
No! Horror gives me insight, accursed harmony!
Every kiss is a presage of fresh agony....
I see, I see afloat, fleeing the flesh's dignity,
The embittered myriads of impotent shades....
No no, breaths, sighs, tender gazes...my fellows,
Race all athirst for me, begging you may live,
No, from me you will not have life....Be gone,
Spectres, groans the night exhales in vain,
Go and join the impalpable throngs of the dead!
I will not concede light to shadows, I keep
Remote from you a mind ominous and clear....
No! Not from my lips will you get the lightning!...
And then...my heart too refuses you its fire.
I pity all of us, oh eddyings of dust!

Grands Dieux ! Je perds en vous mes pas déconcertés !

Je n'implorerai plus que tes faibles clartés,
Longtemps sur mon visage envieuse de fondre,
Très imminente larme, et seule à me répondre,
Larme qui fais trembler à mes regards humains
Une variété de funèbres chemins;
Tu procèdes de l'âme, orgueil du labyrinthe.
Tu me portes du cœur cette goutte contrainte,
Cette distraction de mon suc précieux
Qui vient sacrifier mes ombres sur mes yeux,
Tendre libation de l'arrière-pensée !
D'une grotte de crainte au fond de moi creusée
Le sel mystérieux suinte muette l'eau.
D'où nais-tu? Quel travail toujours triste et nouveau
Te tire avec retard, larme, de l'ombre amère?
Tu gravis mes degrés de mortelle et de mère,
Et déchirant ta route, opiniâtre faix,
Dans le temps que je vis, les lenteurs que tu fais
M'étouffent...Je me tais, buvant ta marche sûre...
— Qui t'appelle au secours de ma jeune blessure?

Mais blessures, sanglots, sombres essais, pourquoi?
Pour qui, joyaux cruels, marquez-vous ce corps froid,
Aveugle aux doigts ouverts évitant l'espérance !
Où va-t-il, sans répondre à sa propre ignorance,
Ce corps dans la nuit noire étonné de sa foi?
Terre trouble...et mêlée à l'algue, porte-moi,
Porte doucement moi...Ma faiblesse de neige
Marchera-t-elle tant qu'elle trouve son piège?
Où traîne-t-il, mon cygne, où cherche-t-il son vol?
...Dureté précieuse...O sentiment du sol,

Great Gods, in you I am losing my baffled way!

I shall beg no more than your feeble inklings,
For so long striving to melt on my face,
Tear most imminent, sole response to me,
Tear setting a-quiver in my mortal gaze
A whole diversity of funereal paths;
You come from the soul, pride of the labyrinth.
You bring me from the heart this extracted drop,
This extrusion of my own precious essence
Rising to immolate my phantoms on my eyes,
A fond libation of my thought's reserve!
From a grotto of fear hollowed in my depths
Mutely the salt of mystery oozes moisture.
Whence born? What labor ever solemn and new
Draws you unwilling, tear, from the bitter dark?
You mount on my mortal and mothering rungs,
A wilful burden, and rending yourself a path
Through the time I live, your long delays
Stifle me....Dumb, I drink your steady pace....
—Who summons you to the aid of my youthful wound?

But why, oh wounds, sobs, dark probings, why?
Heartless jewels, for whom do you mark this cold body,
Blind, with stretched fingers groping away from hope!
Where bound, answerless to its own self-ignorance,
This body in black night amazed by its faith?
Troublous earth...and mingled with slime, bear me
Gently, gently bear me....Will my snowy weakness
Be able to walk until it find its snare?
Where is my swan trailing, seeking his flight?
...Precious hardness....Oh feel of firm earth,

Mon pas fondait sur toi l'assurance sacrée !
Mais sous le pied vivant qui tâte et qui la crée
Et touche avec horreur à son pacte natal,
Cette terre si ferme atteint mon piédestal.
Non loin, parmi ces pas, rêve mon précipice...
L'insensible rocher, glissant d'algues, propice
À fuir, (comme en soi-même ineffablement seul),
Commence...Et le vent semble au travers d'un linceul
Ourdir de bruits marins une confuse trame,
Mélange de la lame en ruine, et de rame...
Tant de hoquets longtemps, et de râles heurtés,
Brisés, repris au large...et tous les sorts jetés
Éperdument divers roulant l'oubli vorace...

Hélas ! de mes pieds nus qui trouvera la trace
Cessera-t-il longtemps de ne songer qu'à soi ?

Terre trouble, et mêlée à l'algue, porte-moi !

Mystérieuse MOI, pourtant, tu vis encore !
Tu vas te reconnaître au lever de l'aurore
Amèrement la même...
               Un miroir de la mer
Se lève...Et sur la lèvre, un sourire d'hier
Qu'annonce avec ennui l'effacement des signes,
Glace dans l'orient déjà les pâles lignes
De lumière et de pierre, et la pleine prison
Où flottera l'anneau de l'unique horizon...
Regarde : un bras très pur est vu, qui se dénude.
Je te revois, mon bras...Tu portes l'aube...
                           O rude

On you my tread founded its sacred surety!
But under the living, groping foot that creates it
And strikes its native treaty with terror,
This so firm earth mines at my pedestal!
Nearby, amid these steps, my precipice dreams....
The gradual rock, slippery with seaweed, aid
To vanishing (as in one's sole ineffable self)
Begins....And through a shroud the wind seems
To weave a mazy plot of marine noises,
Blend of breakers falling in ruins, and oars....
Prolonged gulps and wallowings, hurtling rattles,
Broken, re-echoed in the deep...and all the cast lots,
Wildly at odds rolling greedy oblivion....

Ah, whoever finds the print of my bare feet,
Will he cease for long to think only of himself?

Troublous earth, and mingled with slime, bear me!

Thing of mystery, ME, are you living yet!
When dawn's curtain lifts, you will recognize
Your same bitter self....
                   A mirror is rising
From the sea....And on its lip a smile of yesterday
Heralded by the weary extinction of the signs,
Already in the east fixes the faint lines
Of light and stone, and the ample prison
Where will float the ring of the single horizon....
Look: a purest arm is seen baring itself,
My arm: I see you again....You bear the dawn....
                             Rude

Réveil d'une victime inachevée... et seuil
Si doux... si clair, que flatte, affleurement d'écueil,
L'onde basse, et que lave une houle amortie !...
L'ombre qui m'abandonne, impérissable hostie,
Me découvre vermeille à de nouveaux désirs,
Sur le terrible autel de tous mes souvenirs.

Là, l'écume s'efforce à se faire visible;
Et là, titubera sur la barque sensible
À chaque épaule d'onde, un pêcheur éternel.
Tout va donc accomplir son acte solennel
De toujours reparaître incomparable et chaste,
Et de restituer la tombe enthousiaste
Au gracieux état du rire universel.

Salut ! Divinités par la rose et le sel,
Et les premiers jouets de la jeune lumière,
Îles !... Ruches bientôt, quand la flamme première
Fera que votre roche, îles que je prédis,
Ressente en rougissant de puissants paradis;
Cimes qu'un feu féconde à peine intimidées,
Bois qui bourdonnerez de bêtes et d'idées,
D'hymnes d'hommes comblés des dons du juste éther,
Îles ! dans la rumeur des ceintures de mer,
Mères vierges toujours, même portant ces marques,
Vous m'êtes à genoux de merveilleuses Parques:
Rien n'égale dans l'air les fleurs que vous placez,
Mais, dans la profondeur, que vos pieds sont glacés !

De l'âme les apprêts sous la tempe calmée,
Ma mort, enfant secrète et déjà si formée,

Waking of a victim undispatched...and sill
So gentle...bright, soothed level with the reef
By the low wave, and washed by a deadened surf!...
The darkness that sheds me, indestructible victim,
Unveils me rosy to newborn desires
On the terrible altar of all my memories.

There, the foam strives to become visible,
And there, reels swaying in a boat that gives
With every shouldering wave, an eternal fisher.
So all is about to fulfil its solemn decree
Of forever reappearing, incomparable, untouched,
And of restoring the eager cenotaph
To a state of grace in the universal laugh.

Hail! Deities in virtue of rose and salt,
And earliest playthings of the infant light,
Islands!...Hives soon to be, when the first flame
Will see that your rocks, islands I foretell,
Again feel the red flush of powerful paradises;
Summits no sooner daunted than quickened by
The fire, woods that will hum with creatures and moods,
With hymns of men loaded with heaven's just gifts,
Islands! in the murmur of the girdling sea,
Mothers still virgin, even bearing these proofs,
To me you are marvels, kneeling Destinies:
Nothing matches the flowers you lift in air,
But how icy in the depths your feet are!

Preparatives of the soul beneath the quieted temples,
My death, secret child already fully formed,

Et vous, divins dégoûts qui me donniez l'essor,
Chastes éloignements des lustres de mon sort,
Ne fûtes-vous, ferveur, qu'une noble durée?
Nulle jamais des dieux plus près aventurée
N'osa peindre à son front leur souffle ravisseur,
Et de la nuit parfaite implorant l'épaisseur,
Prétendre par la lèvre au suprême murmure...

   Je soutenais l'éclat de la mort toute pure
Telle j'avais jadis le soleil soutenu...
Mon corps désespéré tendait le torse nu
Où l'âme, ivre de soi, de silence et de gloire,
Prête à s'évanouir de sa propre mémoire,
Écoute, avec espoir, frapper au mur pieux
Ce cœur, — qui se ruine à coups mystérieux,
Jusqu'à ne plus tenir que de sa complaisance
Un frémissement fin de feuille, ma présence...

Attente vaine, et vaine...Elle ne peut mourir
Qui devant son miroir pleure pour s'attendrir.

Ô n'aurait-il fallu, folle, que j'accomplisse
Ma merveilleuse fin de choisir pour supplice
Ce lucide dédain des nuances du sort?
   Trouveras-tu jamais plus transparente mort
Ni de pente plus pure où je rampe à ma perte
Que sur ce long regard de victime entr'ouverte,
Pâle, qui se résigne et saigne sans regret?
Que lui fait tout le sang qui n'est plus son secret?
Dans quelle blanche paix cette pourpre la laisse,
À l'extrême de l'être, et belle de faiblesse!

And you, divine revulsions that gave me wings,
Chaste estrangements from the lustra of my lot,
Ardency, were you only a noble interlude?
None ever who ventured thus near to the gods
Dared picture on her brow their ravishers' breath,
Nor, praying for the stupor of total night,
Dared let her lips lay claim to the final murmur....

   I withstood the dazzle of death in its purity
As I formerly had withstood the sun....
My body desperate stretched its naked torso
Where the soul, crazed with self, silence, and glory
Ready to faint away from its own memory
Listens, in hope, to this heart knocking against
The pious wall, with a secret, self-destroying beat,
Till only from sheer compliance does it keep up
This thin quivering of a leaf, my presence....

Vain the suspense, vain...She cannot die
Who weeps in her own mirror from self-pity.

Oh fool, ought I not to have fulfilled
My marvelous aim, choosing for self-torture
My lucid contempt for fate's varying moods?
   Will you ever light on a death more translucent,
On a purer slope whereby to creep to perdition
Than by that long gaze of the victim laid open,
Pale, resigned, bleeding away without regret?
What matters that blood, now no more her secret?
In what a snowy calm does the purple leave her
On the furthest edge of being, lovely in weakness!

Elle calme le temps qui la vient abolir,
Le moment souverain ne la peut plus pâlir,
Tant la chair vide baise une sombre fontaine !...
Elle se fait toujours plus seule et plus lointaine...
Et moi, d'un tel destin, le cœur toujours plus près,
Mon cortège, en esprit, se berçait de cyprès...
　　Vers un aromatique avenir de fumée,
Je me sentais conduite, offerte et consumée,
Toute, toute promise aux nuages heureux !
Même, je m'apparus cet arbre vaporeux,
De qui la majesté légèrement perdue
S'abandonne à l'amour de toute l'étendue.
L'être immense me gagne, et de mon cœur divin
L'encens qui brûle expire une forme sans fin...
Tous les corps radieux tremblent dans mon essence !...

Non, non !...N'irrite plus cette réminiscence !
Sombre lys ! Ténébreuse allusion des cieux,
Ta vigueur n'a pu rompre un vaisseau précieux...
Parmi tous les instants tu touchais au suprême...
— Mais qui l'emporterait sur la puissance même,
Avide par tes yeux de contempler le jour
Qui s'est choisi ton front pour lumineuse tour?

Cherche, du moins, dis-toi, par quelle sourde suite
La nuit, d'entre les morts, au jour t'a reconduite?
Souviens-toi de toi-même, et retire à l'instinct
Ce fil (ton doigt doré le dispute au matin),
Ce fil dont la finesse aveuglément suivie
Jusque sur cette rive a ramené ta vie...
Sois subtile...cruelle...ou plus subtile !...Mens
Mais sache !...Enseigne-moi par quels enchantements,

She quiets the time as it comes to annul her,
The supreme moment cannot increase her pallor,
The void flesh so kisses a dark fountain!...
Ever lonelier she feels, and more remote....
In my own mind I felt my heart nearer and nearer
To such a fate, my funeral train swaying in cypress....
 Towards a future of aromatic vapor
I felt I was being led, offered up, consumed,
To the happy clouds I was promised entire!
I even saw myself changed to that misty tree
Whose majesty diaphanously lost
Surrenders to the love of infinite space.
Immense being invades me, the burning incense
Of my divine heart breathes a shape without end....
All the forms of light quiver in my essence!...

No, no!...No longer chafe that reminiscence,
Lily of darkness! Gloomy allusion of the skies,
Your vigor could not break a precious vessel....
Amid all possible moments you touched on the ultimate....
—But who could win mastery over the very power
That is greedy, through your eyes, to contemplate
The day which chose your brow for its tower of light?

Seek at least, and declare by what sly paths
Night restored you to day from among the dead?
Recall self to self, reclaim from instinct
That thread (your golden finger vies for it with morning)
That thread whose fine-spun trace blindly followed
Has led your life again back to this shore....
Be subtle...or cruel...or more subtle still!...
Cheat, but find out!...Tell me by what wiles,

Lâche que n'a su fuir sa tiède fumée,
Ni le souci d'un sein d'argile parfumée,
Par quel retour sur toi, reptile, as-tu repris
Tes parfums de caverne et tes tristes esprits?

Hier la chair profonde, hier, la chair maîtresse
M'a trahie...Oh! sans rêve, et sans une caresse!...
Nul démon, nul parfum ne m'offrit le péril
D'imaginaires bras mourant au col viril;
Ni, par le Cygne-Dieu, de plumes offensée
Sa brûlante blancheur n'effleura ma pensée...

Il eût connu pourtant le plus tendre des nids!
Car toute à la faveur de mes membres unis,
Vierge, je fus dans l'ombre une adorable offrande...
Mais le sommeil s'éprit d'une douceur si grande,
Et nouée à moi-même au creux de mes cheveux,
J'ai mollement perdu mon empire nerveux.
Au milieu de mes bras, je me suis faite une autre...
Qui s'aliène?...Qui s'envole?...Qui se vautre?...
À quel détour caché, mon cœur s'est-il fondu?
Quelle conque a redit le nom que j'ai perdu?
Le sais-je, quel reflux traître m'a retirée
De mon extrémité pure et prématurée,
Et m'a repris le sens de mon vaste soupir?
Comme l'oiseau se pose, il fallut m'assoupir.

Ce fut l'heure, peut-être, où la devineresse
Intérieure s'use et se désintéresse:
Elle n'est plus la même...Une profonde enfant
Des degrés inconnus vainement se défend,

Coward whom her own warm breath could not relinquish,
Nor the fond love of a breast of perfumed clay,
By what self-recollection, reptile, did you
Resume your cavernous savor and your glooms?

Yesterday, the insidious, the masterful flesh
Betrayed me....Oh, not by a dream or caress!
No demon, no perfume proffered me the risk
Of imagined arms a-swoon on a virile neck;
Nor, in a feathery onset, did the Swan-God
Even graze my thought with his snowy fires....

And yet...he would have known the tenderest nest!
For, thanks to the smooth oneness of my limbs,
A shaded virgin, I was a worshipful offering....
But sleep grew enamored of such sweetness,
And wrapped upon myself in my hollowed hair
Weakly I surrendered my nervous sway.
Amid my own arms, I became another....
Who is estranged?...Who is vanishing?...Wallowing?...
In what blind turning did my heart melt away?
What shell echoed to the name I had given up?
Can I guess what treacherous ebb withdrew me
From my naked and untimely extremity,
And took away the sense of my huge sigh?
As a bird alights, I had to fall asleep.

It may be it was the hour when the inner
Prophetess grows worn, loses interest:
No longer is she herself....A child far within
Against the unknown descent struggles in vain,

Et redemande au loin ses mains abandonnées.
Il faut céder aux vœux des mortes couronnées
Et prendre pour visage un souffle...
                          Doucement,
Me voici: mon front touche à ce consentement...
   Ce corps, je lui pardonne, et je goûte à la cendre.
Je me remets entière au bonheur de descendre,
Ouverte aux noirs témoins, les bras suppliciés,
Entre des mots sans fin, sans moi, balbutiés...
Dors, ma sagesse, dors. Forme-toi cette absence;
Retourne dans le germe et la sombre innocence.
Abandonne-toi vive aux serpents, aux trésors...
Dors toujours! Descends, dors toujours! Descends, dors,
     dors!
(*La porte basse c'est une bague...où la gaze*
Passe...Tout meurt, tout rit dans la gorge qui jase...
L'oiseau boit sur ta bouche et tu ne peux le voir...
Viens plus bas, parle bas...Le noir n'est pas si noir...)

Délicieux linceuls, mon désordre tiède,
Couche où je me répands, m'interroge et me cède,
Où j'allai de mon cœur noyer les battements,
Presque tombeau vivant dans mes appartements,
Qui respire, et sur qui l'éternité s'écoute.
Place pleine de moi qui m'avez prise toute,
Ô forme de ma forme et la creuse chaleur
Que mes retours sur moi reconnaissaient la leur,
Voici que tant d'orgueil qui dans vos plis se plonge
À la fin se mélange aux bassesses du songe!
Dans vos nappes, où lisse elle imitait sa mort
L'idole malgré soi se dispose et s'endort,

And pleads from far for its own surrendered hands....
The pleas of dead crowned women, give way to them,
Let the face become a breathing....
                        Gently,
I am come: my brow is at one with this consent.
   This body, I forgive it, I am tasting ash.
I am wholly given to the bliss of falling,
Exposed to dark witnesses, my arms twisted,
Among endless words muttered without my will....
Sleep, my prudence, sleep. Shape this absence;
Turn back to the seed, into dark innocence.
Give yourself up alive to the dragons, treasures....
Sleep still! Down, sleep still! Down, sleep, sleep!
(*The low door is a ring...where gauze filters....*
All dies away, laughs, in the babbling throat....
The bird sips from your mouth, you cannot see it....
Come lower, speak low....The dark is not so dark....)

Shrouds delectable, warm disarray,
Couch where I spread, question, yield to myself,
Where I set out to drown my beating heart,
Living tomb almost within my dwelling,
Breathing, on which eternity is conscious,
Shape that is filled by me and takes me whole,
Oh, form of my form, and hollow warmth
Which my returning senses knew as theirs,
Now all the pride that plunges in your folds
Is confused in the end with the low shallows of dreams!
In your sheets where smooth she simulated
Her death, the reluctant idol lies drowsing,

Lasse femme absolue, et les yeux dans ses larmes,
Quand, de ses secrets nus les antres et les charmes,
Et ce reste d'amour qui se gardait le corps
Corrompirent sa perte et ses mortels accords.

Arche toute secrète, et pourtant si prochaine,
Mes transports, cette nuit, pensaient briser ta chaîne;
Je n'ai fait que bercer de lamentations
Tes flancs chargés de jour et de créations !
Quoi ! mes yeux froidement que tant d'azur égare
Regardent là périr l'étoile fine et rare,
Et ce jeune soleil de mes étonnements
Me paraît d'une aïeule éclairer les tourments,
Tant sa flamme aux remords ravit leur existence,
Et compose d'aurore une chère substance
Qui se formait déjà substance d'un tombeau !...
Ô, sur toute la mer, sur mes pieds, qu'il est beau !
Tu viens !...Je suis toujours celle que tu respires,
Mon voile évaporé me fuit vers tes empires...

...Alors, n'ai-je formé, vains adieux si je vis,
Que songes?...Si je viens, en vêtements ravis,
Sur ce bord, sans horreur, humer la haute écume,
Boire des yeux l'immense et riante amertume,
L'être contre le vent, dans le plus vif de l'air,
Recevant au visage un appel de la mer;
Si l'âme intense souffle, et renfle furibonde
L'onde abrupte sur l'onde abattue, et si l'onde
Au cap tonne, immolant un monstre de candeur,
Et vient des hautes mers vomir la profondeur
Sur ce roc, d'où jaillit jusque vers mes pensées
Un éblouissement d'étincelles glacées,

Weary, absolute woman, eyes sunk in her tears,
Since the grottoes and charms of her naked secrets
And that relic of love which possessed her body
Undid her ruin, and her mortal pact.

All-secret ark, and yet so intimate,
My night's delirium thought to snap your moorings,
But all I did was rock with my laments
Your sides thronged with day and created things!
What! coldly my eyes bewildered by so much blue
Can watch the faint, rare star there as it fades,
And this young sun of my astonishment
Seems to light up the woes of an ancestress,
Its flames so rob remorse of its existence,
Reshaping with the dawn a precious substance
That had already shaped itself to a tomb!...
Ah, lovely over all the sea, on my feet, the sun!
You are here!...I am still she whom you breathe,
My dizzy veil flies out to your empires....

...So then—vain farewells if I live—did I only
Dream?...If I come in windswept garments
To this edge, unafraid, inhaling the high foam,
My eyes drinking the immense salt laughter,
My being into the wind, in the keenest air
Receiving the sea's challenge on my face;
If the intense soul snuffs and furious swells
The sheer on the shattered wave, and if the headland
Breaker thunders, immolating a snowy monster
Come from the open sea to vomit the deeps
Over this rock, whence leaps to my very thought
A dazzling burst of icy sparks, and over

Et sur toute ma peau que morde l'âpre éveil,
Alors, malgré moi-même, il le faut, ô Soleil,
Que j'adore mon cœur où tu te viens connaître,
Doux et puissant retour du délice de naître,

Feu vers qui se soulève une vierge de sang
Sous les espèces d'or d'un sein reconnaissant !

All my skin, stung awake by the harsh shock,
Then, even against my will, I must, oh Sun,
Worship this heart where you seek to know yourself,
Strong, sweet renewal of birth's own ecstasy,

Fire to which a virgin of blood uplifts herself
Beneath the gold coinage of a grateful breast!

CHARMES

Deducere carmen

CHARMS

Deducere carmen

Aurore

À Paul Poujaud

La confusion morose
Qui me servait de sommeil,
Se dissipe dès la rose
Apparence du soleil.
Dans mon âme je m'avance,
Tout ailé de confiance:
C'est la première oraison !
À peine sorti des sables,
Je fais des pas admirables
Dans les pas de ma raison.

Salut ! encore endormies
À vos sourires jumeaux,
Similitudes amies
Qui brillez parmi les mots !
Au vacarme des abeilles
Je vous aurai par corbeilles,
Et sur l'échelon tremblant
De mon échelle dorée,
Ma prudence évaporée
Déjà pose son pied blanc.

Quelle aurore sur ces croupes
Qui commencent de frémir !
Déjà s'étirent par groupes
Telles qui semblaient dormir:
L'une brille, l'autre bâille;

Dawn

To Paul Poujaud

The morose confusion
That served me for sleep
Disperses at the rosy
Apparition of the sun.
I step forth in my own mind
Fully fledged with confidence.
Now is the first orison!
Scarcely emerged from the quicksands
I am making admirable strides
In the paces of my reason.

Hail! Still sleeping ones,
To your coupled smiles,
Friendly similitudes
That gleam in the midst of words.
To the uproar of the bees
I shall have you in basketfuls,
And on the quivering rung
Of my golden stepladder
My prudence, lightheaded,
Already sets her white foot.

What a dawning over those croups
That are now beginning to quiver!
Already there are stretching groups
Of such as seemed to be asleep.
One gleams, another yawns,

Et sur un peigne d'écaille
Égarant ses vagues doigts,
Du songe encore prochaine,
La paresseuse l'enchaîne
Aux prémisses de sa voix.

Quoi! c'est vous, mal déridées!
Que fîtes-vous, cette nuit,
Maîtresses de l'âme, Idées,
Courtisanes par ennui?
— Toujours sages, disent-elles,
Nos présences immortelles
Jamais n'ont trahi ton toit!
Nous étions non éloignées,
Mais secrètes araignées
Dans les ténèbres de toi!

Ne seras-tu pas de joie
Ivre! à voir de l'ombre issus
Cent mille soleils de soie
Sur tes énigmes tissus?
Regarde ce que nous fîmes:
Nous avons sur tes abîmes
Tendu nos fils primitifs,
Et pris la nature nue
Dans une trame ténue
De tremblants préparatifs...

Leur toile spirituelle,
Je la brise, et vais cherchant
Dans ma forêt sensuelle
Les oracles de mon chant.

And on a comb of tortoiseshell
Letting her vague fingers roam,
Still a neighbor to the dream,
The lazy girl enchains it
To the preludings of her voice.

Can it be you? Half-drowsy ones!
What did you do, this night,
Soul's mistresses, Ideas,
Courtesans through boredom?
—Wise as always, they reply,
Our immortal presences
Have never betrayed your roof!
We were no distance off
But secret spiders we
In the shadows of yourself!

From joy will you not be
Wild! to see out of darkness issued
A hundred thousand silken suns
Spun across your mysteries?
Consider what we have made:
Over your abysses we
Have stretched out our primal threads
And caught nature naked
In a tenuous woof
Of tremulous initiatives. . . .

These spiritual toils of theirs
I break, and set out seeking
Within my sensuous forest
For the oracles of my song.

Être ! Universelle oreille !
Toute l'âme s'appareille
À l'extrême du désir...
Elle s'écoute qui tremble
Et parfois ma lèvre semble
Son frémissement saisir.

Voici mes vignes ombreuses,
Les berceaux de mes hasards !
Les images sont nombreuses
À l'égal de mes regards...
Toute feuille me présente
Une source complaisante
Où je bois ce frêle bruit...
Tout m'est pulpe, tout amande,
Tout calice me demande
Que j'attende pour son fruit.

Je ne crains pas les épines !
L'éveil est bon, même dur !
Ces idéales rapines
Ne veulent pas qu'on soit sûr:
Il n'est pour ravir un monde
De blessure si profonde
Qui ne soit au ravisseur
Une féconde blessure,
Et son propre sang l'assure
D'être le vrai possesseur.

J'approche la transparence
De l'invisible bassin
Où nage mon Espérance

Being! Universal Ear!
The soul becomes a fit compeer
For the extremes of desire....
She listens to her own tremors
And at times my lip seems
To seize upon her shudderings.

And here are my shadowy vines
The cradles of my guesses!
Images are in numbers
The equals of my glances....
Every leaf offers me
A spring of compliance
Where I drink that frail rumor....
All is flesh to me, all almond,
Every chalice implores me
That I await its fruit.

I do not shrink from the thorns!
Awaking is good, even if hard.
Such ideal depredations
Insist that one be none too sure:
For ravishing a world there is
No wound however profound
That is not to the ravisher
A fecund wound,
And his own blood approves him
To be the true possessor.

I approach the transparency
Of the invisible pool
Where my Hope is swimming,

Que l'eau porte par le sein.
Son col coupe le temps vague
Et soulève cette vague
Que fait un col sans pareil...
Elle sent sous l'onde unie
La profondeur infinie,
Et frémit depuis l'orteil.

The water bearing up her breast.
Her neck cleaves vague time
And raises such a wave as only
A neck unparalleled can make....
Under the watery oneness she
Feels the deep's infinity
And shivers upwards from the toe.

Au platane

À André Fontainas

Tu penches, grand Platane, et te proposes nu,
    Blanc comme un jeune Scythe,
Mais ta candeur est prise, et ton pied retenu
    Par la force du site.

Ombre retentissante en qui le même azur
    Qui t'emporte, s'apaise,
La noire mère astreint ce pied natal et pur
    À qui la fange pèse.

De ton front voyageur les vents ne veulent pas;
    La terre tendre et sombre,
Ô Platane, jamais ne laissera d'un pas
    S'émerveiller ton ombre!

Ce front n'aura d'accès qu'aux degrés lumineux
    Où la sève l'exalte;
Tu peux grandir, candeur, mais non rompre les nœuds
    De l'éternelle halte!

Pressens autour de toi d'autres vivants liés
    Par l'hydre vénérable;
Tes pareils sont nombreux, des pins aux peupliers,
    De l'yeuse à l'érable,

Qui, par les morts saisis, les pieds échevelés
    Dans la confuse cendre,
Sentent les fuir les fleurs, et leurs spermes ailés
    Le cours léger descendre.

The Plane Tree

To André Fontainas

You lean, great plane, and proffer yourself stripped,
    White as a young Scythian,
But your candor is trapped, and your foot held in
    By the strength of its site.

Reverberating shadow where the selfsame blue
    Transporting you, grows calm,
The dark mother constrains that pure and native foot
    Heavy with the loam.

The winds throw aside your traveling top;
    The dark and tender ground,
Oh Plane tree, will never let your shadow marvel
    At a solitary step!

That brow can only accede to those luminous heights
    Where the sap exalts it;
Grow you may, candid one, but never break the knots
    Of the eternal halt.

Sense all about you the lives of others bound
    By the venerable hydra;
Your equals are many, from the pine to the poplar,
    From ilex to maple

Who, by the dead seized tight, their feet disheveled
    In the chaos of dust,
Feel the flowers fleeing them, and their light-winged seeds
    Glide down the easy way.

Le tremble pur, le charme, et ce hêtre formé
    De quatre jeunes femmes,
Ne cessent point de battre un ciel toujours fermé,
    Vêtus en vain de rames.

Ils vivent séparés, ils pleurent confondus
    Dans une seule absence,
Et leurs membres d'argent sont vainement fendus
    À leur douce naissance.

Quand l'âme lentement qu'ils expirent le soir
    Vers l'Aphrodite monte,
La vierge doit dans l'ombre, en silence, s'asseoir,
    Toute chaude de honte.

Elle se sent surprendre, et pâle, appartenir
    À ce tendre présage
Qu'une présente chair tourne vers l'avenir
    Par un jeune visage...

Mais toi, de bras plus purs que les bras animaux
    Toi qui dans l'or les plonges,
Toi qui formes au jour le fantôme des maux
    Que le sommeil fait songes,

Haute profusion de feuilles, trouble fier
    Quand l'âpre tramontane
Sonne, au comble de l'or, l'azur du jeune hiver
    Sur tes harpes, Platane,

Ose gémir!...Il faut, ô souple chair du bois,
    Te tordre, te détordre,
Te plaindre sans te rompre, et rendre aux vents la voix
    Qu'ils cherchent en désordre!

The pure aspen, the hornbeam, and that beech composed
      Of four young women,
Beat without ceasing on a heaven forever closed,
      Armed with their oars in vain.

Separated they live, they weep altogether
      Blended in a sole absence;
And their silvery limbs are cleft all in vain
      At their tender birth.

When slowly the soul they exhale in the evening
      Mounts towards Aphrodite,
Let the young virgin in the shade sit down silently
      Warm with bashful shame.

Taken by surprise, and pale, she feels herself assigned
      To that fond foreboding
Which a present flesh turns towards the future
      In a youthful face.

But you, with your purer than animal arms,
      You who bathe them in gold,
Who form by day the phantoms of the troubles
      That sleep turns into dreams,

Lofty abundance of leaves, disdainful commotion
      When the rough tramontane
Rings, refined gold, the azure of young winter
      On your harps, Oh Plane,

Dare to groan !...Oh lithe flesh of timber, you must
      Twist and untwist,
Grieve without breaking, give the winds back that voice
      They seek in their riot.

Flagelle-toi !...Parais l'impatient martyr
    Qui soi-même s'écorche,
Et dispute à la flamme impuissante à partir
    Ses retours vers la torche !

Afin que l'hymne monte aux oiseaux qui naîtront,
    Et que le pur de l'âme
Fasse frémir d'espoir les feuillages d'un tronc
    Qui rêve de la flamme,

Je t'ai choisi, puissant personnage d'un parc,
    Ivre de ton tangage,
Puisque le ciel t'exerce, et te presse, ô grand arc,
    De lui rendre un langage !

Ô qu'amoureusement des Dryades rival,
    Le seul poète puisse
Flatter ton corps poli comme il fait du Cheval
    L'ambitieuse cuisse !...

— *Non, dit l'arbre. Il dit:* Non ! *par l'étincellement*
    De sa tête superbe,
Que la tempête traite universellement
    Comme elle fait une herbe !

Whip yourself!...Appear the intolerant martyr
      Who flays his own flesh,
And vie with the flame that can never escape
      Its homings to the torch!

So that the hymn may rise to birds yet to be born,
      And that the pure of soul
May set hope trembling in the leafage of a trunk
      Dreaming of the flame,

I have elected you, powerful presence of a park,
      Drunk with your own heaving,
Seeing that the sky tests and forces you, giant bow,
      To give it back a tongue!

Oh as a lover, rival to the dryads,
      Let the poet alone
Caress your polished body as he would the Horse's
      Self-vaunting thigh!...

—No, the tree says. He says: No! *by the glittering*
      Of his splendid head,
Which the storm treats universally
      As it would a grass-blade!

Cantique des colonnes

À Léon-Paul Fargue

Douces colonnes, aux
Chapeaux garnis de jour,
Ornés de vrais oiseaux
Qui marchent sur le tour,

Douces colonnes, ô
L'orchestre de fuseaux !
Chacun immole son
Silence à l'unisson.

— Que portez-vous si haut,
Égales radieuses ?
— Au désir sans défaut
Nos grâces studieuses !

Nous chantons à la fois
Que nous portons les cieux !
Ô seule et sage voix
Qui chantes pour les yeux !

Vois quels hymnes candides !
Quelle sonorité
Nos éléments limpides
Tirent de la clarté !

Si froides et dorées
Nous fûmes de nos lits
Par le ciseau tirées,
Pour devenir ces lys !

Song of the Columns

To Léon-Paul Fargue

Tender columns, whose
Hats the light garnishes,
Adorned with real birds
Walking about the brim,

Tender columns, Oh
Orchestra of spindles !
Each one sacrificing
Its silence to unison.

—What is it you bear so high,
Equals in radiance?
—To the faultless desire
Our studious graces.

We sing in one measure
How we carry the sky.
Oh voice wise and single
Singing for the eyes !

See what candid hymns,
What a sonority
Our limpid elements
Draw from clarity !

Thus cold and thus golden
Out of our beds we
Were drawn by the chisel
To become these lilies !

De nos lits de cristal
Nous fûmes éveillées,
Des griffes de métal
Nous ont appareillées.

Pour affronter la lune,
La lune et le soleil,
On nous polit chacune
Comme ongle de l'orteil !

Servantes sans genoux,
Sourires sans figures,
La belle devant nous
Se sent les jambes pures.

Pieusement pareilles,
Le nez sous le bandeau
Et nos riches oreilles
Sourdes au blanc fardeau,

Un temple sur les yeux
Noirs pour l'éternité,
Nous allons sans les dieux
À la divinité !

Nos antiques jeunesses,
Chair mate et belles ombres,
Sont fières des finesses
Qui naissent par les nombres !

Filles des nombres d'or,
Fortes des lois du ciel,
Sur nous tombe et s'endort
Un dieu couleur de miel.

From our crystal beds
We were awakened,
Claws of metal
Fashioned us alike.

To stare back at the moon,
The moon and the sun,
We were polished each one
Like the nail on the toe !

Servants unbending,
Smiles with no faces,
Beauty before us
Feels her own limbs pure.

Devoutly of a kind,
Nose hid by the bandeau,
And our rich ears
Deaf to the white load,

A temple upon eyes
Dark for eternity,
Without the gods we go
Towards divinity.

Our ancient youthfulness,
Pale flesh and noble shadows,
Takes pride in the subtleties
That are born of numbers !

Daughters of the golden numbers,
Strong in heaven's laws,
There falls and sleeps on us
A honey-colored god.

Il dort content, le Jour,
Que chaque jour offrons
Sur la table d'amour
Étale sur nos fronts.

Incorruptibles sœurs,
Mi-brûlantes, mi-fraîches,
Nous prîmes pour danseurs
Brises et feuilles sèches,

Et les siècles par dix,
Et les peuples passés,
C'est un profond jadis,
Jadis jamais assez !

Sous nos mêmes amours
Plus lourdes que le monde
Nous traversons les jours
Comme une pierre l'onde !

Nous marchons dans le temps
Et nos corps éclatants
Ont des pas ineffables
Qui marquent dans les fables...

He sleeps content, the Day
We offer every day
On the table of love
Moveless upon our brows.

Incorruptible sisters,
Half-burning, half-cool,
We took as dancing partners
Breezes and dry leaves,

And centuries in tens,
And peoples that have passed.
A deep long since it is,
Never long since enough!

Under our equal loves
Heavier than the world
We traverse the days
As through water a stone!

Our walking is in time
And our dazzling bodies
Have paces ineffable
That leave their prints in fables....

L'Abeille

À Francis de Miomandre

Quelle, et si fine, et si mortelle,
Que soit ta pointe, blonde abeille,
Je n'ai, sur ma tendre corbeille,
Jeté qu'un songe de dentelle.

Pique du sein la gourde belle,
Sur qui l'Amour meurt ou sommeille,
Qu'un peu de moi-même vermeille
Vienne à la chair ronde et rebelle !

J'ai grand besoin d'un prompt tourment :
Un mal vif et bien terminé
Vaut mieux qu'un supplice dormant !

Soit donc mon sens illuminé
Par cette infime alerte d'or
Sans qui l'Amour meurt ou s'endort !

The Bee

To Francis de Miomandre

What and how keen and mortal soever
Your sting may be, blond bee,
Over my tender basket I've thrown
Only a mere dream of lace.

Prick the gourd of the lovely breast
Where love lies dead or asleep,
So that a little of my red
May rise in the round resistant flesh !

I greatly need an instant pang:
A vivid and a clear-cut pain
Is better than a drowsy torment.

So let my senses be illumined
By that tiniest golden alert
For lack of which Love dies or sleeps !

Poésie

Par la surprise saisie,
Une bouche qui buvait
Au sein de la Poésie
En sépare son duvet:

— Ô ma mère Intelligence,
De qui la douceur coulait,
Quelle est cette négligence
Qui laisse tarir son lait !

À peine sur ta poitrine,
Accablé de blancs liens,
Me berçait l'onde marine
De ton cœur chargé de biens;

À peine, dans ton ciel sombre,
Abattu sur ta beauté,
Je sentais, à boire l'ombre,
M'envahir une clarté !

Dieu perdu dans son essence,
Et délicieusement
Docile à la connaissance
Du suprême apaisement,

Je touchais à la nuit pure,
Je ne savais plus mourir,
Car un fleuve sans coupure
Me semblait me parcourir...

Poesy

Arrested by surprise,
A mouth that was drinking
At the breast of Poesy
Draws away its downy lip:

—Oh mothering Intelligence,
From whom sweetness flowed,
What negligence is this
That allows its milk to cease!

Scarcely upon your breast,
Loaded with white bands
I was rocked on the sea wave
Of your boon-laden heart;

Scarcely, within your somber heaven
Making your beauty my prey,
I could feel, as I drank the shadow,
A clarity invade me!

A god immersed in his essence,
And delectably
Docile to the awareness
Of being appeased to the uttermost,

On the verge of pure night
I had forgotten how to die,
For a river uninterrupted
Seemed to traverse me through....

Dis, par quelle crainte vaine,
Par quelle ombre de dépit,
Cette merveilleuse veine
À mes lèvres se rompit?

Ô rigueur, tu m'es un signe
Qu'à mon âme je déplus!
Le silence au vol de cygne
Entre nous ne règne plus!

Immortelle, ta paupière
Me refuse mes trésors,
Et la chair s'est faite pierre
Qui fut tendre sous mon corps!

Des cieux même tu me sèvres,
Par quel injuste retour?
Que seras-tu sans mes lèvres?
Que serai-je sans amour?

Mais la Source suspendue
Lui répond sans dureté:
— Si fort vous m'avez mordue
Que mon cœur s'est arrêté!

Tell me what vain fear it was,
What shadow of resentment
That made this marvelous vein
Break off at my lips?

Oh severity, you are a sign
That I have failed to please my soul,
The swan-flight of silence
Between us can no longer reign!

Immortal one, your eyelid
Now denies me my store,
And the flesh is turned to stone
That was so soft beneath my body.

From heaven itself you cut me off
By what unjust change of heart?
What will you be without my lips?
What shall I be without love?

But the suspended Spring
Without unkindness replies:
—You have bitten me so deep
That my heart came to a stop!

Les Pas

Tes pas, enfants de mon silence,
Saintement, lentement placés,
Vers le lit de ma vigilance
Procèdent muets et glacés.

Personne pure, ombre divine,
Qu'ils sont doux, tes pas retenus !
Dieux !. . .tous les dons que je devine
Viennent à moi sur ces pieds nus !

Si, de tes lèvres avancées,
Tu prépares pour l'apaiser,
À l'habitant de mes pensées
La nourriture d'un baiser,

Ne hâte pas cet acte tendre,
Douceur d'être et de n'être pas,
Car j'ai vécu de vous attendre,
Et mon cœur n'était que vos pas.

The Footsteps

Your footsteps, children of my silence,
With gradual and saintly pace
Towards the bed of my watchfulness,
Muted and frozen, approach.

Pure one, divine shadow,
How gentle are your cautious steps!
Gods!...all the gifts that I can guess
Come to me on those naked feet!

If, with your lips advancing,
You are preparing to appease
The inhabitant of my thoughts
With the sustenance of a kiss,

Do not hasten the tender act,
Bliss of being and not being,
For I have lived on waiting for you,
And my heart was only your footsteps.

La Ceinture

Quand le ciel couleur d'une joue
Laisse enfin les yeux le chérir
Et qu'au point doré de périr
Dans les roses le temps se joue,

Devant le muet de plaisir
Qu'enchaîne une telle peinture,
Danse une Ombre à libre ceinture
Que le soir est près de saisir.

Cette ceinture vagabonde
Fait dans le souffle aérien
Frémir le suprême lien
De mon silence avec ce monde...

Absent, présent...Je suis bien seul,
Et sombre, ô suave linceul.

The Girdle

When the sky flushed like a cheek
At last lets the eye linger on it,
And at the golden moment of dying
Time gambols among the roses,

Before one who is mute with pleasure,
Riveted by such a painting,
Dances a Shade in a loose girdle
Which evening is about to snatch.

That vagabonding girdle
In the aerial breath of sky
Sets trembling the ultimate bond
Of my silence with this world. . . .

Absent, present. . .I am all alone,
And in the gloom, ah gentle shroud.

La Dormeuse

À Lucien Fabre

Quels secrets dans son cœur brûle ma jeune amie,
Âme par le doux masque aspirant une fleur?
De quels vains aliments sa naïve chaleur
Fait ce rayonnement d'une femme endormie?

Souffle, songes, silence, invincible accalmie,
Tu triomphes, ô paix plus puissante qu'un pleur,
Quand de ce plein sommeil l'onde grave et l'ampleur
Conspirent sur le sein d'une telle ennemie

Dormeuse, amas doré d'ombres et d'abandons,
Ton repos redoutable est chargé de tels dons,
Ô biche avec langueur longue auprès d'une grappe,

Que malgré l'âme absente, occupée aux enfers,
Ta forme au ventre pur qu'un bras fluide drape,
Veille; ta forme veille, et mes yeux sont ouverts.

A Sleeping Girl

To Lucien Fabre

What secrets in her heart is my young friend burning,
Soul through the tender mask inhaling a flower?
From what vain aliments does her naïve warmth
Create this radiance of a sleeping woman?

Breath, dreams, silence, lull invincible,
You triumph, oh tranquillity keener than a tear,
When the solemn wave, the breadth of that full slumber
Conspire on the breast of such an enemy.

Sleeper, golden mass of shadows and surrenders,
Your formidable quiet is loaded with such powers
—Oh fawn languid with length alongside a vine-cluster—

That though the soul is absent, absorbed in the underworld,
Your form with the pure belly draped by a fluid arm
Is awake: it watches, and my eyes are open.

Fragments du Narcisse

Cur aliquid vidi?

I

Que tu brilles enfin, terme pur de ma course !

Ce soir, comme d'un cerf, la fuite vers la source
Ne cesse qu'il ne tombe au milieu des roseaux,
Ma soif me vient abattre au bord même des eaux.
Mais, pour désaltérer cette amour curieuse,
Je ne troublerai pas l'onde mystérieuse:
Nymphes ! si vous m'aimez, il faut toujours dormir !
La moindre âme dans l'air vous fait toutes frémir;
Même, dans sa faiblesse, aux ombres échappée,
Si la feuille éperdue effleure la napée,
Elle suffit à rompre un univers dormant...
Votre sommeil importe à mon enchantement,
Il craint jusqu'au frisson d'une plume qui plonge !
Gardez-moi longuement ce visage pour songe
Qu'une absence divine est seule à concevoir !
Sommeil des nymphes, ciel, ne cessez de me voir !

Rêvez, rêvez de moi !...Sans vous, belles fontaines,
Ma beauté, ma douleur, me seraient incertaines.
Je chercherais en vain ce que j'ai de plus cher,
Sa tendresse confuse étonnerait ma chair,
Et mes tristes regards, ignorants de mes charmes,
À d'autres que moi-même adresseraient leurs larmes...

Vous attendiez, peut-être, un visage sans pleurs,
Vous calmes, vous toujours de feuilles et de fleurs,
Et de l'incorruptible altitude hantées,

Fragments of the Narcissus

Why did I see something?
Ovid: *Tristia*, II.

I

How you finally gleam, pure goal of the race I run!

This evening, the flight towards the pool, like a stag's,
Has no cease till it drops in the midst of the reeds.
My thirst brings me down on the very water's edge.
But, to quench the thirst of this inquisitive love,
I shall not trouble the mysterious surface:
Nymphs, you must sleep still, if you love me!
The merest ghost in air can make you all shudder;
Even if, in its weakness, unleashed from the shade,
The bewildered leaf grazes the napaea,
It is enough to shatter a sleeping universe....
Your slumber is vital to my enchantment,
It dreads even the shiver of a swooping feather!
Keep and guard long for me that face as a dream
Which a divine absence alone can conceive!
Sleep of the nymphs, sky, never cease from seeing me!

Dream, dream of me!...But for you, lovely founts,
My beauty, my sorrow, would be uncertain to me.
I would search in vain for what I have most dear,
Its vague tenderness would astonish my flesh,
And my mournful gazes, ignorant of my charms,
Would address their tears to others than myself....

Perhaps you were awaiting a tearless face,
You who are calm, you still by leaves and flowers
And by the incorruptible heights haunted,

Ô Nymphes !... Mais docile aux pentes enchantées
Qui me firent vers vous d'invincibles chemins,
Souffrez ce beau reflet des désordres humains !

Heureux vos corps fondus, Eaux planes et profondes !
Je suis seul !... Si les Dieux, les échos et les ondes
Et si tant de soupirs permettent qu'on le soit !
Seul !... mais encor celui qui s'approche de soi
Quand il s'approche aux bords que bénit ce feuillage...
Des cimes, l'air déjà cesse le pur pillage;
La voix des sources change, et me parle du soir;
Un grand calme m'écoute, où j'écoute l'espoir.
J'entends l'herbe des nuits croître dans l'ombre sainte,
Et la lune perfide élève son miroir
Jusque dans les secrets de la fontaine éteinte...
Jusque dans les secrets que je crains de savoir,
Jusque dans le repli de l'amour de soi-même,
Rien ne peut échapper au silence du soir...
La nuit vient sur ma chair lui souffler que je l'aime.
Sa voix fraîche à mes vœux tremble de consentir;
À peine, dans la brise, elle semble mentir,
Tant le frémissement de son temple tacite
Conspire au spacieux silence d'un tel site.

Ô douceur de survivre à la force du jour,
Quand elle se retire enfin rose d'amour,
Encore un peu brûlante, et lasse, mais comblée,
Et de tant de trésors tendrement accablée
Par de tels souvenirs qu'ils empourprent sa mort,
Et qu'ils la font heureuse agenouiller dans l'or,
Puis s'étendre, se fondre, et perdre sa vendange,
Et s'éteindre en un songe en qui le soir se change.

Nymphs!...But, obedient to the enchanted slopes
That blazed me irresistible paths towards you,
Endure this lovely reflex of mortal disquiet!

Happy your blended bodies, level and deep Waters.
I am alone!...If the Gods, the echoes, and ripples
And such abundance of sighs admit loneliness!
Alone!...and yet he who can approach himself
In approaching the verges this leafage makes holy....
In the heights, the air already ceases its pure pillage;
The voice of the springs changes, speaks to me of evening;
A great calm, where I listen to hope, listens to me.
I hear the night grass growing in the sacred gloom,
And the traitorous moon lifts up her mirror
Even into the secrets of the extinct fountain....
Even into the secrets I dread to know,
Even into the deep recesses of self-love.
Nothing can escape the evening silence....
Night comes whispering on my flesh that I love her.
Her cool voice tremblingly consents to my vows;
She seems, in the breeze, scarcely even to be lying,
So deeply does the quivering of her tacit temple
Conspire with the spacious silence of this scene.

Oh the bliss of surviving the day's rigor
When she retires at last, rosy with love,
Still on fire a little, but weary and fulfilled,
And with such store of treasures tenderly overwhelmed
By memories of a kind that empurple her dying,
So that she kneels down happy in the gold,
And then lies, and melts, squandering her vintage,
And fades into a dream that transforms to evening.

Quelle perte en soi-même offre un si calme lieu !
L'âme, jusqu'à périr, s'y penche pour un Dieu
Qu'elle demande à l'onde, onde déserte, et digne
Sur son lustre, du lisse effacement d'un cygne...
　À cette onde jamais ne burent les troupeaux !
D'autres, ici perdus, trouveraient le repos,
Et dans la sombre terre, un clair tombeau qui s'ouvre...
Mais ce n'est pas le calme, hélas ! que j'y découvre !
Quand l'opaque délice où dort cette clarté,
Cède à mon corps l'horreur du feuillage écarté,
Alors, vainqueur de l'ombre, ô mon corps tyrannique,
Repoussant aux forêts leur épaisseur panique,
Tu regrettes bientôt leur éternelle nuit !
Pour l'inquiet Narcisse, il n'est ici qu'ennui !
Tout m'appelle et m'enchaîne à la chair lumineuse
Que m'oppose des eaux la paix vertigineuse !

Que je déplore ton éclat fatal et pur,
Si mollement de moi, fontaine environnée,
Où puisèrent mes yeux dans un mortel azur,
Les yeux mêmes et noirs de leur âme étonnée !

Profondeur, profondeur, songes qui me voyez,
　　　　Comme ils verraient une autre vie,
Dites, ne suis-je pas celui que vous croyez,
　　　　Votre corps vous fait-il envie?

Cessez, sombres esprits, cet ouvrage anxieux
　　　　Qui se fait dans l'âme qui veille;
Ne cherchez pas en vous, n'allez surprendre aux cieux
　　　　Le malheur d'être une merveille:
Trouvez dans la fontaine un corps délicieux...

To be lost in oneself how this calm place urges !
The soul, to perishing-point, leans out for a God,
Demanding him of the water, empty and glossed,
Worthy the sleek self-effacement of a swan.. . .
Never did the herds drink from this fountain !
Others, losing themselves, might find rest here,
And in the gloomy ground, a clear tomb opening.. . .
But calm here is not what I find, alas !
When the opaque bliss where this clarity sleeps
Yields to my body the horror of foliage pushed aside,
Then, victor over shadow, oh my tyrannous body,
Thrusting their panic density in the forests' face,
Soon you will long once again for their eternal night !
Nothing but tedium here for restless Narcissus !
All urges and chains me to the luminous flesh
Which the dizzy peace of the water offers up to me !

How much I rue your pure and fatal glitter,
Fountain so softly all-surrounded by me,
Where my eyes imbibed in the mortal ether
The same eyes, darkened, of their astonished ghost !

Deeps, deeps of dreams that can see me,
      As they might see another life,
Tell me, am I not the one you imagine,
      Do you yearn for your own body?

Relinquish, dark moods, the anxious laborings
      That prevail in a soul awake;
Do not seek in yourselves, nor startle in the heavens
      The woe of being a thing of wonder:
Find in the fountain a body delectable.

Prenant à vos regards cette parfaite proie,
Du monstre de s'aimer faites-vous un captif;
Dans les errants filets de vos longs cils de soie
Son gracieux éclat vous retienne pensif;

Mais ne vous flattez pas de le changer d'empire.
Ce cristal est son vrai séjour;
Les efforts mêmes de l'amour!
Ne le sauraient de l'onde extraire qu'il n'expire...

PIRE.
Pire?...
Quelqu'un redit *Pire*...Ô moqueur!
Écho lointaine est prompte à rendre son oracle
De son rire enchanté, le roc brise mon cœur,
Et le silence, par miracle,
Cesse!...parle, renaît, sur la face des eaux...

Pire?...
Pire destin!...Vous le dites, roseaux,
Qui reprîtes des vents ma plainte vagabonde!
Antres, qui me rendez mon âme plus profonde,
Vous renflez de votre ombre une voix qui se meurt...
Vous me le murmurez, ramures!...Ô rumeur
Déchirante, et docile aux souffles sans figure,
Votre or léger s'agite, et joue avec l'augure....
Tout se mêle de moi, brutes divinités!
Mes secrets dans les airs sonnent ébruités,
Le roc rit; l'arbre pleure; et par sa voix charmante,
Je ne puis jusqu'aux cieux que je ne me lamente
D'appartenir sans force à d'éternels attraits!
Hélas! entre les bras qui naissent des forêts,

Entrapping in your gazes this ideal prey,
Make the monster of self-love a captive;
In the straying toils of your silk lashes
Let its glorious grace keep you still pensive;

But never hope that you can change its empire.
That crystal is its true domain:
Even the very strivings of love
Could not draw it from the water except to a dire...

DIRE.
Dire?...
Someone repeats *dire*...O mocker!
Remote Echo is quick to deliver her oracle!
With its magic laughter the rock breaks my heart
And the silence miraculously
Ceases!...talks, is reborn on the face of the waters...

Dire?...
A fate more dire! Such is your word, reeds,
Catching from the winds my wandering lament.
Caverns who give me back my deeper soul,
You swell with your shadow an expiring voice....
Branchage, you rustle it! O rending
Rumor, and pliant to faceless breaths,
Your light gold quivers, and frolics with the augury...
All meddles with me, brute divinities!
My secrets ring noised abroad in the air,
Rock laughs; tree weeps; and through that enchanted voice
Even to the sky itself I cannot but lament
That I am bound resistless to perpetual charms!
Alas! between the limbs that reach out of the woods

Une tendre lueur d'heure ambiguë existe...
Là, d'un reste du jour, se forme un fiancé,
Nu, sur la place pâle où m'attire l'eau triste,
Délicieux démon désirable et glacé!

Te voici, mon doux corps de lune et de rosée,
Ô forme obéissante à mes yeux opposée!
Qu'ils sont beaux, de mes bras les dons vastes et vains!
Mes lentes mains, dans l'or adorable se lassent
D'appeller ce captif que les feuilles enlacent;
Mon cœur jette aux échos l'éclat des noms divins!...

Mais que ta bouche est belle en ce muet blasphème!

Ô semblable!...Et pourtant plus parfait que moi-même,
Éphémère immortel, si clair devant mes yeux,
Pâles membres de perle, et ces cheveux soyeux,
Faut-il qu'à peine aimés, l'ombre les obscurcisse,
Et que la nuit déjà nous divise, ô Narcisse,
Et glisse entre nous deux le fer qui coupe un fruit!
Qu'as-tu?
              Ma plainte même est funeste?...
                                                 Le bruit
Du souffle que j'enseigne à tes lèvres, mon double,
Sur la limpide lame a fait courir un trouble!...
Tu trembles!...Mais ces mots que j'expire à genoux
Ne sont pourtant qu'une âme hésitante entre nous,
Entre ce front si pur et ma lourde mémoire...
Je suis si près de toi que je pourrais te boire,
Ô visage!...Ma soif est un esclave nu...
    Jusqu'à ce temps charmant je m'étais inconnu,
Et je ne savais pas me chérir et me joindre!

A tender gleam of time ambiguous exists....
There, from an ember of day, is fashioned a betrothed,
Naked, on the pale space where the sad lake draws me,
Delicious demon, desirable and icy !

I see you there, my soft body of moon and dew,
Form compliant, still adamant to my wishes !
How beautiful the vast and vain givings of my arms !
My slow hands weary in the adorable gilt
Of enticing that captive bound among the leaves;
My heart flings to the echoes the shock of holy names....

But your mouth is lovely in that dumb blasphemy !

O like !...And yet more perfect than myself,
Ephemeral immortal, so lucid to my gaze,
Pale, pearly limbs, and that silky hair,
Must they, barely loved, be hidden by the dark,
Must night already divide us, Narcissus,
And slide between us a knife halving a fruit !
What ails you?
              Even my complaint is baleful ?
                                    The ruffle
Of the breath I teach your lips, Oh my double,
On the limpid sheet has set coursing a ripple !
You tremble !...Yet these words I breathe out on my knees
Are nothing but a spirit hesitating between us,
Between that so pure brow and my loaded memory....
I am so close to you that I could drink you,
O face !...My thirst is a naked slave....
   Till this bewitching time I never knew myself,
And had no way to cherish and to reach me !

Mais te voir, cher esclave, obéir à la moindre
Des ombres dans mon cœur se fuyant à regret,
Voir sur mon front l'orage et les feux d'un secret,
Voir, ô merveille, voir ! ma bouche nuancée
Trahir...peindre sur l'onde une fleur de pensée,
Et quels événements étinceler dans l'œil !
J'y trouve un tel trésor d'impuissance et d'orgueil,
Que nulle vierge enfant échappée au satyre,
Nulle ! aux fuites habiles, aux chutes sans émoi,
Nulle des nymphes, nulle amie, ne m'attire
Comme tu fais sur l'onde, inépuisable Moi !...

II

Fontaine, ma fontaine, eau froidement présente,
Douce aux purs animaux, aux humains complaisante
Qui d'eux-mêmes tentés suivent au fond la mort,
Tout est songe pour toi, Sœur tranquille du Sort !
À peine en souvenir change-t-il un présage,
Que pareille sans cesse à son fuyant visage,
Sitôt de ton sommeil les cieux te sont ravis !
Mais si pure tu sois des êtres que tu vis,
Onde, sur qui les ans passent comme les nues,
Que de choses pourtant doivent t'être connues,
Astres, roses, saisons, les corps et leurs amours !

Claire, mais si profonde, une nymphe toujours
Effleurée, et vivant de tout ce qui l'approche,
Nourrit quelque sagesse à l'abri de sa roche,
À l'ombre de ce jour qu'elle peint sous les bois.
Elle sait à jamais les choses d'une fois...

Ô présence pensive, eau calme qui recueilles
Tout un sombre trésor de fables et de feuilles,
L'oiseau mort, le fruit mûr, lentement descendus,

But to see you, dear slave, submissive to the finest
Shades evading each other ruefully in my heart,
To see on my brow the storm and fires of a secret,
To see, Oh miracle, see my mouth faintly shaping,
Betray...limn on the water a blossom of thought,
And what events to be, glittering in the eye!
There I find such a store of powerlessness and pride,
That no child virgin escaped from the satyr,
Not one! cunning in flight, unflurried in her falls,
Not one of the nymphs, no friendly one, draws me
As you do on the water, my inexhaustible Self!...

II

Fountain, my fountain, water coldly present,
Sweet to the purely animal, compliant to humans
Who self-tempted pursue death into the depths,
To you all is dream, tranquil Sister of Fate!
Barely does it alter an omen to recollection
When, ceaselessly reflecting its fugitive face,
At once the skies are ravished from your slumber!
But pure as you may be of the beings you have seen,
Water where the years drift by like clouds,
How many things, nevertheless, you must know,
Stars, roses, seasons, bodies and their amours!

Clear, but how deep, a nymph continually
Ruffled, and drawing her life from all that approaches,
Must nurse some wisdom in the shelter of her rock,
In the shadowy light she paints beneath the woods.
She knows for all time things that happened once....

O thinking presence, calm water collecting
A whole dark store of legends and leafage,
The dead bird, the ripe fruit, gradually submerged,

Et les rares lueurs des clairs anneaux perdus.
Tu consommes en toi leur perte solennelle;
Mais, sur la pureté de ta face éternelle,
L'amour passe et périt...

              Quand le feuillage épars
Tremble, commence à fuir, pleure de toutes parts,
Tu vois du sombre amour s'y mêler la tourmente,
L'amant brûlant et dur ceindre la blanche amante,
Vaincre l'âme...Et tu sais selon quelle douceur
Sa main puissante passe à travers l'épaisseur
Des tresses que répand la nuque précieuse,
S'y repose, et se sent forte et mystérieuse;
Elle parle à l'épaule et règne sur la chair.

   Alors les yeux fermés à l'éternel éther
Ne voient plus que le sang qui dore leurs paupières;
Sa pourpre redoutable obscurcit les lumières
D'un couple aux pieds confus qui se mêle, et se ment.
Ils gémissent...La Terre appelle doucement
Ces grands corps chancelants, qui luttent bouche à bouche,
Et qui, du vierge sable osant battre la couche,
Composeront d'amour un monstre qui se meurt...
Leurs souffles ne font plus qu'une heureuse rumeur,
L'âme croit respirer l'âme toute prochaine,
Mais tu sais mieux que moi, vénérable fontaine,
Quels fruits forment toujours ces moments enchantés !

   Car, à peine les cœurs calmes et contentés
D'une ardente alliance expirée en délices,
Des amants détachés tu mires les malices,
Tu vois poindre des jours de mensonges tissus,
Et naître mille maux trop tendrement conçus !

   Bientôt, mon onde sage, infidèle et la même,
Le Temps mène ces fous qui crurent que l'on aime

And the fitful gleamings of bright lost rings.
Within yourself you consume their solemn loss,
But on your purely everlasting face
Love passes and perishes....
                              When the scattered foliage
Quivers, begins to fly, and showers every way,
There you see hidden love mingling its turmoil,
The burning, hard lover girdling his white love,
Vanquishing the will....And you know how gently
His powerful hand passes through all the density
Of tresses streaming from the precious nape,
Resting there, feeling its own mystery and force;
It speaks to the shoulder and rules over the flesh.
    Then the eyes shut to the eternal ether
Are blind to all but the blood glazing their lids;
That redoubtable crimson darkens the seeing
Of a couple with feet entwined, mixed in a mutual lie.
They groan....The Earth tenderly draws down
The heavy staggering bodies, wrestling mouth to mouth,
And they, daring to press the couch of virgin sand,
Will make a monster of love, but a mortal one....
Now their breaths are no more than a blissful murmur,
Soul feels it breathes in a neighboring soul,
But better than I, venerable fountain, you know
What fruits these enchanted moments always form!
    For no sooner are their hearts calmed and satisfied
From an ardent union dying away in raptures,
Than you mirror the spites of the detached lovers,
You see the days woven of lies about to dawn,
And births of a thousand ills too tenderly begot!
    Soon, my wise pool, faithless and constant,
Time brings back the fools who thought they could love

Redire à tes roseaux de plus profonds soupirs !
Vers toi, leurs tristes pas suivent leurs souvenirs...
   Sur tes bords, accablés d'ombres et de faiblesse,
Tout ébloui d'un ciel dont la beauté les blesse
Tant il garde l'éclat de leurs jours les plus beaux,
Ils vont des biens perdus trouver tous les tombeaux...
« Cette place dans l'ombre était tranquille et nôtre ! »
« L'autre aimait ce cyprès, se dit le cœur de l'autre »,
« Et d'ici, nous goûtions le souffle de la mer ! »
Hélas ! la rose même est amère dans l'air...
Moins amers les parfums des suprêmes fumées
Qu'abandonnent au vent les feuilles consumées !...
   Ils respirent ce vent, marchent sans le savoir,
Foulent aux pieds le temps d'un jour de désespoir...
Ô marche lente, prompte, et pareille aux pensées
Qui parlent tour à tour aux têtes insensées !
La caresse et le meurtre hésitent dans leurs mains,
Leur cœur, qui croit se rompre au détour des chemins,
Lutte, et retient à soi son espérance étreinte.
Mais leurs esprits perdus courent ce labyrinthe
Où s'égare celui qui maudit le soleil !
Leur folle solitude, à l'égal du sommeil,
Peuple et trompe l'absence ; et leur secrète oreille
Partout place une voix qui n'a point de pareille.
Rien ne peut dissiper leurs songes absolus ;
Le soleil ne peut rien contre ce qui n'est plus !
Mais s'ils traînent dans l'or leurs yeux secs et funèbres,
Ils se sentent des pleurs défendre leurs ténèbres
Plus chères à jamais que tous les feux du jour !
Et dans ce corps caché tout marqué de l'amour
Que porte amèrement l'âme qui fut heureuse,
Brûle un secret baiser qui la rend furieuse...

To re-echo ever deeper sighs to your reeds!
Towards you their mournful steps follow their memories...
    On your verges, weighted down with glooms and weakness,
Dazzled blind by a sky whose beauty wounds them,
For it glitters still as bright as their happiest days,
They will discover all the tombs of blessings lost....
"This nook in the shade was calm, and our own!"
"The other loved this cypress," says the heart of each.
"And from here we could savor the breath of the sea!"
Alas, even the rose is bitter on the air....
Less bitter are the scents of the final fumes
Which the burnt leaves surrender to the winds!...
    They breathe this wind, walking unawares,
Treading underfoot a whole despairing day....
How slow, how abrupt the step, like the thoughts
That speak by turns in their maddened brains!
The hands hesitate between murder and a caress,
Their hearts, ready to break at a turn in the path,
Wrestle, and hold on to a clinging hope.
But their minds distraught course through the labyrinth
Where he who curses the sun loses himself!
Their crazed loneliness, like a dreaming sleep,
Peoples and cheats emptiness, their secret ear
Everywhere fixes a voice that has no fellow.
Nothing can dispel their all-powerful dreams;
The sun cannot prevail over what is no more!
But, if they scan the gold with dry, funereal eyes,
They feel tears within protecting that inner gloom
Forever dearer than all the day's fires!
And in that body's hidden places, love-bruised,
Still bitterly borne by a soul once happy,
There burns a secret kiss that maddens....

Mais moi, Narcisse aimé, je ne suis curieux
       Que de ma seule essence;
Tout autre n'a pour moi qu'un cœur mystérieux,
       Tout autre n'est qu'absence.
Ô mon bien souverain, cher corps, je n'ai que toi !
Le plus beau des mortels ne peut chérir que soi. . .
    Douce et dorée, est-il une idole plus sainte,
De toute une forêt qui se consume, ceinte,
Et sise dans l'azur vivant par tant d'oiseaux?
Est-il don plus divin de la faveur des eaux,
Et d'un jour qui se meurt plus adorable usage
Que de rendre à mes yeux l'honneur de mon visage?
Naisse donc entre nous que la lumière unit
De grâce et de silence un échange infini !

    Je vous salue, enfant de mon âme et de l'onde,
Cher trésor d'un miroir qui partage le monde !
Ma tendresse y vient boire, et s'enivre de voir
Un désir sur soi-même essayer son pouvoir !

    Ô qu'à tous mes souhaits, que vous êtes semblable !
Mais la fragilité vous fait inviolable,
Vous n'êtes que lumière, adorable moitié
D'une amour trop pareille à la faible amitié !

    Hélas ! la nymphe même a séparé nos charmes !
Puis-je espérer de toi que de vaines alarmes?
Qu'ils sont doux les périls que nous pourrions choisir !
Se surprendre soi-même et soi-même saisir,
Nos mains s'entremêler, nos maux s'entre-détruire,
Nos silences longtemps de leurs songes s'instruire,
La même nuit en pleurs confondre nos yeux clos,
Et nos bras refermés sur les mêmes sanglots
Étreindre un même cœur, d'amour prêt à se fondre. . .
    Quitte enfin le silence, ose enfin me répondre,

But I, loved Narcissus, my only quest
    Is for my own sole essence.
Any other's heart for me is mere mystery,
    Another is mere absence.
O my sovereign boon, dear body, all I have!
The loveliest mortal can love only himself....
    Sweetly gilded, is there an idol more holy,
By an entire self-consuming forest framed,
And set against a blue alive with so many birds?
Is there gift more divine, by the water's favor,
A more adorable purpose for a day dying
Than to honor my eyes with the tribute of my face?
So let there be, between us whom light makes one,
An infinite interchange of silence and grace!
    I greet you, child of my soul and of the wave,
Dear treasure of a mirror dividing the universe!
My tenderness comes to be quenched, wild to see
How a desire can prove its power upon itself!
    Ah, how one you are with all my wishes!
But made inviolable by fragility,
You are merest light, adorable moiety
Of a love all too akin to a pale friendship!
    Alas, the very nymph has cleft our charms apart!
What can I hope from you but shadows of fright?
How sweet the risks are, could we but choose!
To take unawares and seize on one's very self,
With intermingling hands soothing each other's ills,
Our long silences learning each other's dreams,
The same night of tears confounding our closed eyes,
And our locked arms over the same griefs
Pressing the same heart, ready to melt with love....
    Quit this silence, dare finally to respond,

Bel et cruel Narcisse, inaccessible enfant,
Tout orné de mes biens que la nymphe défend...

III

...Ce corps si pur, sait-il qu'il me puisse séduire?
De quelle profondeur songes-tu de m'instruire,
Habitant de l'abîme, hôte si spécieux
D'un ciel sombre ici-bas précipité des cieux?...
　　Ô le frais ornement de ma triste tendance
Qu'un sourire si proche, et plein de confidence,
Et qui prête à ma lèvre une ombre de danger
Jusqu'à me faire craindre un désir étranger!
Quel souffle vient à l'onde offrir ta froide rose!...
J'aime...J'aime!...Et qui donc peut aimer autre chose
Que soi-même?...
　　　　　　　　Toi seul, ô mon corps, mon cher corps,
Je t'aime, unique objet qui me défends des morts!
. . . .

Formons, toi sur ma lèvre, et moi, dans mon silence,
Une prière aux dieux qu'émus de tant d'amour
Sur sa pente de pourpre ils arrêtent le jour!...
Faites, Maîtres heureux, Pères des justes fraudes,
Dites qu'une lueur de rose ou d'émeraudes
Que des songes du soir votre sceptre reprit,
Pure, et toute pareille au plus pur de l'esprit,
Attende, au sein des cieux, que tu vives et veuilles,
Près de moi, mon amour, choisir un lit de feuilles,
Sortir tremblant du flanc de la nymphe au cœur froid,
Et sans quitter mes yeux, sans cesser d'être moi,
Tendre ta forme fraîche, et cette claire écorce...
Oh! te saisir enfin!...Prendre ce calme torse

Lovely and cruel Narcissus, child inaccessible,
Decked out with my favors that the nymph forbids....

III

...A body thus pure, can it know it charms me?
Out of what deeps do you think to teach me,
Abyss-haunter, specious denizen
Of a dark heaven flung down here from the heavens?...
　　Ah, the cool flourish on my sadness outstretched,
That smile so close and full of confidence,
Lending my lip a velleity of risk,
Making me even afraid of an alien desire!
What breath rises offering your cold rose to the surface?
I love, I love. And who can love any other
Than himself?...
　　　　　　You only, body mine, my dear body
I love, the one alone who shields me from the dead!

.　　ˋ　　.　　.　　.　　.　　.　　.　　.

Let us shape, you on my lip, I on my silence,
A prayer to the gods that, moved by such love,
They make the day stand still on its purple slope!...
Lords of happiness, Fathers of just connivance,
Decree that a gleam of rose or emerald
Reflected in your wand by evening's dreams,
Pure semblance of the purest reach of the mind,
Be stayed in the sky's breast, until you live and deign
To choose, close by me, my love, a bed of leaves.
Rise trembling from the flank of the cold-hearted nymph,
And never quitting my eyes, nor ceasing to be me,
Offer your cool form, and that radiant skin....
Ah, to seize you at last! Grip that calm torso

Plus pur que d'une femme et non formé de fruits...
Mais, d'une pierre simple est le temple où je suis,
Où je vis...Car je vis sur tes lèvres avares!...
    Ô mon corps, mon cher corps, temple qui me sépares
De ma divinité, je voudrais apaiser
Votre bouche...Et bientôt, je briserais, baiser,
Ce peu qui nous défend de l'extrême existence,
Cette tremblante, frêle, et pieuse distance
Entre moi-même et l'onde, et mon âme, et les dieux!...
    Adieu...Sens-tu frémir mille flottants adieux?
Bientôt va frissonner le désordre des ombres!
L'arbre aveugle vers l'arbre étend ses membres sombres,
Et cherche affreusement l'arbre qui disparaît...
Mon âme ainsi se perd dans sa propre forêt,
Où la puissance échappe à ses formes suprêmes...
L'âme, l'âme aux yeux noirs, touche aux ténèbres mêmes,
Elle se fait immense et ne rencontre rien...
Entre la mort et soi, quel regard est le sien!

    Dieux! de l'auguste jour, le pâle et tendre reste
Va des jours consumés joindre le sort funeste;
Il s'abîme aux enfers du profond souvenir!
Hélas! corps misérable, il est temps de s'unir...
Penche-toi...Baise-toi. Tremble de tout ton être!
L'insaisissable amour que tu me vins promettre
Passe, et dans un frisson, brise Narcisse, et fuit...

Purer than a woman's and formed without fruits. . . .
But of a single stone is the temple I am
And inhabit. . . .For I live on your miserly lips! . . .
    Oh body of mine, dear body, temple dividing
Me from my god, I long to bring peace
To your mouth. . . .And soon let me break, kiss,
This frail defense against uttermost being,
This quivering, fragile and holy distance
Between me and the surface, my soul, and the gods! . . .
    Farewell. . .You hear a thousand floating farewells?
Soon the confusion of shades will begin to shiver,
Blind tree stretches to tree its somber limbs,
Fearfully groping for the vanishing tree.
My soul alike dislimns in its own forest,
Where power now eludes its ultimate shapes. . . .
The soul, the dark-eyed soul, touches on pure gloom.
Larger and larger it grows, and encounters nothing. . . .
Between death and the self, what a look is there!

    Gods! The pale and tender remnant of the sublime day
Approaches the drear lot of days consumed,
Sinks to the underworld of memory's deeps!
Ah miserable body, be one without delay. . . .
Lean, lean. . . .And kiss. Quiver with all your being!
The unseizable love you came promising me
Passes, and in a shudder breaks Narcissus, and flees. . . .

La Pythie

À Pierre Louÿs

Hæc effata silet; pallor simul occupat ora.
Virgile, *Æn.*, IV

La Pythie exhalant la flamme
De naseaux durcis par l'encens,
Haletante, ivre, hurle!...l'âme
Affreuse, et les flancs mugissants!
Pâle, profondément mordue,
Et la prunelle suspendue
Au point le plus haut de l'horreur,
Le regard qui manque à son masque
S'arrache vivant à la vasque,
À la fumée, à la fureur!

Sur le mur, son ombre démente
Où domine un démon majeur,
Parmi l'odorante tourmente
Prodigue un fantôme nageur,
De qui la transe colossale,
Rompant les aplombs de la salle,
Si la folle tarde à hennir,
Mime de noirs enthousiasmes,
Hâte les dieux, presse les spasmes
De s'achever dans l'avenir!

Cette martyre en sueurs froides,
Ses doigts sur ses doigts se crispant,
Vocifère entre les ruades

The Pythoness

To Pierre Louÿs

*She had spoken, and was silent; at once
a pallor came over her face.*
Virgil, *Aeneid* IV.

The Pythoness exhaling flame
From nostrils hardened by the incense,
Gasping, crazed, howls !. . .Her soul
Fearful, her flanks roaring !
Pale, corroded to her depths,
The pupil of her eye hung
On the highest point of horror,
The gaze vacant from her mask
Is wrenched away alive from the font,
From the fury, from the smoke !

On the wall her demented shadow
A giant daemon dominates,
Among the whirling eddies of scent
Lavishes a phantom swimmer
In whom the enormous trance,
Rending the chamber out of plumb,
If she holds back her mad whinnying,
Mimics a black enthusiasm,
Hurrying the gods, jostling the spasm
To achieve itself in the future !

A martyr in her icy sweats,
Her fingers wrenching at her fingers,
She vociferates at each kick

D'un trépied qu'étrangle un serpent:
—Ah! maudite!...Quels maux je souffre!
Toute ma nature est un gouffre!
Hélas! Entr'ouverte aux esprits,
J'ai perdu mon propre mystère!...
Une Intelligence adultère
Exerce un corps qu'elle a compris!

Don cruel! Maître immonde, cesse
Vite, vite, ô divin ferment,
De feindre une vaine grossesse
Dans ce pur ventre sans amant!
Fais finir cette horrible scène!
Vois de tout mon corps l'arc obscène
Tendre à se rompre pour darder,
Comme son trait le plus infâme,
Implacablement au ciel l'âme
Que mon sein ne peut plus garder!

Qui me parle, à ma place même?
Quel écho me répond: Tu mens!
Qui m'illumine?...Qui blasphème?
Et qui, de ces mots écumants,
Dont les éclats hachent ma langue,
La fait brandir une harangue
Brisant la bave et les cheveux
Que mâche et trame le désordre
D'une bouche qui veut se mordre
Et se reprendre ses aveux?

Dieu! Je ne me connais de crime
Que d'avoir à peine vécu!...

Of the snake-knotted tripod:
—Oh I am cursed!...The agony!
My whole being is an abyss.
Woe! Laid open to the spirits,
I have lost my own mystery!
An adulterous Intelligence
Has found me out and plies my body!

Cruel gift! Unclean mastery, cease,
O holy ferment, quickly, quickly,
From simulating a pregnant void
In this womb pure of any lover!
Put an end to the hideous scene!
See how my body's squalid bow
Is stretched to breaking point to draw
And shoot, as its wickedest arrow,
Implacably skywards the soul
My own breast can no longer hold!

Who speaks to me in place of me?
What echo is it answers: Liar!
Who illuminates?...Who blasphemes?
And who, with this slavering speech
Whose outbreaks hack my very tongue,
Makes it brandish a harangue
To rend through the saliva and hair
Mashed and twisted by the riot
Of a mouth that would bite itself,
Swallowing back its own utterance?

Gods, I am guiltless of any crime
Except—to have scarcely lived!

Mais si tu me prends pour victime
Et sur l'autel d'un corps vaincu
Si tu courbes un monstre, tue
Ce monstre, et la bête abattue,
Le col tranché, le chef produit
Par les crins qui tirent les tempes,
Que cette plus pâle des lampes
Saisisse de marbre la nuit !

Alors, par cette vagabonde
Morte, errante, et lune à jamais,
Soit l'eau des mers surprise, et l'onde
Astreinte à d'éternels sommets !
Que soient les humains faits statues,
Les cœurs figés, les âmes tues,
Et par les glaces de mon œil,
Puisse un peuple de leurs paroles
Durcir en un peuple d'idoles
Muet de sottise et d'orgueil !

Eh ! Quoi !...Devenir la vipère
Dont tout le ressort de frissons
Surprend la chair que désespère
Sa multitude de tronçons !...
Reprendre une lutte insensée !...
Tourne donc plutôt ta pensée
Vers la joie enfuie, et reviens,
Ô mémoire, à cette magie
Qui ne tirait son énergie
D'autres arcanes que des tiens !

Mon cher corps...Forme préférée,
Fraîcheur par qui ne fut jamais

But if you choose me for your victim,
And on the vanquished body's altar
If you lay out a monster, kill
That monster, and the slaughtered beast
Beheaded, and the head held up
By its temple-dragging hair,
Let that ghastliest of all lamps
Transfix darkness itself to marble!

Then let that vagabond, that waif,
Dead and forever to wander moon,
Astonish the sea's waters, compel
Each wave to an everlasting summit!
Let humankind be turned to statues,
Hearts transfixed and souls struck dumb,
And may the freezings of my eye
Harden a people from their babble
Into a population of idols
Dumb with stupidity and pride!

What!...So I am to be the viper
Whose whole sprung system of shivers
Shocks the flesh made desperate by
The multiplicity of its sections!...
Begin once again a meaningless struggle?
Better to turn back my mind
On vanished happiness, and restore,
Memory, that other magic
Drawing all its energy
From no mystery but yours.

Precious body...Form of my choice,
Coolness that never gave itself

Aphrodite désaltérée,
Intacte nuit, tendres sommets,
Et vos partages indicibles
D'une argile en îles sensibles,
Douce matière de mon sort,
Quelle alliance nous vécûmes,
Avant que le don des écumes
Ait fait de toi ce corps de mort !

Toi, mon épaule, où l'or se joue
D'une fontaine de noirceur,
J'aimais de te joindre ma joue
Fondue à sa même douceur !...
Ou, soulevée à mes narines,
Ouverte aux distances marines,
Les mains pleines de seins vivants,
Entre mes bras aux belles anses
Mon abîme a bu les immenses
Profondeurs qu'apportent les vents !

Hélas ! ô roses, toute lyre
Contient la modulation !
Un soir, de mon triste délire
Parut la constellation !
Le temple se change dans l'antre,
Et l'ouragan des songes entre
Au même ciel qui fut si beau !
Il faut gémir, il faut atteindre
Je ne sais quelle extase, et ceindre
Ma chevelure d'un lambeau !

Ils m'ont connue aux bleus stigmates
Apparus sur ma pauvre peau;

To quench an Aphrodite's thirst,
Night untouched, summits of softness,
With your unsayable dividings
Of clay into isles of feelings,
Sweet substance of my fate,
How we lived in our alliance
Until you were gifted with these foamings
That turned you to a body of death!

You, my shoulder, where gold frolics
Within a fountain pool of darkness,
I loved to press my cheek on you,
Melting it into the same softness. . . .
Or, lifted breathing to my nostrils,
Laid wide to the sea's expanses,
My hands filled with my living breasts
Between my arms of lovely inlets,
My abyss drew in the immense
Depths carried to it by the winds!

Alas, oh roses, every lyre
Is pent with modulations!
One evening there dawned the dire
Star-cluster of my deliriums!
The temple changes to a cave,
And the hurricane of dreams
Invades the same once-shining heaven!
Now must begin the groans to attain
Unspeakable ecstasy, now I must
Tie my hair in a rag of flesh!

They knew me by the blue bruises
Emerging on my hapless skin:

Ils m'assoupirent d'aromates
Laineux et doux comme un troupeau;
Ils ont, pour vivant amulette,
Touché ma gorge qui halète
Sous les ornements vipérins;
Étourdie, ivre d'empyreumes,
Ils m'ont, au murmure des neumes,
Rendu des honneurs souterrains.

Qu'ai-je donc fait qui me condamne
Pure, à ces rites odieux?
Une sombre carcasse d'âne
Eût bien servi de ruche aux dieux!
Mais une vierge consacrée,
Une conque neuve et nacrée
Ne doit à la divinité
Que sacrifice et que silence,
Et cette intime violence
Que se fait la virginité!

Pourquoi, Puissance Créatrice,
Auteur du mystère animal,
Dans cette vierge pour matrice,
Semer les merveilles du mal!
Sont-ce les dons que tu m'accordes?
Crois-tu, quand se brisent les cordes
Que le son jaillisse plus beau?
Ton plectre a frappé sur mon torse,
Mais tu ne lui laisses la force
Que de sonner comme un tombeau!

Sois clémente, sois sans oracles!
Et de tes merveilleuses mains,

They dulled me with aromatics
Woolly and soft as flocks of sheep;
They, as a live amulet,
Fingered my palpitating throat
Under its viperine ornaments;
Stunned and drunk with charring fumes,
They, with ritual choric moans,
Paid me subterranean honors.

What have I done to be condemned
Pure, to abominable rites?
The gloom within a donkey's carcase
As fit a place for the gods to swarm!
But a dedicated virgin,
A new shell all mother-of-pearl,
What it may owe the divinity
Can only be offerings and silence
—Besides that inner violence
Virginity must do to itself!

Why, Creative Power and maker
Of the animal mystery,
Choose this virgin for a matrix
To breed miracles of evil?
Are these the gifts you grant to me?
You think that when the strings are snapped
They release a jet of finer sound?
My torso is stricken by your plectrum,
But you leave it with no more strength
Than to ring hollow as a tomb!

Be merciful, no oracles!
And, with your marvelous hands

171

Change en caresses les miracles,
Retiens les présents surhumains !
C'est en vain que tu communiques
À nos faibles tiges, d'uniques
Commotions de ta splendeur !
L'eau tranquille est plus transparente
Que toute tempête parente
D'une confuse profondeur !

Va, la lumière la divine
N'est pas l'épouvantable éclair
Qui nous devance et nous devine
Comme un songe cruel et clair !
Il éclate !. . .Il va nous instruire !. . .
Non !. . .La solitude vient luire
Dans la plaie immense des airs
Où nulle pâle architecture,
Mais la déchirante rupture
Nous imprime de purs déserts !

N'allez donc, mains universelles,
Tirer de mon front orageux
Quelques suprêmes étincelles !
Les hasards font les mêmes jeux !
Le passé, l'avenir sont frères
Et par leurs visages contraires
Une seule tête pâlit
De ne voir où qu'elle regarde
Qu'une même absence hagarde
D'îles plus belles que l'oubli.

Noirs témoins de tant de lumières
Ne cherchez plus. . .Pleurez, mes yeux !. . .

Change prodigies into caresses,
Hold back all superhuman gifts !
Only in vain can you entrust
Our feeble stems with vortices
Unprecedented of your splendor !
Still water is far clearer
Than all the storms that are ancestors
To unfathomable confusion !

Light, you know, light the divine
Is a long way from the lightning terror
Outrunning and seeing us through
Like a clear and cruel nightmare !
It explodes !. . .Is about to reveal !
But no. . .Only solitude gleams
In the immense wound of the air
Where no ghostly architecture,
Nothing but rending and rupture
Prints pure desert on our minds !

So do not, universal hands,
Extract from my brow of storms
A few uttermost lightning sparks !
Chance can play at the same games !
The past, the future are twins,
And, through their opposing faces
A solitary head grows pale
To see wherever she gazes, nothing
But a same bewildered absence
Of lovelier isles than oblivion.

Black witnesses of so many stars,
My eyes, search no further. . . .Weep !

Ô pleurs dont les sources premières
Sont trop profondes dans les cieux !...
Jamais plus amère demande !...
Mais la prunelle la plus grande
De ténèbres se doit nourrir !...
Tenant notre race atterrée,
La distance désespérée
Nous laisse le temps de mourir !

Entends, mon âme, entends ces fleuves !
Quelles cavernes sont ici ?
Est-ce mon sang ?... Sont-ce les neuves
Rumeurs des ondes sans merci ?
Mes secrets sonnent leurs aurores !
Tristes airains, tempes sonores,
Que dites-vous de l'avenir !
Frappez, frappez, dans une roche,
Abattez l'heure la plus proche...
Mes deux natures vont s'unir !

Ô formidablement gravie,
Et sur d'effrayants échelons,
Je sens dans l'arbre de ma vie
La mort monter de mes talons !
Le long de ma ligne frileuse,
Le doigt mouillé de la fileuse
Trace une atroce volonté !
Et par sanglots grimpe la crise
Jusque dans ma nuque où se brise
Une cime de volupté !

Ah ! brise les portes vivantes !
Fais craquer les vains scellements,

O tears, whose ultimate fountains
Are hidden in heavens far too deep !...
Never was a bitterer quest !...
But the pupil of the hugest eye
Can feed only on darknesses !...
Holding all our kind earthbound,
Distance, beyond all hope,
Just allows us time to die !

But listen, my soul, listen to
The torrents. What caverns are these?
Is it my blood?...Are these new
Thunderings of pitiless waves?
My hidden places sound their dawns.
Doleful gongs, booming temples,
Of what's to come what can you tell?
Strike, strike, into a rock,
Shoot, bring down this hour in flight....
Soon my two beings will be one !

Oh, formidably climbed,
Rung upon terrifying rung,
I can feel in my tree of life
Death, mounting from my heels !
Along my shuddering life-line
The spinner with her moistened finger
Traces an atrocious will !
And sob by sob the climbing crisis
Rises to my nape where it breaks
Into a peak of pure bliss !

Ah, let the live doors burst open !
Let all the useless fastenings crack,

Épais troupeau des épouvantes,
Hérissé d'étincellements !
Surgis des étables funèbres
Où te nourrissaient mes ténèbres
De leur fabuleuse foison !
Bondis, de rêves trop repue,
Ô horde épineuse et crépue,
Et viens fumer dans l'or, Toison !

*

Telle, toujours plus tourmentée,
Déraisonne, râle et rugit
La prophétesse fomentée
Par les souffles de l'or rougi.
Mais enfin le ciel se déclare !
L'oreille du pontife hilare
S'aventure dans le futur :
Une attente sainte la penche,
Car une voix nouvelle et blanche
Échappe de ce corps impur.

*

Honneur des Hommes, Saint LANGAGE,
Discours prophétique et paré,
Belles chaînes en qui s'engage
Le dieu dans la chair égaré,
Illumination, largesse !
Voici parler une Sagesse
Et sonner cette auguste Voix
Qui se connaît quand elle sonne
N'être plus la voix de personne
Tant que des ondes et des bois !

Muddled herd of thronging panics,
Your hides bristling with lightning sparks,
Surge from the funereal stables
Where my darknesses nourished you
With their fabulous abundance !
Replete with dreams, gambol, skip,
Oh prickly and crisp-wooled crew,
And rise, steaming...a fleece, in gold !

*

Thus, in ever-increasing torment,
With throat rattling, booms and raves
The prophetess, fomented still
By the reddening gold's hot breaths.
But now at last heaven speaks its will !
The ear of the jubilant archpriest
Listens, exploring into the future:
She is borne over by a holy
Suspense, for now a new and snowy
Voice breaks from that impure body.

*

Honor of Mankind, Sacred LANGUAGE,
Ordered and prophetic speech,
Chains of beauty that enwind
The god bewildered in the flesh,
Illumination, and largess !
Now a Wisdom makes utterance,
And rings out in that sovereign voice
Which when it rings can only know
It is no longer anyone's
So much as the woods' and the waters' voice !

Le Sylphe

Ni vu ni connu
Je suis le parfum
Vivant et défunt
Dans le vent venu !

Ni vu ni connu,
Hasard ou génie?
À peine venu
La tâche est finie !

Ni lu ni compris?
Aux meilleurs esprits
Que d'erreurs promises !

Ni vu ni connu,
Le temps d'un sein nu
Entre deux chemises !

The Sylph

Nor seen nor known
I am the perfume
Alive, dead and gone
In the wind as it comes!

Nor seen nor known,
Genius or chance?
The moment I'm come
The task is done!

Nor read, nor divined?
To the keenest minds
What hints of illusions!

Nor seen nor known,
A bare breast glimpsed
Between gown and gown!

L'Insinuant

Ô Courbes, méandre,
Secrets du menteur,
Est-il art plus tendre
Que cette lenteur?

Je sais où je vais,
Je t'y veux conduire,
Mon dessein mauvais
N'est pas de te nuire...

(Quoique souriante
En pleine fierté,
Tant de liberté
La désoriente!)

Ô Courbes, méandre,
Secrets du menteur,
Je veux faire attendre
Le mot le plus tendre.

The Sly One

O Windings, meanders,
Wiles of the deceiver,
What art more tender
Than this in its slowness?

I know where I go,
To where I will take you,
My wicked designings
Will do you no harm.....

(Smile though she may
In the fullness of pride,
So much freedom
Sets her wits astray!)

O Windings, meanders,
Wiles of the deceiver,
I must hold in suspense
The word the most tender.

La Fausse Morte

Humblement, tendrement, sur le tombeau charmant,
    Sur l'insensible monument,
Que d'ombres, d'abandons, et d'amour prodiguée,
    Forme ta grâce fatiguée,
Je meurs, je meurs sur toi, je tombe et je m'abats,
Mais à peine abattu sur le sépulcre bas,
Dont la close étendue aux cendres me convie,
Cette morte apparente, en qui revient la vie,
Frémit, rouvre les yeux, m'illumine et me mord,
Et m'arrache toujours une nouvelle mort
    Plus précieuse que la vie.

She Only Seems Dead

Humbly, tenderly, upon the charming tomb,
    Unfeeling monument
Made of shadows, surrenders and lavishments of love,
    Shaped by your weary grace,
I am dying, dying over you, I fall, abandoned,
But no sooner do I sink on the deep sepulcher
Whose confined space urges me to ashes,
Than she, the seemingly dead, in whom life returns,
Shivers, opens her eyes, fills me with light, and bites me,
And continues to wrench from me an ever newer death
    More precious than life itself.

Ébauche d'un serpent

À Henri Ghéon

Parmi l'arbre, la brise berce
La vipère que je vêtis;
Un sourire, que la dent perce
Et qu'elle éclaire d'appétits,
Sur le Jardin se risque et rôde,
Et mon triangle d'émeraude
Tire sa langue à double fil...
Bête je suis, mais bête aiguë,
De qui le venin quoique vil
Laisse loin la sage ciguë !

Suave est ce temps de plaisance !
Tremblez, mortels ! Je suis bien fort
Quand jamais à ma suffisance,
Je bâille à briser le ressort !
La splendeur de l'azur aiguise
Cette guivre qui me déguise
D'animale simplicité;
Venez à moi, race étourdie !
Je suis debout et dégourdie,
Pareille à la nécessité !

Soleil, soleil !...Faute écaltante !
Toi qui masques la mort, Soleil,
Sous l'azur et l'or d'une tente
Où les fleurs tiennent leur conseil;
Par d'impénétrables délices,
Toi, le plus fier de mes complices,

Silhouette of a Serpent

To Henri Ghéon

In the tree's midst, the breeze rocks
The viper whose vesture I put on;
A smile, which the tooth pricks
Lighting it up with appetites,
Ventures and roves over the Garden.
And my triangle of emerald
Juts its tongue with double file... .
Beast I am, but a sharp one,
Whose venom however vile
Can far out-vie the hemlock's wisdom!

How suave is this leisurely weather!
Mortals, beware! I'm in full vigor
When, never yawning wide enough,
My jaw gapes fit to break the lock!
The blue sky in its splendor sharpens
This wyvern who disguises me
In animal simplicity;
Come unto me, ye thoughtless ones.
I am erect and all-alert,
Exactly like necessity!

Sun!...Oh Sun, you glaring error!
You who are death's own lifemask, Sun,
Under the or and azure pavilion
That tents the flowers holding council;
By way of delights impenetrable
You, my proudest accomplice,

Et de mes pièges le plus haut,
Tu gardes les cœurs de connaître
Que l'univers n'est qu'un défaut
Dans la pureté du Non-être !

Grand Soleil, qui sonnes l'éveil
À l'être, et de feux l'accompagnes,
Toi qui l'enfermes d'un sommeil
Trompeusement peint de campagnes,
Fauteur des fantômes joyeux
Qui rendent sujette des yeux
La présence obscure de l'âme,
Toujours le mensonge m'a plu
Que tu répands sur l'absolu,
Ô roi des ombres fait de flamme !

Verse-moi ta brute chaleur,
Où vient ma paresse glacée
Rêvasser de quelque malheur
Selon ma nature enlacée...
Ce lieu charmant qui vit la chair
Choir et se joindre m'est très cher !
Ma fureur, ici, se fait mûre;
Je la conseille et la recuis,
Je m'écoute, et dans mes circuits,
Ma méditation murmure...

Ô Vanité ! Cause Première !
Celui qui règne dans les Cieux,
D'une voix qui fut la lumière
Ouvrit l'univers spacieux.
Comme las de son pur spectacle,

And loftiest of all my snares,
You protect all hearts from knowing
That the universe is merely a blot
On the pure void of Non-being!

Great Sun, sounding the reveille
To being, and clothing it with fire,
You who fence it in a slumber
Painted about with cheating landscapes,
Fomenter of the gay phantoms
Who enslave to the eye's seeing
The uncertain presence of the soul,
I have always enjoyed the lie
You throw across the absolute,
O king of shadows made of flame!

Pour me out your brutish heat,
Where my icy idleness
May daydream of some evil or other
Appropriate to my knotted being....
How dear to me these charming purlieus
That saw flesh fall and join together!
Here my fury grows mature,
I counsel it and mull it over,
I listen to me, and in my coils
Hear my meditations murmur....

O Vanity! Very First Cause!
The Other who reigns in the Heavens,
With the word that was light itself
Opened the spacious universe.
As though bored with the pure theater

Dieu lui-même a rompu l'obstacle
De sa parfaite éternité;
Il se fit Celui qui dissipe
En conséquences, son Principe,
En étoiles, son Unité.

Cieux, son erreur ! Temps, sa ruine !
Et l'abîme animal, béant !. . .
Quelle chute dans l'origine
Étincelle au lieu de néant !. . .
Mais, le premier mot de son Verbe,
moi !. . .Des astres le plus superbe
Qu'ait parlés le fou créateur,
Je suis !. . .Je serai !. . .J'illumine
La diminution divine
De tous les feux du Séducteur !

Objet radieux de ma haine,
Vous que j'aimais éperdument,
Vous qui dûtes de la géhenne
Donner l'empire à cet amant,
Regardez-vous dans ma ténèbre !
Devant votre image funèbre,
Orgueil de mon sombre miroir,
Si profond fut votre malaise
Que votre souffle sur la glaise
Fut un soupir de désespoir !

En vain, Vous avez, dans la fange,
Pétri de faciles enfants,
Qui de Vos actes triomphants
Tout le jour Vous fissent louange !

Of Self, God broke the barrier
Of his perfect eternity:
He became He who fritters away
His Primal Cause in consequences,
And in stars his Unity.

Skies, his blunder! Time, his undoing!
And the animal abyss agape!
What a collapse into origin,
Glitters in place of total void!...
But the first syllable of his Word
Was me!...The proudest of the stars
Uttered by the besotted maker,
I am!...Shall be!...I illuminate
How divinity was diminished
By all the fires of the Seducer!

Radiant target of my hate
Whom I once desperately loved,
You who had to give dominion
Over Gehenna to this your lover,
See yourself in my mirroring gloom!
Faced with your own funereal image,
Glory of my darkling glass,
So profound was your distress
That when you breathed over the clay
It was a sign of hopelessness!

All in vain You, out of the mud,
Molded these infants, facile toys,
So that Your triumphant deeds
Be lauded day-long by their praise!

Sitôt pétris, sitôt soufflés,
Maître Serpent les a sifflés,
Les beaux enfants que Vous créâtes !
Holà ! dit-il, nouveaux venus !
Vous êtes des hommes tout nus,
Ô bêtes blanches et béates !

À la ressemblance exécrée,
Vous fûtes faits, et je vous hais !
Comme je hais le Nom qui crée
Tant de prodiges imparfaits !
Je suis Celui qui modifie,
Je retouche au cœur qui s'y fie,
D'un doigt sûr et mystérieux !...
Nous changerons ces molles œuvres,
Et ces évasives couleuvres
En des reptiles furieux !

Mon Innombrable Intelligence
Touche dans l'âme des humains
Un instrument de ma vengeance
Qui fut assemblé de tes mains !
Et ta Paternité voilée,
Quoique, dans sa chambre étoilée,
Elle n'accueille que l'encens,
Toutefois l'excès de mes charmes
Pourra de lointaines alarmes
Troubler ses desseins tout-puissants !

Je vais, je viens, je glisse, plonge,
Je disparais dans un cœur pur !
Fut-il jamais de sein si dur

No sooner molded and set to breathe
Than Snake applauded with a hiss
The pretty infants You had made!
Hi there, said I, you new arrivals,
You know you are human, and stark naked,
Oh snow-white sanctimonious beasts!

In the likeness of the accursed
You were made, and you I hate
As I hate the Name that creates
All these imperfect prodigies!
I am He who modifies,
I re-touch the incautious heart
With a sure, mysterious finger!...
We'll transform these tender products,
These self-effacing little snakes
Into reptiles of pure fury!

My Numberless Intelligence
Finds in the souls of human things
A playable instrument of my vengeance
Put together by your hands!
And though your Paternity,
Veiled aloft in its starry chamber,
May receive nothing but incense,
Still my overpowering charms
Can disturb its almighty designs
With the remotest of alarms!

I come, I go, I glide, I plunge
Vanishing into the pure of heart!
Was there ever a soul so tough

Qu'on n'y puisse loger un songe !
Qui que tu sois, ne suis-je point
Cette complaisance qui poind
Dans ton âme, lorsqu'elle s'aime?
Je suis au fond de sa faveur
Cette inimitable saveur
Que tu ne trouves qu'à toi-même !

Ève, jadis, je la surpris,
Parmi ses premières pensées,
La lèvre entr'ouverte aux esprits
Qui naissaient des roses bercées.
Cette parfaite m'apparut,
Son flanc vaste et d'or parcouru
Ne craignant le soleil ni l'homme;
Tout offerte aux regards de l'air,
L'âme encore stupide, et comme
Interdite au seuil de la chair.

Ô masse de béatitude,
Tu es si belle, juste prix
De la toute sollicitude
Des bons et des meilleurs esprits !
Pour qu'à tes lèvres ils soient pris
Il leur suffit que tu soupires !
Les plus purs s'y penchent les pires,
Les plus durs sont les plus meurtris...
Jusques à moi, tu m'attendris,
De qui relèvent les vampires !

Oui ! De mon poste de feuillage
Reptile aux extases d'oiseau,

As to leave no lodgment for a dream?
Whoever you be, whatever am I
If not the connivance that begins
In your mind when it pleases itself?
In the depths of that very pleasure
I'm the inimitable flavor
You find that you alone possess!

Eve, long since, I took by surprise
In the depths of her dawning mind,
Her lip just opened to the ideas
Inspired by the rocking roses.
That perfection greeted my gaze,
Her spacious flank overrun with golden
Light, fearless of sun or man;
All exposed to the watching air,
Her soul still stupid, as it were,
Nonplussed on the sill of the flesh.

Oh, mass of beatitude,
How lovely you are, a just reward
For the total solicitude
Of good—and even superior minds!
To make them captive of your lips
All you need do is breathe!
The purest are smitten the worst,
The toughest are the most deeply bitten....
Yes, even me, you soften the heart
From whence the vampires arose!

True! In my leafy post of vantage,
Reptile ecstatic as a bird,

Cependant que mon babillage
Tissait de ruses le réseau,
Je te buvais, ô belle sourde !
Calme, claire, de charmes lourde,
Je dominais furtivement,
L'œil dans l'or ardent de ta laine,
Ta nuque énigmatique et pleine
Des secrets de ton mouvement !

J'étais présent comme une odeur,
Comme l'arôme d'une idée
Dont ne puisse être élucidée
L'insidieuse profondeur !
Et je t'inquiétais, candeur,
Ô chair mollement décidée,
Sans que je t'eusse intimidée,
À chanceler dans la splendeur !
Bientôt, je t'aurai, je parie,
Déjà ta nuance varie !

(La superbe simplicité
Demande d'immenses égards !
Sa transparence de regards,
Sottise, orgueil, félicité,
Gardent bien la belle cité !
Sachons lui créer des hasards,
Et par ce plus rare des arts,
Soit le cœur pur sollicité;
C'est là mon fort, c'est là mon fin,
À moi les moyens de ma fin !)

While my innocent warblings wove
Their web of ruses, lovely one,
All unawares I was drinking you in !
Calm, clear, loaded with charms,
I was slily taking command
Of the eye in your bright gold fleece,
Your enigmatic nape, charged
With the secrets of your moves !

I was immanent like a scent,
The aroma of an idea
Whose deep insidious element
Nothing can quite elucidate !
And I was troubling your candor,
O flesh, just inclining to weakness
(Though never offering you a threat)
You tottered in that blaze of glory !
Soon I'll have you, I lay a bet,
Already your mood begins to vary !

(Glorious simplicity
Calls for the immensest care !
Its transparency of gaze,
Stupidity, pride, self-content,
Are guardians of the citadel !
Let us invent some risks for it,
And by this rarest of all arts
Let the pure heart be solicited;
That's my forte, that's my craft,
I make my means to fit my ends !)

Or, d'une éblouissante bave,
Filons les systèmes légers
Où l'oisive et l'Ève suave
S'engage en de vagues dangers !
Que sous une charge de soie
Tremble la peau de cette proie
Accoutumée au seul azur !...
Mais de gaze point de subtile,
Ni de fil invisible et sûr,
Plus qu'une trame de mon style !

Dore, langue ! dore-lui les
Plus doux des dits que tu connaisses !
Allusions, fables, finesses,
Mille silences ciselés,
Use de tout ce qui lui nuise:
Rien qui ne flatte et ne l'induise
À se perdre dans mes desseins,
Docile à ces pentes qui rendent
Aux profondeurs des bleus bassins
Les ruisseaux qui des cieux descendent !

Ô quelle prose non pareille,
Que d'esprit n'ai-je pas jeté
Dans le dédale duveté
De cette merveilleuse oreille !
Là, pensais-je, rien de perdu;
Tout profite au cœur suspendu !
Sûr triomphe ! si ma parole,
De l'âme obsédant le trésor,
Comme une abeille une corolle
Ne quitte plus l'oreille d'or !

So, out of a dazzling slime
Let's weave systems of gossamer
Where Eve the idle and the smooth
Involves herself in doubt and danger!
May it, under a weight of silk,
Tremble, this victim whose skin
Is used to nothing but blue air!...
For of gauze there's none so fine,
No thread so invisible and strong
As the filament of my style!

Tongue, embroider, gild for her
The softest sayings that you know.
Allusions, fables, finest fancies,
A thousand chiseled silences,
Using anything that may injure:
All that may flatter and guide
Her to perdition in my designs;
Docile to the slopes restoring
To the depths of the blue lakes
The streams that shower from the skies!

Ah, what a prose unparalleled,
What wit did I spare to throw
In the dedal downy windings
Of that most delightful ear!
Nothing, thought I, is wasted there,
All works on an undecided heart!
Triumph is certain, if my speech
Besieging the treasury of the soul,
Like a bee in a flower-bell,
Never quits that ear of gold.

197

«Rien, lui soufflais-je, n'est moins sûr
Que la parole divine, Ève !
Une science vive crève
L'énormité de ce fruit mûr !
N'écoute l'Être vieil et pur
Qui maudit la morsure brève !
Que si ta bouche fait un rêve,
Cette soif qui songe à la sève,
Ce délice à demi futur,
C'est l'éternité fondante, Ève !»

Elle buvait mes petits mots
Qui bâtissaient une œuvre étrange;
Son œil, parfois, perdait un ange
Pour revenir à mes rameaux.
Le plus rusé des animaux
Qui te raille d'être si dure,
Ô perfide et grosse de maux,
N'est qu'une voix dans la verdure !
— Mais sérieuse l'Ève était
Qui sous la branche l'écoutait !

«Âme, disais-je, doux séjour
De toute extase prohibée,
Sens-tu la sinueuse amour
Que j'ai du Père dérobée?
Je l'ai, cette essence du Ciel,
À des fins plus douces que miel
Délicatement ordonnée...
Prends de ce fruit...Dresse ton bras !
Pour cueillir ce que tu voudras
Ta belle main te fut donnée !»

"Nothing," I prompted, "is more unsure
Than the divine pronouncement, Eve!
A live knowledge will soon burst
The enormity of that ripe fruit.
Don't heed the ancient Puritan
Who laid a curse on the briefest bite.
For if your mouth holds a daydream,
A thirst, musing upon a savor,
That just-about-to-be delight
Is melt-in-the-mouth eternity, Eve!"

She drank in my casual words,
As they built a curious edifice;
Her eye would quit an angel's flight
To turn back towards my bower.
The craftiest of animal kind
Teasing you for being so hard,
Oh traitorous one, big with evils,
Is a bodiless voice in the greenery!
—But solemn she stood, this Eve,
Under the bough, listening hard!

"Soul," I murmured, "tender retreat
Of all prohibited ecstasy,
Can you divine the sinuous love
Which from the Father I've purloined?
That very essence of Heaven
To a purpose sweeter than honey
I have delicately devised....
Try this fruit.... Stretch your arm...!
To choose and pick whatever you will
Is why you were given that lovely hand!"

Quel silence battu d'un cil !
Mais quel souffle sous le sein sombre
Que mordait l'Arbre de son ombre !
L'autre brillait comme un pistil !
— *Siffle, siffle !* me chantait-il !
Et je sentais frémir le nombre,
Tout le long de mon fouet subtil,
Des ces replis dont je m'encombre :
Ils roulaient depuis le béryl
De ma crête, jusqu'au péril !

Génie ! Ô longue impatience !
À la fin, les temps sont venus,
Qu'un pas vers la neuve Science
Va donc jaillir de ces pieds nus !
Le marbre aspire, l'or se cambre !
Ces blondes bases d'ombre et d'ambre
Tremblent au bord du mouvement !...
Elle chancelle, la grande urne,
D'où va fuir le consentement
De l'apparente taciturne !

Du plaisir que tu te proposes
Cède, cher corps, cède aux appâts !
Que ta soif de métamorphoses
Autour de l'Arbre du Trépas
Engendre une chaîne de poses !
Viens sans venir ! forme des pas
Vaguement comme lourds de roses...
Danse, cher corps...Ne pense pas !
Ici les délices sont causes
Suffisantes au cours des choses !...

A silence stricken by an eyelash beat!
But such a heave of breath in the dark
Breast bitten by the Tree's shadow!
The other breast shone like a pistil.
—*Whistle, hiss!* It hummed to me.
I felt a quiver throughout the number,
The whole length of my slender whip,
Of all the coils I am burdened with,
Rippling downwards from the beryl
Of my crest to my tip of peril!

Genius! Oh tedious impatience!
Now at last the moment comes
When a step towards the new Science
Will issue from those naked feet!
The marble yearns, the gold stretches,
Those fair foundations of shadow and amber
Tremble on the brink of movement!...
She is tilting, the great urn
Whence will trickle the consent
Of the seemingly wordless one!

The pleasure that your mind proposes,
Yield, dear body, yield to its charms!
Let your thirst for transformations
All around the Tree of Death
Give birth to a chain of poses.
Come without seeming to! making paces
As vague as though loaded with roses....
Dear body, dance....With never a thought!
Here is where delights are causes
Sufficient to the course of events!...

Ô follement que je m'offrais
Cette infertile jouissance:
Voir le long pur d'un dos si frais
Frémir la désobéissance!...
Déjà délivrant son essence
De sagesse et d'illusions,
Tout l'Arbre de la Connaissance
Échevelé de visions,
Agitait son grand corps qui plonge
Au soleil, et suce le songe!

Arbre, grand Arbre, Ombre des Cieux,
Irrésistible Arbre des arbres,
Qui dans les faiblesses des marbres,
Poursuis des sucs délicieux,
Toi qui pousses tels labyrinthes
Par qui les ténèbres étreintes
S'iront perdre dans le saphir
De l'éternelle matinée,
Douce perte, arôme ou zéphir,
Ou colombe prédestinée,

Ô Chanteur, ô secret buveur
Des plus profondes pierreries,
Berceau du reptile rêveur
Qui jeta l'Ève en rêveries,
Grand Être agité de savoir,
Qui toujours, comme pour mieux voir,
Grandis à l'appel de ta cime,
Toi qui dans l'or très pur promeus
Tes bras durs, tes rameaux fumeux,
D'autre part, creusant vers l'abîme,

Ah how madly I coveted
That copulation with barrenness:
To see the pure length of that cool spine
Quiver with disobedience!...
Already surrendering its essence
Of wisdom and illusions,
Throughout itself the Tree of Knowledge
Shaken, dishevelled with visions,
Shivered its huge body that plunges
Into the sun, and sucks at nightmares!

Tree, great Tree, Shadow of Heaven,
Irresistible Tree of trees,
Who find even in marble's weakness
A way to pursue the sap's sweet courses,
You whose labyrinthine growths
Are such as constrain the darknesses
To rise and be lost in the sapphire blue
Of the everlasting morning,
—Sweet the shedding of scent or zephyr,
Or else the predestined dove—

Oh Singer, and secret drinker
Of the deepest hidden stones,
Cradling the dreamy reptile
Who tossed his reveries to Eve,
Great Being, restless with knowing,
Forever, as though to enhance your seeing,
Growing towards your urging summit,
You who promote into purest gold
Your hard boughs, your misty branches,
While digging the abyss, its opposite,

Tu peux repousser l'infini
Qui n'est fait que de ta croissance,
Et de la tombe jusqu'au nid
Te sentir toute Connaissance !
Mais ce vieil amateur d'échecs,
Dans l'or oisif des soleils secs,
Sur ton branchage vient se tordre;
Ses yeux font frémir ton trésor.
Il en cherra des fruits de mort,
De désespoir et de désordre !

Beau serpent, bercé dans le bleu,
Je siffle, avec délicatesse,
Offrant à la gloire de Dieu
Le triomphe de ma tristesse...
Il me suffit que dans les airs,
L'immense espoir de fruits amers
Affole les fils de la fange...
— Cette soif qui te fit géant,
Jusqu'à l'Être exalte l'étrange
Toute-Puissance du Néant !

You can press back the infinite,
It's only made of your increase,
And every inch from tomb to nest
Feel you are the all of Knowledge!
But this old amateur of checkers,
In the sun's dry and lazy gold,
Comes a-winding in your branchage;
In his gaze your treasure flickers.
Fruits of death it will let fall,
Of desperation, and chaos!

Lovely serpent, rocked in the blue,
With all delicacy I hiss
Offering God's glory the due
Triumph of my balefulness....
Enough for me if, in the air,
The giant promise of bitter fruits
Should madden the children of clay....
—The very thirst that made you huge
Can raise to the power of Being the strange
All-probing force of Nothingness!

Les Grenades

Dures grenades entr'ouvertes
Cédant à l'excès de vos grains,
Je crois voir des fronts souverains
Éclatés de leurs découvertes !

Si les soleils par vous subis,
Ô grenades entre-bâillées,
Vous ont fait d'orgueil travaillées
Craquer les cloisons de rubis,

Et que si l'or sec de l'écorce
À la demande d'une force
Crève en gemmes rouges de jus,

Cette lumineuse rupture
Fait rêver une âme que j'eus
De sa secrète architecture.

Pomegranates

Tough pomegranates half-opening
Yielding to your intemperate seeds,
I see you as brows of sovereign minds
Bursting with their discoveries!

If the suns that you've endured,
Oh pomegranates agape,
Have made you overworked with pride
Crack open your partitioned rubies,

And if the parched gold of the rind
Responding to a certain force
Explodes in gems ruddy with juice,

That illuminating rupture
Recalls a dream to a soul I had
About its secret architecture.

Le Vin perdu

J'ai, quelque jour, dans l'Océan,
(Mais je ne sais plus sous quels cieux),
Jeté, comme offrande au néant,
Tout un peu de vin précieux...

Qui voulut ta perte, ô liqueur?
J'obéis peut-être au devin?
Peut-être au souci de mon cœur,
Songeant au sang, versant le vin?

Sa transparence accoutumée
Après une rose fumée
Reprit aussi pure la mer...

Perdu ce vin, ivres les ondes!...
J'ai vu bondir dans l'air amer
Les figures les plus profondes...

The Lost Wine

Once on a day, in the open Sea
(Under what skies I cannot recall),
I threw, as oblation to vacancy,
More than a drop of precious wine....

Who decreed your waste, oh potion?
Did I perhaps obey some divine?
Or else the heart's anxiety,
Dreaming blood, spilling the wine?

Its habitual clarity
After a mist of rosiness
Returned as pure again to the sea....

The wine lost, drunken the waves!...
I saw leaping in the salt air
Shapes of the utmost profundity....

Intérieur

Une esclave aux longs yeux chargés de molles chaînes
Change l'eau de mes fleurs, plonge aux glaces prochaines,
Au lit mystérieux prodigue ses doigts purs;
Elle met une femme au milieu de ces murs
Qui, dans ma rêverie errant avec décence,
Passe entre mes regards sans briser leur absence,
Comme passe le verre au travers du soleil,
Et de la raison pure épargne l'appareil.

Interior

A slave girl, her long eyes laden with soft chains,
Changes the water of my flowers, sinks in the nearby
    mirrors,
Busies her pure fingers about the mysterious bed;
Situates a woman in the midst of these walls
Who, deferently straying to and fro in my daydream,
Passes between my gazes without breaking their absence,
As a windowpane traverses the sunshine,
Leaving intact the appliances of pure reason.

Le Cimetière marin

Μή, φίλα ψυχά, βίον ἀθάνατον
σπεῦδε, τὰν δ'ἔμπρακτον ἄντλει μαχανάν.
Pindare, *Pythiques*

Ce toit tranquille, où marchent des colombes,
Entre les pins palpite, entre les tombes;
Midi le juste y compose de feux
La mer, la mer, toujours recommencée!
Ô récompense après une pensée
Qu'un long regard sur le calme des dieux!

Quel pur travail de fins éclairs consume
Maint diamant d'imperceptible écume,
Et quelle paix semble se concevoir!
Quand sur l'abîme un soleil se repose,
Ouvrages purs d'une éternelle cause,
Le Temps scintille et le Songe est savoir.

Stable trésor, temple simple à Minerve,
Masse de calme, et visible réserve,
Eau sourcilleuse, Œil qui gardes en toi
Tant de sommeil sous un voile de flamme,
Ô mon silence!...Édifice dans l'âme,
Mais comble d'or aux mille tuiles, Toit!

Temple du Temps, qu'un seul soupir résume,
À ce point pur je monte et m'accoutume,
Tout entouré de mon regard marin;
Et comme aux dieux mon offrande suprême,
La scintillation sereine sème
Sur l'altitude un dédain souverain.

The Graveyard by the Sea

My soul, do not seek immortal life,
but exhaust the realm of the possible.
Pindar, *Pythian Odes.*

Quiet that roof, where the doves are walking,
Quivers between the pines, between the tombs;
Justicer Noon out there compounds with fires
The sea, the sea perpetually renewed!
Ah what a recompense, after a thought,
A prolonged gazing on the calm of gods!

What lucid toil of pure lightings consumes
Many a diamond of imperceptible foams,
And what a stillness seems to beget itself.
For while a sun hangs over the abyss,
Pure workings of an eternal cause,
Time scintillates, and the Dream is knowledge.

Store of sameness, temple sheer to Minerva,
Massively tranquil, visibly contained,
Supercilious deep, Eye keeping your secret
Of all that slumber in a veil of flame,
My own silence!...The soul's edifice...
But towering gold, Roof of a thousand tiles!

Time's temple, summed up in a breath,
Having reached this pure height, I grow used
To my marine gaze, all around,
And as my ultimate offering to the gods,
The serene scintillation over the height
Disseminates a sovereign disdain.

Comme le fruit se fond en jouissance,
Comme en délice il change son absence
Dans une bouche où sa forme se meurt,
Je hume ici ma future fumée
Et le ciel chante à l'âme consumée
Le changement des rives en rumeur.

Beau ciel, vrai ciel, regarde-moi qui change !
Après tant d'orgueil, après tant d'étrange
Oisiveté, mais pleine de pouvoir,
Je m'abandonne à ce brillant espace,
Sur les maisons des morts mon ombre passe
Qui m'apprivoise à son frêle mouvoir.

L'âme exposée aux torches du solstice,
Je te soutiens, admirable justice
De la lumière aux armes sans pitié !
Je te rends pure à ta place première:
Regarde-toi !...Mais rendre la lumière
Suppose d'ombre une morne moitié.

Ô pour moi seul, à moi seul, en moi-même,
Auprès d'un cœur, aux sources du poème,
Entre le vide et l'événement pur,
J'attends l'écho de ma grandeur interne,
Amère, sombre et sonore citerne,
Sonnant dans l'âme un creux toujours futur !

Sais-tu, fausse captive des feuillages,
Golfe mangeur de ces maigres grillages,
Sur mes yeux clos, secrets éblouissants,
Quel corps me traîne à sa fin paresseuse,
Quel front l'attire à cette terre osseuse ?
Une étincelle y pense à mes absents.

As a fruit dissolves into a taste,
Changing its absence to deliciousness
Within a palate where its shape must die,
Here I can savor my own future smoke,
And the sky sings to the soul consumed
The changing of the shores into a sigh.

Clear heaven, true heaven, look at me, I change !
After so much pride, after so much strange
Idleness, and yet instilled with power,
I give myself up to this shining space,
And over the houses of the dead my shadow
Passes, taming me to that frail mover.

With soul stripped to the torches of the solstice,
I can withstand you, admirable justice
Of light itself, with your pitiless blades !
I give you back pure to your primal place,
Look at yourself !. . .But to reflect the light
Bespeaks another half of mournful shade.

Ah for myself, to my own self within,
Close by a heart, at the sources of the poem,
Between emptiness and the pure event,
I await my grandeur's echo from within,
That bitter, gloomy and resounding cistern
Ringing in the soul a still future void !

Can you tell, sham prisoner of the leaves,
Gulf devouring these flimsy rails,
On my closed eyes, dazzling secrecy,
What body drags me to its lazy end,
What brow attracts it to this bony ground?
A spark within there thinks of absent ones.

Fermé, sacré, plein d'un feu sans matière,
Fragment terrestre offert à la lumière,
Ce lieu me plaît, dominé de flambeaux,
Composé d'or, de pierre et d'arbres sombres,
Où tant de marbre est tremblant sur tant d'ombres;
La mer fidèle y dort sur mes tombeaux!

Chienne splendide, écarte l'idolâtre!
Quand solitaire au sourire de pâtre,
Je pais longtemps, moutons mystérieux,
Le blanc troupeau de mes tranquilles tombes,
Éloignes-en les prudentes colombes,
Les songes vains, les anges curieux!

Ici venu, l'avenir est paresse.
L'insecte net gratte la sécheresse;
Tout est brûlé, défait, reçu dans l'air
À je ne sais quelle sévère essence...
La vie est vaste, étant ivre d'absence,
Et l'amertume est douce, et l'esprit clair.

Les morts cachés sont bien dans cette terre
Qui les réchauffe et sèche leur mystère.
Midi là-haut, Midi sans mouvement
En soi se pense et convient à soi-même...
Tête complète et parfait diadème,
Je suis en toi le secret changement.

Tu n'as que moi pour contenir tes craintes!
Mes repentirs, mes doutes, mes contraintes
Sont le défaut de ton grand diamant...
Mais dans leur nuit toute lourde de marbres,
Un peuple vague aux racines des arbres
A pris déjà ton parti lentement.

Shut in, sacred, crammed with bodiless fire,
A patch of ground offered up to the light,
Crowned with flambeaux, this purlieu pleases me,
Compact of gilt, stone, and solemn trees
Where so much marble quivers on so many shadows;
The faithful sea's asleep there on my tombs!

Glorious bitch-hound, keep out the idolater!
While solitary, smiling like a shepherd,
I graze for hours my mysterious
Sheep, the white flock of my peaceful tombs,
Keep far away from here the cautious doves,
The vain dreams, the prying angels!

Once here, the future is an idleness,
The clear-cut insect scratches at the dryness;
Everything's burned, dispelled, received in air
Into I know not what impartial essence....
Life is immense, being drunk with its own absence,
And bitterness is sweet, the mind clear.

The dead concealed lie easy in this earth
That keeps them warm, drying their mystery.
And Noon up there, Noon the motionless,
Thinks its own thought approving its own self....
Total head, and perfect diadem,
I am the secret changing in your mind.

I am all you have to contain your fears!
My doubts, my strivings, my repentances,
These are the flaw in your great diamond....
But in their darkness under a marble load
An empty people among the tree roots
Have gradually come to take your side.

Ils ont fondu dans une absence épaisse,
L'argile rouge a bu la blanche espèce,
Le don de vivre a passé dans les fleurs!
Où sont des morts les phrases familières,
L'art personnel, les âmes singulières?
La larve file où se formaient des pleurs.

Les cris aigus des filles chatouillées,
Les yeux, les dents, les paupières mouillées,
Le sein charmant qui joue avec le feu,
Le sang qui brille aux lèvres qui se rendent,
Les derniers dons, les doigts qui les défendent,
Tout va sous terre et rentre dans le jeu!

Et vous, grande âme, espérez-vous un songe
Qui n'aura plus ces couleurs de mensonge
Qu'aux yeux de chair l'onde et l'or font ici?
Chanterez-vous quand serez vaporeuse?
Allez! Tout fuit! Ma présence est poreuse,
La sainte impatience meurt aussi!

Maigre immortalité noire et dorée,
Consolatrice affreusement laurée,
Qui de la mort fais un sein maternel,
Le beau mensonge et la pieuse ruse!
Qui ne connaît, et qui ne les refuse,
Ce crâne vide et ce rire éternel!

Pères profonds, têtes inhabitées,
Qui sous le poids de tant de pelletées,
Êtes la terre et confondez nos pas,
Le vrai rongeur, le ver irréfutable
N'est point pour vous qui dormez sous la table,
Il vit de vie, il ne me quitte pas!

They have melted into a dense unbeing,
The red clay has drained the paler kind,
The gift of living has passed into flowers!
Where now are the singular souls of the dead,
Their personal ways, the tricks of speech they had?
The worm channels its way where tears formed.

The piercing cries of girls being tickled,
The eyes, the teeth, the moistened eyelids,
The enchanting breast that frolics with the flame,
The blood glistening in yielding lips,
The ultimate boons, the fingers that defend...
All goes to earth and back into the game!

And you, great soul, still hoping for a dream
That will be delivered from these lying colors
Which sun and wave make here for eyes of flesh?
Will you sing, when you are vaporous?
Go on! Time flies! My presence here is porous,
Holy impatience also dies the death!

Skinny immortality, black and gilt-lettered,
Hideously laurel-crowned she-comforter,
Trying to make death a maternal lap,
—A pretty fiction, and a pious ruse!—
Who cannot know, and who cannot refuse
That empty skull, the eternal grinning gape!

Fathers deep-laid, heads uninhabited,
Who under the weight of so many spade-loads,
Are earth itself and who confound our steps,
The real canker, the irrefutable worm
Is not for you asleep under the table,
He lives on life, it's me he never quits!

Amour, peut-être, ou de moi-même haine?
Sa dent secrète est de moi si prochaine
Que tous les noms lui peuvent convenir!
Qu'importe! Il voit, il veut, il songe, il touche!
Ma chair lui plaît, et jusque sur ma couche,
À ce vivant je vis d'appartenir!

Zénon! Cruel Zénon! Zénon d'Élée!
M'as-tu percé de cette flèche ailée
Qui vibre, vole, et qui ne vole pas!
Le son m'enfante et la flèche me tue!
Ah! le soleil...Quelle ombre de tortue
Pour l'âme, Achille immobile à grands pas!

Non, non!...Debout! Dans l'ère successive!
Brisez, mon corps, cette forme pensive!
Buvez, mon sein, la naissance du vent!
Une fraîcheur, de la mer exhalée,
Me rend mon âme...Ô puissance salée!
Courons à l'onde en rejaillir vivant!

Oui! Grande mer de délires douée,
Peau de panthère et chlamyde trouée
De mille et mille idoles du soleil,
Hydre absolue, ivre de ta chair bleue,
Qui te remords l'étincelante queue
Dans un tumulte au silence pareil,

Le vent se lève!...Il faut tenter de vivre!
L'air immense ouvre et referme mon livre,
La vague en poudre ose jaillir des rocs!
Envolez-vous, pages tout éblouies!
Rompez, vagues! Rompez d'eaux réjouies
Ce toit tranquille où picoraient des focs!

Love, it may be, or else self-hatred?
Its secret tooth is so my intimate
That any name you choose to give could fit!
No matter what! It sees, wants, dreams and touches,
It likes my flesh, and even on my bed
My life's possessed by that undying one!

Zeno, Zeno, the cruel, Elean Zeno!
You've truly fixed me with that feathered arrow
Which quivers as it flies and never moves!
The sound begets me and the arrow kills!
Ah, sun!...What a tortoise shadow for the soul,
Achilles motionless in his giant stride!

No, no! Up! And away into the next era!
Break, body, break this pensive mold,
Lungs, drink in the beginnings of the wind!
A coolness, exhalation of the sea,
Gives me my soul back!...Ah, salt potency,
Into the wave with us, and out alive!

Yes, gigantic sea delirium-dowered,
Panther-hide, and chlamys filled with holes
By thousands of the sun's dazzling idols,
Absolute hydra, drunk with your blue flesh,
Forever biting your own glittering tail
In a commotion that is silence's equal,

The wind is rising!...We must try to live!
The immense air opens and shuts my book,
A wave dares burst in powder over the rocks.
Pages, whirl away in a dazzling riot!
And break, waves, rejoicing, break that quiet
Roof where foraging sails dipped their beaks!

Ode secrète

Chute superbe, fin si douce,
Oubli des luttes, quel délice
Que d'étendre à même la mousse
Après la danse, le corps lisse !

Jamais une telle lueur
Que ces étincelles d'été
Sur un front semé de sueur
N'avait la victoire fêté !

Mais touché par le Crépuscule,
Ce grand corps qui fit tant de choses,
Qui dansait, qui rompit Hercule,
N'est plus qu'une masse de roses !

Dormez, sous les pas sidéraux,
Vainqueur lentement désuni,
Car l'Hydre inhérente au héros
S'est éployée à l'infini...

Ô quel Taureau, quel Chien, quelle Ourse,
Quels objets de victoire énorme,
Quand elle entre aux temps sans ressource
L'âme impose à l'espace informe !

Fin suprême, étincellement
Qui, par les monstres et les dieux,
Proclame universellement
Les grands actes qui sont aux Cieux !

Secret Ode

Glorious the fall, the end so soft,
The wrestling over, the bliss
Of stretching on the naked moss
The sleek body, after the dance !

Never was there such a gleam
As these sparking drops of summer
On a brow sprinkled with sweat
A victory to celebrate !

But, at the touch of Twilight,
The great body of many a feat,
Who danced, who broke a Hercules,
Is no more than a heap of roses.

Sleep, beneath the sidereal paces,
Conqueror, in slow disunity,
For the Hydra inherent in the hero
Is unfolded to infinity. . . .

Ah, what Bull, what Dog, or Bear,
What trophies of victory immense,
Once embarked on resourceless time
The soul imposes on formless space !

Supreme the end, the glittering
Proclaiming by way of divinities
And monsters, to the universe
The giant acts that are in the skies !

Le Rameur

À André Lebey

Penché contre un grand fleuve, infiniment mes rames
M'arrachent à regret aux riants environs;
Âme aux pesantes mains, pleines des avirons,
Il faut que le ciel cède au glas des lentes lames.

Le cœur dur, l'œil distrait des beautés que je bats,
Laissant autour de moi mûrir des cercles d'onde,
Je veux à larges coups rompre l'illustre monde
De feuilles et de feu que je chante tout bas.

Arbres sur qui je passe, ample et naïve moire,
Eau de ramages peinte, et paix de l'accompli,
Déchire-les, ma barque, impose-leur un pli
Qui coure du grand calme abolir la mémoire.

Jamais, charmes du jour, jamais vos grâces n'ont
Tant souffert d'un rebelle essayant sa défense:
Mais, comme les soleils m'ont tiré de l'enfance,
Je remonte à la source où cesse même un nom.

En vain, toute la nymphe énorme et continue
Empêche de bras purs mes membres harassés;
Je romprai lentement mille liens glacés
Et les barbes d'argent de sa puissance nue.

Ce bruit secret des eaux, ce fleuve étrangement
Place mes jours dorés sous un bandeau de soie;
Rien plus aveuglément n'use l'antique joie
Qu'un bruit de fuite égale et de nul changement.

The Rower

To André Lebey

Stooped on the great river, continually my strokes
Pull me regretful on through laughing surroundings;
Soul of the heavy hands, laden with the oars,
Make the sky yield to the slow, knelling blades.

Hardhearted, the eye drawn to the beauties I beat off,
Leaving circles of ripples to ripen all round me,
With wide thrusts I have to break the shining world
Of foliage and fire, though it sings low within me.

Trees I float over, ample, ingenuous silk,
Water painted with branchage, and placidly complete,
Rend, rend it, my boat, drive into it a cleft
Whose running will erase memory's giant quiet.

Never, day's delights, never have your graces
Suffered so from a rebel in his own defense:
But, as the daily suns have drawn me out of childhood,
I am returning to the source where even names cease.

In vain the entire, immense and continuous nymph
Strives to hinder my harassed limbs with her pure arms;
Piece by piece I shall break a thousand icy bonds,
And the silvery barbs of her naked potency.

This noise of secret waters, this river curiously
Lays my golden days under a silken band;
Nothing more blindly wears away at primal joy
Than the unchanging sound of even, gliding flight.

Sous les ponts annelés, l'eau profonde me porte,
Voûtes pleines de vent, de murmure et de nuit,
Ils courent sur un front qu'ils écrasent d'ennui,
Mais dont l'os orgueilleux est plus dur que leur porte.

Leur nuit passe longtemps. L'âme baisse sous eux
Ses sensibles soleils et ses promptes paupières,
Quand, par le mouvement qui me revêt de pierres,
Je m'enfonce au mépris de tant d'azur oiseux.

Under the rings of bridges the deep water carries me,
Vaults filled with winds and rumorous darkness,
They run above a head they oppress with weariness
But whose proud bone is tougher than their gates.

Slowly their night passes. Beneath them the mind
Lowers its sensitive suns, its ready eyelids,
Until with a leap that clothes me with jewels
I plunge into the disdain of all that idle azure.

Palme

À Jeannie

De sa grâce redoutable
Voilant à peine l'éclat,
Un ange met sur ma table
Le pain tendre, le lait plat;
Il me fait de la paupière
Le signe d'une prière
Qui parle à ma vision:
— Calme, calme, reste calme !
Connais le poids d'une palme
Portant sa profusion !

Pour autant qu'elle se plie
À l'abondance des biens,
Sa figure est accomplie,
Ses fruits lourds sont ses liens.
Admire comme elle vibre,
Et comme une lente fibre
Qui divise le moment,
Départage sans mystère
L'attirance de la terre
Et le poids du firmament !

Ce bel arbitre mobile
Entre l'ombre et le soleil,
Simule d'une sibylle
La sagesse et le sommeil.
Autour d'une même place

228

Palm

To Jeannie

Of his formidable grace
Scarcely veiling the glory,
An angel lays on my table
Tender bread, smooth milk;
With his eyelid he makes
Me the sign of a prayer
That speaks to my seeing:
—Calm, calm, still be calm!
Know the weightiness of a palm
Bearing its profusion.

For as much as it may bend
Under its treasured abundance,
Its form is fulfilled,
Its heavy fruits are its bond.
Wonder at how it sways,
And how a gradual sinew
Dividing a moment of time
Unpretendingly apportions
The attraction of the ground
And the weight of the firmament!

Lovely mobile arbiter
Between the shadow and the sun,
It simulates the wisdom
And the slumber of a sibyl.
Still about the same place

L'ample palme ne se lasse
Des appels ni des adieux...
Qu'elle est noble, qu'elle est tendre !
Qu'elle est digne de s'attendre
À la seule main des dieux !

L'or léger qu'elle murmure
Sonne au simple doigt de l'air,
Et d'une soyeuse armure
Charge l'âme du désert.
Une voix impérissable
Qu'elle rend au vent de sable
Qui l'arrose des ses grains,
À soi-même sert d'oracle,
Et se flatte du miracle
Que se chantent les chagrins.

Cependant qu'elle s'ignore
Entre le sable et le ciel,
Chaque jour qui luit encore
Lui compose un peu de miel.
Sa douceur est mesurée
Par la divine durée
Qui ne compte pas les jours,
Mais bien qui les dissimule
Dans un suc où s'accumule
Toute l'arôme des amours.

Parfois si l'on désespère,
Si l'adorable rigueur
Malgré tes larmes n'opère

The ample palm tree never tires
Of summonses and farewells....
How noble it is, and tender,
How worthy to await
Only the hands of gods !

The frail gold it murmurs
Rings on the air's artless finger,
And with a silky armor
Invests the soul of the desert.
An imperishable voice
Which it gives to the sandy wind
Sprinkling it with its grains,
Serves as its own oracle,
Soothing itself with the miracle
The griefs sing to themselves.

Self-oblivious the while
Between heaven and the sand,
Every day as it still shines
Compounds another mite of honey.
This sweetness is measured out
By the divine durability
That is not counted in days
But rather disguises them
In a juice where accumulates
All the aroma of the loves.

If at times there is despair,
If the adorable strictness,
For all your tears only labors

Que sous ombre de langueur,
N'accuse pas d'être avare
Une Sage qui prépare
Tant d'or et d'autorité:
Par la sève solennelle
Une espérance éternelle
Monte à la maturité!

Ces jours qui te semblent vides
Et perdus pour l'univers
Ont des racines avides
Qui travaillent les déserts.
La substance chevelue
Par les ténèbres élue
Ne peut s'arrêter jamais,
Jusqu'aux entrailles du monde,
De poursuivre l'eau profonde
Que demandent les sommets.

Patience, patience,
Patience dans l'azur!
Chaque atome de silence
Est la chance d'un fruit mûr!
Viendra l'heureuse surprise:
Une colombe, la brise,
L'ébranlement le plus doux,
Une femme qui s'appuie,
Feront tomber cette pluie
Où l'on se jette à genoux!

Qu'un peuple à présent s'écroule,
Palme!...irrésistiblement!

Under the guise of languors,
Do not accuse of miserliness
Her Wisdom as it prepares
So much gold and so much power:
Through the sap's funereal pace
An ever-living hopefulness
Mounts towards its ripening.

These days that seem to you void
And wasted for the universe,
Have their roots of eagerness
That put the deserts to work.
That dense and hairy mass
Allotted to the shades
Never can arrest itself,
Into the world's entrails
Pursuing water in the depths
To satisfy the treetop.

Endurance, endurance,
Endurance, in the sky's blue !
Every atom of silence
Is a chance of ripened fruit !
There will come the happy shock:
A dove, a breath of wind,
An imperceptibly gentle shake,
The touch of a woman as she leans
Will release that fall of rain
That sends us down on our knees !

Let a whole people now fall,
Palm tree !...irresistibly !

Dans la poudre qu'il se roule
Sur les fruits du firmament !
Tu n'as pas perdu ces heures
Si légère tu demeures
Après ces beaux abandons ;
Pareille à celui qui pense
Et dont l'âme se dépense
À s'accroître de ses dons !

Let them wallow in the dust
On the fruits of the firmament!
For you those hours were no loss
Now you are left so light
After such lovely yieldings:
Image of a thinking mind
Where the spirit spends itself
To be increased by what it gives.

PIÈCES DIVERSES DE TOUTE
ÉPOQUE

VARIOUS POEMS OF ALL PERIODS

Neige

Quel silence, battu d'un simple bruit de bêche !...

Je m'éveille, attendu par cette neige fraîche
Qui me saisit au creux de ma chère chaleur.
Mes yeux trouvent un jour d'une dure pâleur
Et ma chair langoureuse a peur de l'innocence.
Oh ! combien de flocons, pendant ma douce absence,
Durent les sombres cieux perdre toute la nuit !
Quel pur désert tombé des ténèbres sans bruit
Vint effacer les traits de la terre enchantée
Sous cette ample candeur sourdement augmentée
Et la fondre en un lieu sans visage et sans voix,
Où le regard perdu relève quelques toits
Qui cachent leur trésor de vie accoutumée
À peine offrant le vœu d'une vague fumée.

Snow

Such silence, stricken only by a spade-stroke!...

I awake, to this fresh snow lying in wait
To snatch at me in the hollow of my cherished warmth.
My eyes discover a light of pallid hardness
And my lazy flesh is scared of innocence.
Ah! how many flakes, while I was softly absent,
Must the somber skies have been shedding all night!
What desert of purity soundlessly dropped from the dark
Came melting the features of the enchanted earth
Under that vast whiteness stealthily increased,
Dissolving it into a place both faceless and voiceless
Where the absent gaze picks out a few roofs
Hoarding their treasure of everyday living
That offers up no tribute but a wraith of smoke.

Sinistre

Quelle heure cogne aux membres de la coque
Ce grand coup d'ombre où craque notre sort?
Quelle puissance impalpable entre-choque
Dans nos agrès des ossements de mort?

Sur l'avant nu, l'écroulement des trombes
Lave l'odeur de la vie et du vin:
La mer élève et recreuse des tombes,
La même eau creuse et comble le ravin.

Homme hideux, en qui le cœur chavire,
Ivrogne étrange égaré sur la mer
Dont la nausée attachée au navire
Arrache à l'âme un désir de l'enfer,

Homme total, je tremble et je calcule,
Cerveau trop clair, capable du moment
Où, dans un phénomène minuscule,
Le temps se brise ainsi qu'un instrument...

Maudit soit-il le porc qui t'a gréée,
Arche pourrie en qui grouille le lest!
Dans tes fonds noirs, toute chose créée
Bat ton bois mort en dérive vers l'Est...

L'abîme et moi formons une machine
Qui jongle avec des souvenirs épars:
Je vois ma mère et mes tasses de Chine,
La putain grasse au seuil fauve des bars;

Je vois le Christ amarré sur la vergue!...
Il danse à mort, sombrant avec les siens;
Son œil sanglant m'éclaire cet exergue:
UN GRAND NAVIRE A PÉRI CORPS ET BIENS!...

Disaster

What hour hurtles at the staves of the hull
That knock of darkness on which our fate cracks?
What force untouchable plays the castanets
In our tackle with a dead man's bones?

On the prow the crumbling of cloudbursts
Washes off the smell of life and wine:
The sea raises and then re-digs tombs,
The same water hollowing piles the ravine.

Atrocious man, your heart within capsizing,
Drunkard, foreigner, astray on the sea
Whose nausea coupled to the ship
Wrenches from the soul a longing for hell,

Total man, I shudder and calculate,
Brain too lucid, capable of this moment
Where, within a phenomenal microcosm
Time is shattered like an instrument....

A curse on that swine who rigged you out,
Ark of rottenness with your moldering ballast,
In your black holds, every created thing
Rattles on your dead timbers drifting East....

I and the abyss make up between us
A machine juggling scattered memories:
I see my mother, and my china cups,
The greasy trull in the bars' lurid doorways.

I see Christ roped to the yardarm!
Dancing to death, foundering with his herd;
His bloodshot eye lights me to this exergue:
A GREAT SHIP GONE DOWN WITH ALL ON BOARD!...

Colloque

(Pour deux flûtes)

À Francis Poulenc, qui a fait
chanter ce colloque

A

D'une Rose mourante
L'ennui penche vers nous;
Tu n'es pas différente
Dans ton silence doux
De cette fleur mourante;
Elle se meurt pour nous...
Tu me sembles pareille
À celle dont l'oreille
Était sur mes genoux,
À celle dont l'oreille
Ne m'écoutait jamais;
Tu me sembles pareille
À l'autre que j'aimais:
Mais de celle ancienne,
Sa bouche était la mienne.

B

Que me compares-tu
Quelque rose fanée?
L'amour n'a de vertu
Que fraîche et spontanée...
Mon regard dans le tien
Ne trouve que son bien:
Je m'y vois toute nue!

Colloquy

(for two flutes)

*To Francis Poulenc, who made
a song of this dialogue*

A

A dying Rose's
Fatigue leans toward us;
You are no other
In your sweet silence
Than this dying flower;
It is dying for us.....
You seem the same
As she who leant
An ear on my knee,
As she whose ear
Never listened to me;
You seem the same
As she whom I loved;
But that earlier one
Had a mouth that was mine.

B

Why compare me
To some faded rose?
Love's only force
Grows new of itself.....
My gaze in yours
Finds all that it wants;
Myself naked I see!

Mes yeux effaceront
Tes larmes qui seront
D'un souvenir venues !...
Si ton désir naquit
Qu'il meure sur ma couche
Et sur mes lèvres qui
T'emporteront la bouche...

My eyes will wipe away
Your tears as they rise
From a memory !...
Let your desire born
Die too on my couch
And on my lips: they
Will bear away your mouth....

La Distraite

Daigne, Laure, au retour de la saison des pluies,
Présence parfumée, épaule qui t'appuies
Sur ma tendresse lente attentive à tes pas,
Laure, très beau regard qui ne regarde pas,
Daigne, tête aux grands yeux qui dans les cieux t'égares,
Tandis qu'à pas rêveurs, tes pieds voués aux mares
Trempent aux clairs miroirs dans la boue arrondis,
Daigne, chère, écouter les choses que tu dis...

The Absent-Minded One

Deign, Laura, now the rainy season is back,
Presence imbued with perfume, shoulder leaning
On my considerate tenderness slackened to your step,
Laura, gaze of loveliness, looking nowhere,
Deign, head in air, with your great eyes,
While with dreamy steps your feet doomed to puddles
Dip in the clear mirrors rounded in the mud,
Deign, dear one, to listen to the things you say....

L'Insinuant II

Folle et mauvaise
Comme une abeille
Ma lèvre baise
L'ardente oreille.

J'aime ton frêle
Étonnement
Où je ne mêle
Qu'un rien d'amant.

Quelle surprise...
Ton sang bourdonne.
C'est moi qui donne
Vie à la brise...

Dans tes cheveux
Tendre et méchante
Mon âme hante
Ce que je veux.

The Sly One II

Wicked and wild,
Like a bee,
My lip caresses
The ardent ear.

I love your frail
Astonishment
Where I mingle a mere
Lover's hint.

What marvel is this?...
Your blood murmurs.
I am what gives
Its life to the breeze....

Within your hair,
Tender, malicious
My soul haunts
What I desire.

Heure

L'HEURE me vient sourire et se faire sirène:
Tout s'éclaire d'un jour que jamais je ne vis:
Danseras-tu longtemps, Rayon, sur le parvis
    De l'âme sombre et souveraine?

Voici L'HEURE, la soif, la source et la sirène.

Pour toi, le passé brûle, HEURE qui m'assouvis;
Enfin, splendeur du seul, ô biens que j'ai ravis,
J'aime ce que je suis: ma solitude est reine!
Mes plus secrets démons, librement asservis
Accomplissent dans l'or de l'air même où je vis
Une sagesse pure aux lucides avis:
    Ma présence est toute sereine.

Voici L'HEURE, la soif, la source et la sirène,

Danseras-tu longtemps, rayon, sur le parvis,
Du soir, devant l'œil noir de ma nuit souveraine?

Hour

The HOUR comes smiling at me, changing into a siren:
All is illumined by a light I never saw;
Will you dance for long, Sunbeam, on the forecourt
 Of the dark and sovereign soul?

Now comes the HOUR, the thirst, the spring and the siren.

For you the past burns up, HOUR fulfilling my need;
At last, glory of the alone, O boons I have ravished,
I love what I am, my solitude is queen!
My innermost demons, willingly enslaved,
Achieve in the gold of the very air I breathe
A wisdom unalloyed, lucid in counsel:
 My presence is totally serene.

Now comes the HOUR, the thirst, the spring and the siren.

Will you dance for long, Sunbeam, on the evening's
Forecourt, in the dark gaze of my sovereign night?

L'Oiseau cruel

L'oiseau cruel toute la nuit me tint
Au point aigu du délice d'entendre
Sa voix qu'adresse une fureur si tendre
Au ciel brûlant d'astres jusqu'au matin.

Tu perces l'âme et fixes le destin
De tel regard qui ne peut se reprendre;
Tout ce qui fut tu le changes en cendre,
Ô voix trop haute, extase de l'instinct...

L'aube dans l'ombre ébauche le visage
D'un jour très beau qui déjà ne m'est rien:
Un jour de plus n'est qu'un vain paysage,

Qu'est-ce qu'un jour sans le visage tien?
Non!...Vers la nuit mon âme retournée
Refuse l'aube et la jeune journée.

The Cruel Bird

The whole night through, the cruel bird held me
At the sheer climax of the bliss of hearing
That voice directed with such tender fury
At a sky on fire with stars until morning.

You pierce the soul, decree the destiny
Of a given look that cannot be taken back;
Everything that was, you change to ashes,
Oh too high voice, instinct's own ecstasy....

Dawn in the shadow outlines the face
Of a lovely day: nothing to me already.
One day more is only an empty landscape,

What is a day without that face of yours?
No!...My mind, turning back night-wards,
Rejects the dawn, and the youthful day.

À l'aurore

À l'aurore, avant la chaleur,
La tendresse de la couleur
À peine éparse sur le monde,
Étonne et blesse la douleur.

Ô Nuit, que j'ai toute soufferte,
Souffrez ce sourire des cieux
Et cette immense fleur offerte
Sur le front d'un jour gracieux.

Grande offrande de tant de roses,
Le mal vous peut-il soutenir
Et voir rougissantes les choses
À leurs promesses revenir?

J'ai vu se feindre tant de songes
Sur mes ténèbres sans sommeil
Que je range entre les mensonges
Même la force du soleil,

Et que je doute si j'accueille
Par le dégoût, par le désir,
Ce jour très jeune sur la feuille
Dont l'or vierge se peut saisir.

At Dawn

At dawn, before the heats begin,
The tenderness of the color
Just impinging on the world
Startles and stabs at pain.

Oh Night I have endured entire,
Endure this smiling of the skies,
The offering of this great blossom
On the brow of a gracious day.

Oblation of so many roses,
Can suffering withstand
And look at all things in the flush
Of their promises renewed?

I've seen so many simulated
Dreams in my sleepless gloom,
That I must range among delusions
Even the power of the sun,

And cannot know whether I welcome
In disgust or in desire,
This day so infant on the leaf
Due to be snatched by the virgin gold.

Équinoxe

Élégie

To look...

Je change...Qui me fuit?...Ses feuilles immobiles
　　Accablent l'arbre que je vois...
Ses bras épais sont las de bercer mes sibylles:
　　Mon silence a perdu ses voix.

Mon âme, si son hymne était une fontaine
　　Qui chantait de toutes ses eaux,
N'est plus qu'une eau profonde où la pierre lointaine
　　Marque la tombe des oiseaux.

Au lit simple d'un sable aussi fin que la cendre
　　Dorment les pas que j'ai perdus,
Et je me sens vivant sous les ombres descendre
　　Par leurs vestiges confondus.

Je perds distinctement Psyché la somnambule
　　Dans les voiles trop purs de l'eau
Dont le calme et le temps se troublent d'une bulle
　　Qui se défait de ce tombeau.

À soi-même, peut-être, Elle parle et pardonne,
　　Mais cédant à ses yeux fermés,
Elle me fuit fidèle, et, tendre, m'abandonne
　　À mes destins inanimés.

Equinox

Elegy

To look...

I change....Who glides away from me?...Its motionless
leaves
Weigh down the tree I see....
Its dense arms are weary of lulling my sibyls:
My silence is bereft of its voices.

My mind, supposing its hymn were once a fountain
Singing with all its waters,
Is now a deep lake, where a distant stone marks
The burial place of the birds.

In the sheer bed of sand that is fine as ash
Sleep the footprints I have lost,
And I feel myself living go down under the shades
By way of their intermingled tracks.

Distinctly I feel the loss of the sleepwalking Psyche
Behind the waters' too pure veils,
Its calm and its time disturbed by a bubble
Self-released from this tomb.

Perhaps she talks to herself in self-forgiveness,
But drawn away by her closed eyes,
Faithful still she quits me, and tender, consigns me
To my inanimate dooms.

Elle me laisse au cœur sa perte inexpliquée,
  Et ce cœur qui bat sans espoir
Dispute à Perséphone Eurydice piquée
  Au sein pur par le serpent noir...

Sombre et mourant témoin de nos tendres annales,
  Ô soleil, comme notre amour,
L'invincible douceur des plages infernales
  T'appelle aux rives sans retour.

Automne, transparence ! ô solitude accrue
  De tristesse et de liberté !
Toute chose m'est claire à peine disparue;
  Ce qui n'est plus se fait clarté.

Tandis que je m'attache à mon regard de pierre
  Dans le fixe et le dur «Pourquoi?»,
Un noir frémissement, l'ombre d'une paupière
  Palpite entre moi-même et moi...

Ô quelle éternité d'absence spontanée
  Vient tout à coup de s'abréger?...
Une feuille qui tombe a divisé l'année
  De son événement léger.

Vers moi, restes ardents, feuilles faibles et sèches,
  Roulez votre frêle rumeur,
Et toi, pâle Soleil, de tes dernières flèches,
  Perce-moi ce temps qui se meurt...

Oui, je m'éveille enfin, saisi d'un vent d'automne
  Qui soulève un vol rouge et triste;
Tant de pourpre panique aux trombes d'or m'étonne
  Que je m'irrite et que j'existe !

She leaves me with her loss unexplained in my heart,
  And that heart, beating without hope,
Strives with Persephone for Eurydice stung
  In her breast by the black snake. . . .

Somber, expiring witness of our tender annals,
  Oh sun, as with our love,
Irresistibly gentle, the infernal shores
  Summon you to the banks of no return.

Autumn, translucency! Oh solitude enhanced
  By sorrow and by release!
Once it is gone each thing grows bright to me;
  What no longer is becomes a clarity.

While I am growing fixed into my gaze of stone
  In the stern and unalterable "Why?",
A dark shimmer, the shadow of an eyelid
  Quivers between myself and me. . . .

Ah, what an everlasting, self-willed absence
  Suddenly comes to a halt? . . .
A leaf in falling has divided the year
  With its diaphanous event.

Burning embers, feeble and dried-up leaves, roll
  Your frail whisper towards me,
And you, pale Sun, with your ultimate arrows
  Dispatch for me this dying-away time. . . .

Yes, I awake at last, caught by an autumn wind
  Rising in a red and dreary swarm;
Such a panic of purple in the golden cloudbursts
  Startles my nerves to life, and I am!

La Caresse

Mes chaudes mains, baigne-les
Dans les tiennes...Rien ne calme
Comme d'amour ondulés
Les passages d'une palme.

Tout familiers qu'ils me sont,
Tes anneaux à longues pierres
Se fondent dans le frisson
Qui fait clore les paupières

Et le mal s'étale, tant,
Comme une dalle est polie,
Une caresse l'étend
Jusqu'à la mélancolie.

The Caress

My hot hands, bathe them
In your own.... Nothing calms
Like love's undulating
Passing pressures of a palm.

Familiar as their touch may be,
Your rings with their long jewels
Melt away in the shiver
Persuading the eyelids to close

And the pain thins out, to where,
As a sheet of stone is polished,
A caress diffuses it
To the brink of melancholy.

Chanson à part

Que fais-tu? De tout.
Que vaux-tu? Ne sais,
Présages, essais,
Puissance et dégoût...
Que vaux-tu? Ne sais...
Que veux-tu? Rien, mais tout.

Que sais-tu? L'ennui.
Que peux-tu? Songer.
Songer pour changer
Chaque jour en nuit.
Que sais-tu? Songer
Pour changer d'ennui.

Que veux-tu? Mon bien.
Que dois-tu? Savoir,
Prévoir et pouvoir
Qui ne sert de rien.
Que crains-tu? Vouloir.
Qui es-tu? Mais rien!

Où vas-tu? À mort.
Qu'y faire? Finir,
Ne plus revenir
Au coquin de sort.
Où vas-tu? Finir.
Que faire? Le mort.

Song Sotto Voce

What d'you do? Anything.
What are you good for? Don't know,
Surmises and efforts,
Power and surfeit.
What are you good for? Don't know.…
And you want? Nothing, yet all.

What d'you know? Boredom.
And your talent? For dreaming.
Dreaming of changing
Each day into night.
What d'you know? That dreaming
Can vary the boredom.

And you want? My own good.
What's your duty? To know,
To foresee, to be able,
All to no purpose.
And you fear? To wish.
Who are you? Why, nothing!

Whither bound? For death.
What for? To finish,
And never come back
To this knavish lot.
Whither bound? For the finish.
What to do? To act dead.

Le Philosophe et la Jeune Parque

La Jeune Parque, un jour, trouva son Philosophe:

«Ah, dit-elle, de quelle étoffe
Je saurai donc mon être fait...
À plus d'un je produis l'effet
D'une personne tout obscure;
Chaque mortel qui n'a point cure
De songer ni d'approfondir,
Au seul nom que je porte a tôt fait de bondir.
Quand ce n'est la pitié, j'excite la colère,
Et parmi les meilleurs esprits,
S'il est quelqu'un qui me tolère,
Le reste tient qu'il s'est mépris.
Ces gens disent qu'il faut qu'une muse ne cause
Non plus de peines qu'une rose!
Qui la respire a purement plaisir.
Mais les amours sont les plus précieuses
Qu'un long labeur de l'âme et du désir
Mène à leurs fins délicieuses.
Aux cœurs profonds ne suffit point
D'un regard, qu'un baiser rejoint,
Pour qu'on vole au plus vif d'une brève aventure...
Non!...L'objet vraiment cher s'orne de vos tourments,
Vos yeux en pleurs lui voient des diamants,
L'amère nuit en fait la plus tendre peinture.
C'est pourquoi je me garde et mes secrets charmants.
Mon cœur veut qu'on me force, et vous refuse, Amants
Que rebutent les nœuds de ma belle ceinture.
Mon Père l'a prescrit: j'appartiens à l'effort.

The Philosopher and the Young Fate

One day the Young Fate found her Philosopher:

"Ah," said she, "now I shall know
Of what stuff my being is made....
On more than some I create the effect
Of a character totally obscure;
The mortal who never gives a thought
To considering or finding out,
Is ready to give a start at the very name I bear.
If not condescension, then it's anger I provoke;
And if, among the best of minds,
There's one who finds me tolerable,
The rest maintain he has delusions.
Such people are convinced that a muse ought to raise
No more difficulties than a rose!
Who breathes its scent enjoys it free.
But most precious of all are the loves
Which a long toil of the soul and its desire
Leads to their delectable ends.
Deeper hearts are not satisfied
With a glance, overtaken by a kiss,
Leading at once to the core of a fleeting affair....
No!....A thing truly loved is enhanced by your torments
Your eyes see it in diamonds of tears,
The night of bitterness paints it in the tenderest colors.
That is why I withhold myself and my secret charms.
My heart requires force, and rejects you, Lovers,
Who are put off by the knottings of my lovely girdle.
My Father so decreed: I am the reward of effort.

Mes ténèbres me font maîtresse de mon sort,
Et ne livrent enfin qu'à l'heureux petit nombre
Cette innocente MOI que fait frémir son ombre
Cependant que l'Amour ébranle ses genoux.
CERTES, d'un grand désir je fus l'œuvre anxieuse...
Mais je ne suis en moi pas plus mystérieuse
Que le plus simple d'entre vous...
Mortels, vous êtes chair, souvenance, présage;
Vous fûtes; vous serez; vous portez tel visage:
Vous êtes tout; vous n'êtes rien,
Supports du monde et roseaux que l'air brise,
Vous VIVEZ...Quelle surprise!...
Un mystère est tout votre bien,
Et cet arcane en vous s'étonnerait du mien?
Que seriez-vous, si vous n'étiez mystère?
Un peu de songe sur la terre,
Un peu d'amour, de faim, de soif, qui font des pas
Dont aucun ne fuit le trépas,
Et vous partageriez le pur destin des bêtes
Si les Dieux n'eussent mis, comme un puissant ressort,
Au plus intime de vos têtes,
Le grand don de ne rien comprendre à votre sort.
«Qui suis-je?» dit au jour le vivant qui s'éveille
Et que redresse le soleil.
«Où vais-je?» fait l'esprit qu'immole le sommeil,
Quand la nuit le recueille en sa propre merveille.
Le plus habile est piqué de l'abeille,
Dans l'âme du moindre homme un serpent se remord;
Un sot même est orné d'énigmes par la mort
Qui le pare et le drape en personnage grave,

My obscurities make me mistress of my fate,
Delivering only to the happy few
That innocent ME who trembles at her shadow
The while Love is quivering at the knees.
   TRUE, I was the anxious labor of a great desire,
But in myself I am no more mysterious
      Than the simplest among you.. . .
Mortals, you are made of flesh, of remembering, and
      forebodings;
You were; you shall be; you have a certain face;
   You are everything; and nothing,
  Pillars of the universe, and reeds broken by the wind,
    You are ALIVE.. . .How astonishing !. . .
    A mystery is all you possess,
And that enigma of yours chooses to wonder at mine?
  What would you be, if you were not mystery?
    A little dreaming on the earth,
A little love, hunger, thirst, taking steps
    Not one of which can escape death,
And you would share the simple lot of beasts
If the Gods had not inserted, like a powerful spring,
    Within your inmost heads
The great gift of understanding nothing of your fates.
'Who am I?' says the living to the daylight when he wakes
    Lifted erect by the sun.
'Where am I bound?' thinks the mind consigned to
  slumber,
When night receives him into her own wonders.
    The most astute is stung by this bee,
In the soul of the least of men a serpent bites its tail;
Even a fool is enhanced by the mysteries of death
Draping and laying him out like a weighty personage,

Glacé d'un tel secret qu'il en demeure esclave.

    ALLEZ !—Que tout fût clair, tout vous semblerait vain !
Votre ennui peuplerait un univers sans ombre
D'une impassible vie aux âmes sans levain.
Mais quelque inquiétude est un présent divin.
L'espoir qui dans vos yeux brille sur un seuil sombre
Ne se repose pas sur un monde trop sûr;
De toutes vos grandeurs le principe est obscur.
Les plus profonds humains, incompris de soi-mêmes,
D'une certaine nuit tirent des biens suprêmes
Et les très purs objets de leurs nobles amours.
Un trésor ténébreux fait l'éclat de vos jours:
Un silence est la source étrange des poèmes.
Connaissez donc en vous le fond de mon discours:
C'est de vous que j'ai pris l'ombre qui vous éprouve.
Qui s'égare en soi-même aussitôt me retrouve.
Dans l'obscur de la vie où se perd le regard,
    Le temps travaille, la mort couve,
    Une Parque y songe à l'écart.
C'est MOI...Tentez d'aimer cette jeune rebelle:
    «Je suis noire, mais je suis belle»
Comme chante l'Amante, au Cantique du Roi,
    Et si j'inspire quelque effroi,
Poème que je suis, à qui ne peut me suivre,
    Quoi de plus prompt que de fermer un livre?

    C'est ainsi que l'on se délivre
De ces écrits si clairs qu'on n'y trouve que soi.»

Petrified by a secret that makes him its slave.
GO ON !—If all were clear, all would be futile !
Your boredom would people a shadowless universe
With the inert life of souls devoid of leaven.
But a certain restlessness is the gift of the gods.
The hope in your eyes glittering on a dark threshold
Reposes on a world that is far from secure;
The source of all your greatnesses is none too clear.
The subtlest of humankind, obscure to themselves,
Draw their supreme feats out of a form of darkness
As well as the pure objects of their noblest passions.
A treasure from the glooms makes the glory of your days;
A silence is the alien source of the poem.
Recognize in yourselves the matter of my verse:
It is from you I drew the obscurity that tries you.
Who strays within himself discovers me at once.
In the shadows of life where the eye is bewildered,
  Where time labors, and death broods,
  There a Fate dreams aloof.
That fate is ME....Try to love the young rebel:
  '*I am black, but I am comely*'
As the Beloved sings in the Song of Solomon,
  And if I inspire alarm,
Poem that I am, for him who cannot follow me,
  What could be easier than to shut a book?

  That is how to get rid
Of writings so clear they mirror nothing but oneself."

Le Sonnet d'Irène

par Monsieur de Saint-Ambroyse
1644

De ses divers desirs combien qu'Elle se vante,
Pour mon cœur enchanté Son dire est un détour;
Elle n'ayme qu'un seul, Elle ayme dans l'Amour
Une personne rare, et supresme et sçavante.

Vainement se plaist-Elle à Se feindre mouvante
Et de trop de regards le divin quarrefour;
Cette beauté n'est point pour les galants d'un jour
Qui porte un corps si pur d'éternelle vivante !

Vous m'avez beau parler d'une trouppe d'amants,
Vous parer de desirs comme de diamants,
Et me vouloir au cœur placer plus d'une flèche,

J'en souffre, Irène d'or, mais j'en souffre sans foy,
Instruit qu'en chaque aurore, ô Rose toute fraîche,
Tu ne vis qu'en moy seul et ne Te plays qu'en moy.

Of Irene, a Sonnett

by Monsieur de Saint-Ambroyse,
1644

Of her diverse desyres howsomuch Shee may vaunt,
To my inchanted hearte Her word is but a blinde;
She loveth onlie One, loving in Love alone
A being rare and soveraigne, of cunning minde.

'Tis vanity if She please to feigne Herself a Mover
And meeting-place divine of all-too-thronging gazes;
No Beautie Shee for this or that day's lover,
Who wears a forme thus pure, whom life eternal graces.

In vain You speake to me of a whole troupe of swains,
Be-glistering yourself with desyres as diamonds,
In vain my hearte You seek to pierce with darte on darte,

Aureate Irene, I suffer unbeleeving in my paines,
Knowing that every Dawn, O freshe Rose intire,
You live in mee alone, in me is Your sole pleasure.

Pour votre Hêtre « Suprême »

À M.A.G.

Très noble Hêtre, tout l'été,
Qui retins la splendeur esclave,
Voici ton supplice apprêté
Par un ciel froidement suave.

Cent fois rappelé des corbeaux,
L'hiver te flagelle et t'écorche;
Au vent qui souffle des tombeaux
Les flammes tombent de ta torche !

Ton front, qui cachait l'infini,
N'est plus qu'une claire vigie,
À qui pèse même le nid
Où l'œil perdu se réfugie !

Tout l'hiver, le regard oiseux,
Trahi par la vitre bossue,
Sur la touffe où furent les œufs
Compose un songe sans issue !

Mais — ô Tristesse de saison,
Qui te consumes en toi-même,
Tu ne peux pas que ma raison
N'espère en le Hêtre Suprême !

For your "Supreme" Beech

To M.A.G.

Noblest Beech, all summer long
You who held splendor enslaved,
Now your ordeal is prepared
By a sky coldly benign.

A hundred times summoned by the rooks,
Winter flagellates and flays you;
In a wind blowing from the tombs
The flames are dropping from your torch!

Your brow that masked the infinite
Is now an empty watchtower,
Even a nest is a weight on it
Where the eye dismayed takes refuge!

All winter the idle gaze,
Belied by the embossed windowpane,
On the tuft where eggs once lay
Weaves a dream without issue.

And yet—oh seasonal Sorrow,
Consuming yourself within yourself,
You cannot hold back my reason
From hoping in the Beech Supreme.

Tant de Grâce et de Vénusté !
Se peut-il que toute elle meure,
France, où le moindre nid resté
Balance une fière demeure ?

Mille oiseaux chanteront plus d'un
Souvenir d'atroce tangage,
Quand reverdira par Verdun
Sauvé, notre illustre Langage !

So much grace and comeliness,
Can it possibly quite die?
—France, where the least remaining nest
Rocks a domain of pride?

A thousand birds will sing more than one
Memory of fearful storm-tossings
When grown green after Verdun
Saved will be our glorious language!

À cet éventail

Reviens du large allumé
Le chant des lampes — j'y cause
Distrait du soupir humé
Dans le chaud crêpe où ta pause

Se fait d'une épaule et d'air
Dont la chute d'ombre avive
Loin de mes discours l'éclair
Des feux de l'Inattentive.

Aère l'être rosé
De qui palpites allège
Parmi les ruches osé
La même onde de neige

Aidant les souffles que tu
Inventes sur le cœur tû.

To this Fan

(Written on a fan belonging
to Mme Gabrielle Fontainas-Hérold)

Back from the wide air the song
Of the lamps lit up—I gossip there
Unheeding the sigh inhaled
In the warm crepe where your pause

Is formed of a shoulder and the breath
Whose shadowy fall awakens
Remote from what I say the flash
Of the Heedless One's fires.

Aerate the rosy being
By whom you quiver and ease
Daringly amid the frills
The same surge of snow

Aiding the breaths which you
Devise upon the muted heart.

Petites Choses

Au-dessous d'un portrait

Que si j'étais placé devant cette effigie
Inconnu de moi-même, ignorant de mes traits,
À tant de plis affreux d'angoisse et d'énergie
Je lirais mes tourments et me reconnaîtrais.

*

Sur un éventail

Tantôt caprice et parfois indolence
L'ample éventail entre l'âme et l'ami
Vient dissiper ce qu'on dit à demi
Au vent léger qui le rend au silence.

*

À Juan Ramón Jiménez
que me envió tan preciosas rosas...

...Voici la porte refermée
Prison des roses de quelqu'un?....
La surprise avec le parfum
Me font une chambre charmée...

Seul et non seul, entre ces murs,
Dans l'air les présents les plus purs
Font douceur et gloire muette...
J'y respire un autre poète.

Madrid,
Miércoles 21 de Mayo 1924

Little Things

Inscription for a portrait

Suppose I were confronted by this effigy
Unknown to myself, ignorant of my own face,
By all those lines of anguish, and of force,
I would read my pangs, know who it was.

*

Upon a fan

Now from caprice, and again from indolence,
The ample fan, between mind and friend,
Half dismisses everything that's said
In a waft of air, back to silence.

*

To Juan Ramón Jiménez
que me envió tan preciosas rosas...

And now the door shuts again
Imprisoning roses from someone?...
Scent and astonishment
Create me a room bewitched....

Alone, not alone, between these walls,
The purest of gifts makes a sweetness
A mute glory in the air....
Where I breathe another poet.

Madrid
Miércoles 21 de Mayo 1924

DOUZE POÈMES

TWELVE POEMS

La Jeune Fille

Je suis la jeune fille bleue
Et souple et rose et docte et si
Jolie avec toute une lieue
Marine à l'ombre du sourcil !

Voici ta plus fraîche pensée
Quand mon iris vraiment iris
Pour éphémère fiancée
Te laisse un regret d'oasis.

Tandis que tu songes d'écrire
Ce qu'a vu ton œil voyageur
S'il me voit rougissante rire,
Tu n'oublieras plus ma rougeur.

Et dans la braise et sous la lampe,
Sur la feuille où le doigt posé
Vainement tomba de la tempe,
Reviendra mon rire rosé.

Aux flammes se mêle la souple
Jeune fille vive qui sait
Encor mal garder une couple
De colombes dans son corset.

The Girl

I am the young girl, blue
And supple, rosy, wise and so
Neat and yet with a whole league
Of sea-shadow in my eyelid !

Look, this is your freshest thought,
When my truly rainbow iris
As an ephemeral bride-to-be
Leaves you longing for an oasis.

While you dream of what to write
Of all your traveling eye has seen
If it sees me laugh and redden
My blush you will never forget.

And in the fire-glow, under the lamp,
On the page where the finger lies
Dropped in vain from the temple
My rosy laugh will come again.

Blending with the fire flames
A live and lissom girl there is
Who still cannot learn how to keep
A brace of doves inside her bodice.

Abeille spirituelle

O dieu démon démiurge ou destin
Mon appétit comme une abeille vive
Scintille et sonne environ le festin
Duquel ta grâce a voulu que je vive.

Ici dans l'or la muse a mis ce miel;
Là dans le verre une clarté choisie
Tient froidement la lumière du ciel
Algèbre pure et glacée ambroisie.

Le libre amour du bel entendement
Ô difficile et trop légère abeille
Du même fil se croise et se dément,
Heurte la coupe et manque la corbeille.

Ce point sonore atome le très pur
Chargé de foudre et follement futile
Va-t-il porter la vie unique sur
Le plus beau songe et le plus inutile?

Le diable au corps c'est le recul de Dieu
La flamme court fuyant la cendre pure
Chaque soleil n'est qu'un rien radieux
Qui fait pâlir son aurore future.

Où te poser bourdon de l'absolu
Instant toujours détaché de toi-même?
Tout ce qu'il touche est sûrement élu
Indivisible angoisse du poème.

J'aime l'erreur qui tisse un long chemin
Dans une nuit non avare de mondes
La veille y brille avec son lendemain
Au même sein des ténèbres fécondes.

Spiritual Bee

God demon demiurge or destiny
My appetite like a lively bee
Buzzes and shimmers all about the feast
Which your grace has decreed to nourish me.

Here in day's gold the muse has laid this honey:
There in the glass an elected gleam
Pure algebra and iced ambrosia
Coldly contains light out of the sky.

Carefree love of lovely understanding
Fastidious and all-too-nimble bee
Doubles upon its track, defeats itself,
Missing the flowerbed, hurtles at the cup.

This sounding point of utmost purity
Lightning-charged and crazily futile
Will it bring singular life to bear upon
The finest and most useless dream of all?

Devil in the body is God's recoil
The flame sweeps on leaving behind pure ash
A mere radiant nothing is each sun
Creating the pallor of its future dawn.

Where to place you drone of the absolute
Instant forever separate from yourself?
All that it touches is distinctly chosen
Indivisible anguish of the poem.

I love the straying that weaves a path prolonged
Within a night not miserly of worlds
Evening gleams there with its tomorrow
In the one womb of all-fruitful glooms.

Béatrice

Le moindre pli de cette amour
Inflige la plus grande peine;
Un instant fait noircir un jour,
Un soupir te rend incertaine,

Te fait paraître sans retour.
Et tu me sembles si lointaine
Quand au fond de cette fontaine
Où se reflète mon amour

Je crois voir d'assez tristes signes,
Des ombres de soleils insignes,
Et des reprises de tes yeux;

Et la douce amère parole
Par quoi se fane de mes cieux
La parfaite et pure corolle.

Beatrice

The slightest crossing of this love
Inflicts the greatest suffering;
An instant can darken a day,
A sigh can make your image vague,

Render you inaccessible.
And you seem to me so remote
When in the depths of this pool
Where my love reflects itself

I seem to see omens, signs,
Shadows from memorable suns,
And renewals of your eyes;

And the sweet bitter word
At which there fades the perfect
And pure corolla of my skies.

Le Philosophe

À peine m'eut-elle prédit
Sans parler, mais par l'œil immense,
Magnifiquement la démence
De mon désir approfondi

Que mon extase se perdit
Dans un sourire qui commence
Tel sur les mers l'or est semence
De soleils tombés de midi.

La splendeur à l'enfantillage
Touche par mille doigts dorés
Comme le dieu fait au feuillage;

Trop de bonheur que vous aurez
Jeté du plus haut de votre âme
Brise en l'étincelle la flamme.

The Philosopher

No sooner had she foretold to me
Unspeaking, through her great eye alone
Magnificent, the insanity
Of my desire fulfilled to its depths

Than my ecstasy was lost
In a smiling that begins
As on the seas the gold is seed
From suns fallen at high noon.

Glory toys with childishness
Through a thousand golden fingers
As the god touches the leafage;

Excess of joy that you may fling
From the highest jet of the soul
Within the spark breaks off the flame.

À chaque doigt

À chaque doigt sourd la goutte
Et tu trempes tes mains pour
Mieux feindre sur qui t'écoute
L'onde d'un premier amour

Né limpide flamme ou bulle
D'azur qu'on croit étranger
À tous les sus et sans nulle
Épaule à boire ou manger

Sans se pencher ton visage
Ou l'autre qu'on dirait tel
Vers ses sœurs du paysage
Que le vacarme immortel

Peur de la chèvre camuse
Inonde de cornemuse.

At Every Finger

At every finger oozes a drop
And you dip your hands the more
To simulate on whoever listens
The ripple of an early love

Born a lucent flame or bubble
Of azure we see as alien
To all those known and devoid
Of shoulder to drink or eat

Without leaning your face
Or the other that seems the same
Towards its sisters of the landscape
Whom the immortal din

Fear of the snub-nosed goat
Floods with bagpipe sound.

T'évanouir

T'évanouir — aile ou voilure
Par la brume bue au nadir
Et plus s'enfume la brûlure
Qu'est la mer pour y refroidir

Un vertige igné dont palpite
La ronde odeur d'onde et de pur
Vent de spire où se précipite
Ton vol de cheveux au sel sur.

Pense au plus délicieux gouffre;
Crise du soir même — tu fus
Abondamment celle qui souffre
Aux grises roses de l'Infus

Sourire — comme au vague on glisse
Où meurt la lèvre humide hélice.

For You to Vanish

For you to vanish—wing or sail
By the mist consumed at the nadir
And the more smoky grows the burning
Which is the sea there to cool

A whirling fire that agitates
The rough breath of wave and pure
Spiral wind where plunges
Your flight of hair to the bitter salt.

Muse on the most delicious deeps;
Crisis of evening itself—you were
Abundantly she who suffers
In the grey roses of the Innate

Smile—as one glides to the void
Where the lip dies a moist helix.

À la vitre d'hiver...

À la vitre d'hiver que voile mon haleine
Mon front brûlant demande un glacial appui
Et tout mon corps pensif aux paresses de laine
S'abandonne au ciel vide où vivre n'est qu'ennui.

Sous son faible soleil je vois fondre *aujourd'hui*
Déjà dans la pâleur d'une époque lointaine
Tant je sens que je suis vers ma perte certaine
Le Temps, le sang des jours, qui de mon âme fuit.

Passez, tout ce qui soit! Seul, mon silence existe;
Jusqu'au fond de mon cœur je le veux soutenir,
Et muet, feindre en moi la mort d'un souvenir.

Amour est le secret de cette forme triste
L'absence habite l'ombre où je n'attends plus rien
Que l'ample effacement des choses par le mien.

On the Winter Pane...

On the winter pane veiled by my breath
My brow burning seeks a glacial pressure
And all my thinking body woolly with languors
Sinks into the empty sky where living is tedium.

Under its feeble sun I watch *today* melting
Already into the pallor of a distant era
So deeply I feel I am following to my certain end
Time, the blood of days, oozing from my soul.

Pass, all that may be! My silence alone subsists;
I will maintain it to my heart's very depths,
And dumb, rehearse in me a memory's death.

Love is the secret of this mournful shape
Absence inhabits the ghost where I await
Only the wide annulment of all things by my own.

À des divinités cachées

Des Néréides gîte,
Quand elles ont sommeil,
Grottes où l'onde agite
S'il existe un soleil,
Et vous montagnes, cave
En qui l'écume esclave
Des mets menant le choc
Ébranle l'ombre en butte
Aux bords que répercute
Sonorement le roc !

Sonnez trombes et trompes
Dans votre profondeur
Fêtes d'Éros et pompes
Pures de l'impudeur !
Sonnez, sonnez, secrètes
Conques dans les retraites
De notre liberté !
Sonnez les beaux insultes
Et les tendres tumultes
Des membres concertés.

Tonnez, terre profonde
Sous les vulgaires pas;
Ils marchent sur un monde
Que le ciel ne voit pas !
Mais nos étranges havres
Ne sont pas de cadavres
Mais pleins de dieux vivants

To Hidden Divinities

Lair of the Nereids
When in the mood for slumber,
Grottoes where waves wonder
Whether the sun exists,
And you mountains, vault
Where the foam enslaved
Leading the sea's assault
Shakes the shadow, a prey
To the fringes which the rock
Reverberates thunderously!

Sound, waterspouts, trumps
In your uttermost depths
For banquets of Eros and
Pure, lubricious pomps!
Sound, sound, arcane
Conches in the domains
Of our hidden liberty!
Resound the glorious insults
And the tender tumults
Of limbs in conspiracy.

Thunder, earth, in your depths
Under the vulgar tread;
They walk above a world
Never viewed by heaven!
But our undreamt-of havens
Are thronged not with the drowned
But with living gods

Et des mêmes déesses
De qui fuirent les tresses
Les voiles et les vents !

Sonnez, sonnez, Nuit creuse
Le temps retournera
Vers l'aube bienheureuse
D'un jour que l'on verra !
Ce jour de Janus même
Nouant le diadème
Sur ma double raison
Dira le droit des tombes
À laisser les colombes
Poindre de leur prison !

And companion goddesses
Whose escaping tresses
Stream with veils and wind !

Sound, sound, Night's void,
Time will turn back again
Towards the blessed dawn
Of a day yet to be seen !
That day of Janus himself
Binding the diadem
Over my twofold reason
Will decree the right of graves
To allow the doves
To dawn again from their prison !

Odelette nocturne

Écoute la nuit...
Tout devient merveille:
Le silence éveille
Une ombre de bruit...

Une ombre de voix
N'est-ce point la mienne
Dont l'âme te vienne
Si loin que je sois?

Oh! ne doute point:
C'est moi, c'est moi-même
Le même qui t'aime
Si proche de loin,

Se parle de toi,
Le drap sur la bouche,
Blotti dans sa couche
Et seul avec soi.

Il n'y a plus rien
Qu'une peine tendre
Et le mal d'attendre
On ne sait quel bien.

J'implore tout bas
Dans la nuit obscure
La claire figure
Que tu ne vois pas;

A Little Night-Piece

Listen to the night....
All becomes marvel;
Silence awakes
The ghost of a sound....

A ghost of a voice,
Is it not mine
Whose soul can reach you
Far off though I am?

Ah! have no doubt:
It is, it is me,
The one whose love
Is so close from far off,

Talking of you
Through a sheeted mouth,
Hunched in his bed
Alone with himself.

Nothing is left
But a tender pain
Suspense of waiting
For a boon unknown.

Mute I implore
In the black of night
The shining face
That you cannot see;

J'implore si fort,
Tout est si tranquille,
Qu'à travers la ville
Où tout fait le mort

Une ombre de voix
Qui sera la mienne
Dans l'âme te vienne
Si loin que je sois.

So strong is my prayer,
So quiet is all
That over the city
Where all is dead-still

A ghost of a voice
That can only be mine
Creeps into your soul
Far off though I am.

Fragment

...les morts n'ont point de ces retours étranges
Ils reviennent peut-être en de faibles esprits;
Mais le tien, mais le mien, jamais ne sont repris
Que d'un vivant retour de leur soif de vendanges.

Celle qui sait le goût des choses que tu manges
M'a retiré des mains leurs délices sans prix;
J'ai vu s'évanouir comme il m'avait surpris
Tout l'amour qui le cède au vain orgueil des anges.

Le cœur n'est pas plus pur pour vieillir plus amer;
L'un et l'autre chacun le regard sur la mer
Voient le même regret dans la diverse écume...

Fragment

...the dead do not have these strange recurrences,
It may be they return to weaker spirits;
But yours, and mine, are never caught again
Unless by a revived longing for vintages.

She who knows the savor of the things you eat
Has robbed my hands of their once priceless joys;
I have watched fade as I watched it overwhelm me
All the love that yields to the empty pride of angels.

The heart is none the purer growing bitter as it ages;
One and the other gazing fixedly at the sea
Study the same regret in the varying foam....

Silence

Il ne reste de nous ce soir qu'un grand silence
Vers l'ombre va pencher l'implacable balance;
Bientôt de ce beau jour que j'ai tant attendu
Dans le creux de ma main l'or tiède aura fondu.
La puissance du soir à la fin s'est montrée.
Un grand silence touche à plus d'une contrée !
Le temps qui disparut n'est plus si loin de nous
Ni la mort qui s'éveille et baise nos genoux,
Se fait plus familière avec cette âme sombre.
Nos plus doux souvenirs mordent nos cœurs dans l'ombre
Où les faveurs se font d'implacables refus
Ô quel soupir arrache à celui que je fus
Des temps délicieux les présences funèbres...

Silence

This evening nothing is left of us but a great silence,
The implacable scales are tilting toward darkness;
Soon, of this lovely day I so long awaited
The warm gold will have melted away in my hand.
Evening makes its power felt in the end.
A grand silence encroaches on many a country!
Time vanished is no longer so far from us
And death as it wakens, and kisses our knees,
Is alien no more to this somber mind.
Tenderest memories gnaw at our hearts in the dark
Where favors granted turn to stark rejections.
Oh what a sigh wrenches from him I was
The funereal presence of past ecstasies. . . .

Aux vieux livres

Gardiens, profonds témoins, purs et puissants Pénates,
Conservateurs des dons,
Tombes où sont réduits à leurs vains aromates
Les dieux que nous perdons,

Ors devant qui le temps pleure pour qu'on délivre,
Armés d'un doigt pieux,
De l'immortel ennui de n'être plus qu'un livre
Un mort harmonieux,

Longtemps j'ai détesté, foule dense et dorée,
L'insupportable faix
Que place au front vivant la montagne laurée
Des monuments parfaits !

Quel poids resplendissant sur l'âme vierge, ô Maîtres,
Que vos temples parlants !
Delphes définitive aux masses hexamètres,
Antres étincelants,

Marbres tout murmurants d'âmes récompensées
Car elles ont construit
Leur auguste demeure à de pures pensées
Soustraites à la nuit.

Charmes, mesures d'or, odes nettes et grecques
Splendeur des vieux soleils
Qui se couchent dans l'or mort des bibliothèques
Pour de riches sommeils,

To Old Books

Guardians, deep testifiers, pure and puissant Penates,
　　Keepers of what was given,
Tombs where reside, reduced to their frail aromatic essences,
　　The gods from whom we are riven,

Gold casings faced with which time weeps for the deliverance,
　　By some devout finger,
From the immortal tedium of being no more than a book
　　Some dead harmonious singer,

For long I have hated, serried and gilded ranks,
　　The intolerable load
Laid on a living brow by the laurel mountain
　　Of monuments perfected!

Oh masters, what a dazzling weight on the virgin soul
　　Your speaking temples are!
Delphic oracles defined in hexametric masses,
　　Caves of glittering treasure,

Marble memorials echoing with murmurs of souls satisfied
　　After having built
A majestic dwelling-place for thoughts purified
　　And rescued from the night.

Spells, golden measures, odes concise and Greek,
　　Radiance of ancient suns
Gone to couch in the mortuary gilt of libraries
　　On slumber's rich boons,

Telle qu'on le répand de la Belle enchantée
        Qui close tant de jours
Se plut à tant dormir pour n'être point tentée
        À de viles amours.

Hélas, ce long dormir à la mort s'appareille
        Tant le réveil surseoit !
Des barbares naissants vous n'aurez plus l'oreille
        Si longue qu'elle soit.

Déjà le Cygne cède, et dans la nuit sonore
        S'envolera demain.
Le parfum de Platon lentement s'évapore
        Du souvenir humain.

Radiance such as is rumored of the enchanted Beauty
      Who, rather than fall a prey
To the temptings of base lovers, chose to sleep
      Locked up for many a day.

That long sleeping begins, alas, to look like death's twin,
      So delayed is the waking!
Of barbarians to be however long the ear,
      You will not win its heeding.

Already resigns the Swan, and into sounding night
      Tomorrow flies away.
Slowly the Platonic incense will evaporate
      Out of human memory.

POÈMES PUBLIÉS À PART

UNCOLLECTED POEMS

Testament de Vénitienne

La pompe sereine de la lune
Scelle le bonheur du repos.
Gœthe, *Le Second Faust*

Le jour où je mourrai, courez à ma gondole
Emplissez-la d'œillets, de roses, de jasmins
Couchez-moi sur ces fleurs, croisez mes pâles mains,
Laissez mes yeux ouverts comme ceux d'une idole...

Déposez sur mon front aussi pur que le lait
Un diadème vert de feuilles enlacées,
Mettez un long baiser sur mes lèvres glacées,
Et recouvrez mon corps d'un crêpe violet.

Quand vous aurez fini cette tâche importune,
Oh ! regardez-moi bien blanche au milieu des fleurs...
Regardez, regardez...puis sans soupirs, sans pleurs,
Poussez-moi dans la mer un soir de pleine lune.

...La gondole s'en va...s'en va parmi les flots !
Chantez ! là-bas ! chantez. Je vous entends encore
Oh ! les douces chansons que l'espace dévore...
Que les accords sont lents !...Vos chants sont des sanglots.

Adieu ! moi je m'en vais froide et morte sur l'onde
L'eau me berce et la lune argente ma beauté
La gondole s'avance et puis l'immensité
M'entoure lentement, bleuissante et profonde.

A Venetian Lady's Last Will

The serene ceremony of the moon
Seals the bliss of rest.
Goethe, *Faust*, Part II.

The day I die, haste to my gondola,
Fill it with pinks, roses, and jasmine,
Lay me on the flowers, fold my pale hands,
Leave my eyes open like an idol's eyes....

Lay on my brow pure white as milk
A green diadem of leaves interwound,
Seal with a kiss my frozen lips,
And cover my body with a violet crepe.

When you have finished this weary task,
Oh, gaze at how white I am among the flowers....
Gaze, gaze...then, without sighs or tears,
Launch me out to sea on an evening of full moon.

...Away the gondola goes...away among the waves.
Sing, yonder, sing! I can hear you still.
Ah, the sweet carols that space consumes....
How slow the strains of harmony!...Your songs are
    sobbings.

Adieu! I make my way cold and dead on the wave
The water lulls me and the moon silvers my beauty.
The gondola advances until immensity
Slowly enfolds me, profound and ever more blue.

Pessimisme d'une heure

Il est une douleur sans nom, sans but, sans cause
Qui vient je ne sais d'où, je ne sais trop pourquoi,
Aux heures sans travail, sans désir et sans foi
Où le dégoût amer enfielle toute chose.

Rien ne nous fait penser, rien ne nous intéresse,
On a l'esprit fixé sur un maudit point noir.
Tout est sombre: dedans, dehors, le jour, le soir,
C'est un effondrement dans un puits de tristesse.

C'est surtout vers la nuit, quand s'allume la lampe.
Cet ennui fond sur nous, aussi prompt qu'un vautour.
Le découragement nous guette au coin du jour,
Quand s'élève du sol l'obscurité qui rampe.

Ce n'est pas celui-là qui mène à la rivière
C'est un mauvais moment à passer, voilà tout.
Il nous fait ressortir la joie, ce dégoût
Comme l'obscurité fait aimer la lumière.

An Hour's Black Mood

There is a suffering—nameless, aimless, causeless,
Coming from I know not where, nor can I guess why,
In hours devoid of work, desire, or faith
When sour disgust envenoms everything.

Nothing provokes a thought, nothing affects us,
The mind stays fixed upon a cursed black point.
All is gloomy without, within, by day or night,
It is a subsiding into a pit of sadness.

It is towards night, above all, when the lamp lights,
That this melancholy swoops down on us, swift as a vulture.
At day's corner despondency lies in wait for us,
As rampant shadow rises from the ground.

Not of the sort, this, that leads to the river,
It is an evil moment to be traversed, no more.
It makes joy, this disgust, spring out in relief for us
Just as darkness makes us love the light.

Solitude

Loin du monde, je vis tout seul comme un ermite
Enfermé dans mon cœur mieux que dans un tombeau.
Je raffine mon goût du bizarre et du beau,
Dans la sérénité d'un rêve sans limite.

Car mon esprit, avec un art toujours nouveau,
Sait s'illusionner—quand un désir l'irrite.
L'hallucination merveilleuse l'habite
Et je jouis sans fin de mon propre cerveau...

Je méprise les sens, les vices, et la femme,
Moi qui puis évoquer dans le fond de mon âme
La lumière...le son, la multiple beauté !

Moi qui puis combiner des voluptés étranges
Moi dont le rêve peut fuir dans l'immensité
Plus haut que les vautours, les astres et les anges !...

Solitude

Far from the world, I live all alone like a hermit,
Locked inside my heart more than in a tomb.
I refine my liking for the bizarre and beautiful
In the serenity of a limitless dream.

For my mind, with an art ever new,
Can create its own illusions—whenever a desire stirs it.
Marvellous hallucination inhabits it,
And I draw an endless joy from my own brain....

I scorn the senses, the vices, and woman,
I who in the depth of my soul can evoke
Light...sound, beauty in its complexity!

I who can compound strange, voluptuous joys,
I whose dream can take flight into immensity
High above vultures, stars or angels!...

La Voix des choses

À Monsieur G. F.

C'est ainsi que se font les vers!

Si vous le voulez revenons en ville !
Mais on est si bien sur ce vieux rempart...
L'on ne parle pas !...C'est fort inutile
Et l'on se comprend bien mieux qu'autre part !...

Oui. L'on se comprend sans vaines paroles.
Et sans dissiper par le bruit des voix
Le charme divin des idées folles,
Près du flot battant, une rose aux doigts...

La matière parle et l'homme l'écoute
La vague murmure et la brise geint,
La cloche bourdonne et le vent, sans doute,
Ou bien quelque esprit, dans la nuit se plaint.

Et l'Homme, attentif aux phrases troublantes
Des ondes, des bois, des clochers lointains...
Laisse s'évader des Choses troublantes...
...Et ce sont des vers aux sons argentins.

The Voice of Things

To Monsieur G.F.

This is how verses are made!

If you like, let's go back to town !
But how pleasant it is on this ancient rampart. . . .
No talking ! . . .It is so useless,
And we understand each other far better than elsewhere ! . . .

Yes. Understanding without empty words.
And with no sound of voices to dispel
The charm divine of wild fancies,
By the beating wave, a rose in one's fingers. . . .

Matter speaks and man listens,
The wave murmurs and the breeze whines,
The bell booms and no doubt it's the wind,
Or else some ghost, that complains in the night. . . .

And Man, alert to the uneasy speech
Of the waves, the woods, the distant chimes. . .
Allows troublous Things their escape.
. . .And behold, they are verse of silvery sounds.

Rêve

Je rêve un fort splendide et calme, où la nature
S'endort entre la rive et le flot infini,
Près de palais portant des dômes d'or bruni
Près des vaisseaux couvrant de drapeaux leur mâture.

Vers le large horizon où vont les matelots
Les cloches d'argent fin jettent leurs chants étranges.
L'enivrante senteur des vins et des oranges
Se mêle à la senteur enivrante des flots...

Une lente chanson monte vers les étoiles,
Douce comme un soupir, triste comme un adieu.
Sur l'horizon la lune ouvre son œil de feu
Et jette ses rayons parmi les lourdes voiles.

Brune à la lèvre rose et couverte de fards,
La fille, l'œil luisant comme une girandole,
Sur la hanche roulant ainsi qu'une gondole,
Hideusement s'en va sous les flots blafards.

Et moi, mélancolique amant de l'onde sombre,
Ami des grands vaisseaux noirs et silencieux,
J'erre dans la fraîcheur du vent délicieux
Qui fait trembler dans l'eau des lumières sans nombre.

Dream

I dream a calm and splendid fort, where nature
Slumbers between bank and infinite wave,
Close by palaces bearing domes of burnished gold,
Near the ships that load their rigging with flags.

Out to the wide horizon where the sailors go,
The fine silver chimes fling their strange songs.
The heady scents of wines and oranges
Mingle with the heady scent of the waves. . . .

A slow sing-song rises toward the stars,
Tender as a sigh, sad as a farewell.
On the skyline the moon opens her fiery eye
And darts her rays among the heavy sails.

Brown with lips of rose and loaded with paint,
The prostitute, her eye glittering like a chandelier,
Swaying on her hips like a gondola,
Goes her hideous way under waves of whiteness.

And I, melancholy lover of the gloomy main,
Friend to the great black silent ships,
Saunter in the freshness of the delectable breeze
That sets lights numberless a-quiver in the water.

Repas

Le saltimbanque et sa femelle
À l'ombre de l'âne broutant
Vident sous le ciel éclatant
Une déplorable gamelle.

Mais la nature peu cruelle
Pour le fol et joyeux passant
Met un soleil éblouissant
Dans le fer-blanc de l'écuelle,

Fait fondre un rubis dans le vin
Inspirateur du vieux devin,
Faiseur de tours, mangeur de flamme,

Et verse, pleine de bonté,
Une rasade de gaieté
Dans la tristesse de son âme.

Meal

The strolling showman and his mate,
Shadowed by the browsing donkey,
Empty a miserable platter
Under the dazzling sky.

But nature, not too unkind
To the gay and feckless wayfarer,
Lodges a dazzling sun
In the white tin bowl,

Melts a ruby in the wine
Inspiring the old fortune-teller,
Juggler, and flame-swallower,

And full of kindness pours
A bumper of gaiety
Into the sorrow of his soul.

L'Église

Parmi l'Immensité pesante du Saint lieu
Dans l'ombre inexprimable, effrayante, dorée,
Solennelle, se sent la présence de Dieu
Dans le recueillement de la chose adorée.

L'obscurité confond les pourpres et les ors
Et les lampes d'argent gardiennes des Reliques
Et dans ce sombre éclat plane sur ces trésors
L'âpre mysticité des dogmes catholiques.

Le Grand Christ, constellé de pleurs en diamants
Et de rubis saignants, coulant du coup de lance,
Là-haut semble rêver fermant ses yeux aimants
Dans ce vague parfum d'encens et de silence !

La Vierge byzantine et de massif argent
Demeure hiératique en sa chape orfroisie
Fixant ses yeux de perle aux Cieux, comme songeant
Aux Azurs lumineux et lointaines de l'Asie.

The Church

Amid the weighty Immensity of the Holy precinct,
In the unutterable shadow, awful, gilded,
Solemn, the presence of God can be felt
In the tranquillity of the thing adored.

The gloom mingles the purples and the golds
And the silver lamps that watch over the Relics;
And in the dusky splendor there hovers above these riches
The ruthless mysticism of Catholic dogmas.

The Great Christ, starred with tears as diamonds
And with bleeding rubies streaming from the lance-wound,
Seems to dream aloft, closing his lodestar eyes
In that cloudy perfume of incense and silence !

The Byzantine Virgin, in solid silver,
Remains hieratic in her orphreyed cope,
Fixing her eyes of pearl on Heaven, as if dreaming
Of the remote and luminous blues of Asia.

La Mer

Du zénith le soleil trouant l'azur éclate
Au miroir de la mer orbiculaire et bleu
Les flèches d'or, tombant du haut du ciel en feu,
S'enfoncent pesamment dans l'onde calme et plate.

Et la houle odorante au large se dilate
Sinueuse s'allonge et puis se dresse un peu
Comme un serpent sacré sous l'œil fixe d'un Dieu.
Le jour baisse. Le flot s'infuse, d'écarlate.

Dans l'océan d'émeaux [*sic*] translucides fondu
L'astre, mourant oiseau qui plonge, est descendu
Et l'or du soir se perd dans l'Éternelle tombe.

Une vague s'élève à peine et puis retombe
Cependant que s'étend la belle au crêpe sombre
La nuit mystérieuse avec ses yeux sans nombre.

The Sea

From the zenith piercing the azure the sun glitters
In the sea's orbicular and blue mirror.
The golden arrows hurling from the fiery sky's height
Are heavily engulfed in the calm flat main.

And the odorous swell of the open sea dilates
Sinuously lengthens and then rises slightly
Like a sacred serpent under the fixed gaze of a God.
Day sinks. The surge is steeped in scarlet.

Sunk in the ocean of translucent blazonries
The sun, as a dying bird plunges, has set,
And evening's gold is lost in the Eternal tomb.

A wave scarcely rises and then falls
Whilst the beauty in the gloomy crepe spreads—
Night the mysterious with her numberless eyes.

Pour la nuit

Oh ! quelle chair d'odeur fine aromatisée
Où de l'huile blonde a mis sa molle senteur,
Est plus douce que la Nuit au souffle chanteur,
Et sa brise parmi les roses tamisée?

Quel féminin baiser plus léger que le sien?
Et ses yeux, ses yeux d'or immortels, quelle Femme
Peut égaler ses regards noirs avec leur flamme
Et quelle Voix vaudrait ce vent musicien?...

Adieu donc ! toi qui m'attendais ! L'heure est trop bonn
À l'amour immatériel je m'abandonne
Que me promet ce Soir calme et ce bord de l'eau.

Car, j'aime cette grève où mon ombre s'allonge
Et cette Nuit ! Et cette lune au blanc halo
Et puis la murmurante et triste Mer qui songe !...

To the Night

Oh, what flesh of finely etherized fragrance
Where a sunny oil has mingled its soft scent,
Is sweeter than the Night with her singing breath
And her breeze filtered through the roses?

What feminine kiss lighter than hers?
And her eyes, her immortal golden eyes, what Woman
Can equal her dark gazes with their flame,
And what Voice could vie with that musician wind?...

So goodbye, you who were waiting for me! The hour's too
      fine!
I give myself up to the immaterial love
Promised me by this Evening calm and the water's edge.

For I love this strand where my shadow lengthens,
And this Night! And this moon with blanched halo,
And then the murmurous and mournful Sea, dreaming!...

Conseil d'ami

À Albert Dugrip

Verse en un pur cristal un or fauve et sucré.
Allume un feu. Songe un doux songe et fuis le Monde.
Ferme ta porte à toute amante, brune ou blonde.
Ouvre un livre à la pure extase consacré.

Délicieusement imagine. — Et Calcule
Que Rien peut être, hormis ton Rêve, n'est Réel...
Caresse ton vieux chat, et regarde le Ciel
Dans ses yeux, verts miroirs du rose Crépuscule.

Puis, écoutant parler l'intérieure Voix,
Évoque le Passé. Sommeille, lis ou bois,
Et n'ayant nul chagrin, car tu n'as nulle envie

Sens à travers tes jours paisibles mais divers
À travers les printemps, les étés, les hivers
Paresseusement fuir le fleuve de ta Vie !

A Friend's Advice

To Albert Dugrip

Pour a tawny and sugared gold into a pure crystal.
Light a fire. Dream a sweet dream and shun the world.
Close your doors to every mistress, brown or blonde,
Open a book dedicated to pure ecstasy.

Create delicious fancies.—And Deem
That perhaps Nothing, save your Dream, is Real....
Fondle your old cat and gaze at the Heaven
In his eyes—green mirrors of the rosy Twilight.

Then, listening to what the interior Voice says,
Summon the Past. Doze, read or drink,
And free from care, being free from every wish,

Feel how through your placid but changing days,
Through the springs, the summers, and the winters,
Lazily the river of your Life glides away.

Tu sais?...

Oh ! combien de soirs ensemble hantés
Amis nous ont faits !...amis pour toujours !...
Et combien de vers ensemble chantés
Au pied de tu sais quelles vieilles tours.

La lune a mêlé nos ombres, la nuit.
Nos ombres mystérieuses de songeurs,
De songeurs fuyant l'Éternel Ennui,
Fuyant par les nuits les ennuis rongeurs !

...Frère !...Soit cette Lune qui ruisselle
Le large Sceau d'or à jamais qui scelle
Nos âmes, et nos splendides désirs...

Mon rêve et tes Pensées métaphysiques
S'aiment ! Et nous enlaçons nos plaisirs
Comme le soir — tu sais? — de ces belles musiques !...

Remember?...

Ah, how many haunted evenings together
Have made us friends!...Friends forever!...
And how many poems chanted together
At the foot of ancient towers you recall.

The moon mingled our shadows at night,
Our mysterious shadows of dreamers,
Dreamers in flight from Eternal Care,
Fleeing through the nights the gnawing cares!

Brother!...Let this streaming Moon
Be the great gold Seal forever that binds
Our souls, and our shining desires....

My Dream and your metaphysical Mind
Are in love! And we interweave our pleasures
As on the evening—remember?—of the lovely musics!...

Sur l'eau

Fuir ! sur un fleuve calme et si calme et si lent
Dans l'ivoire incrusté d'argent d'un canot frêle
Qui sur l'eau glisse comme un rêve, — vague et blanc !
Fuir ! avec elle fuir l'heure sous son ombrelle !

Sous les feuilles frôler les riches nénuphars,
Au fil du songe, avec une lenteur suave,
Et boire l'oubli tendre en ces parfums épars
Vaporisés par le doux vent — tel un esclave !...

Puis — le calme et le calme et les magiques ronds
Que font les perles qui tombent des avirons
Et ce pétale fin qui tournoie et qui file !...

Puis, ses Yeux dans les miens cherchant le vrai miroir
De son visage pâle aux baisers difficiles
Où passent des rougeurs délicates — ce Soir...

On the Water

To glide !—on a calm river thus calm and thus slow
In the silver-encrusted ivory of a frail boat
That skims the water like a daydream—vague and white !
To glide, glide away the hour with her under her parasol.

To brush by the rich water lilies under the leaves,
On the stream of dream, with a dulcet slowness,
And drink kind oblivion in the thinned perfumes
Vaporized by the soft wind—like a slave !

And then—the calm, the calm and the magic rings
Made by the pearls falling from the oars
And that lissom petal eddying and sailing off. . . .

And then, her Eyes searching in mine for the true
Mirror of her pale face, hard to kiss,
Where delicate reds evanesce—this Evening. . . .

La Suave Agonie

Pourquoi tes Yeux sont si grands, ce soir?...
Et, dans ces flammes de soleil mortes,
Toi qui vas mourir, que veux-tu voir?

Pourquoi ces baisers purs vers le soir?
Pourquoi de ta main pâle tu portes
Lentement, des sourires secrets,

Comme des fleurs vaguement données
À des vierges aux regards sacrés,
Qui dans l'air passent couronnées?...

Toi, qui verras *ailleurs* le Matin,
Ô ma chère agonisante, admire,
Parmi ces brouillards tendres de myrrhe,

Les Salutaires Voix d'or lointain...

Soothing Death Pangs

Why are your eyes so large, this evening?...
And, in those dead flames of sun,
You who are dying, what do you seek to see?

Why those pure kisses evening-wards,
Why on your pale hand do you bear
Slowly, smiles of secrecy,

Like flowers vaguely given
To virgins with sacred gazes
Who pass by crowned in the air?...

You who will see Morning *elsewhere*,
Wonder, oh my dying one,
Among those tender mists of myrrh

At the remote Beneficent Voices of gold....

Luxurieuse au bain

L'eau se trouble — amoureusement — de Roses vagues
Riantes parmi la mousse et le marbre pur,
Car une chair, illuminant l'humide azur
Vient d'y plonger, avec des ronds d'heureuses vagues !...

...Ô baigneuse !...de ton rire c'est le secret !...
Aux caresses de l'eau, tes mûrs désirs s'apaisent
Tu chéris la clarté fraîche et ces fleurs qui baisent
Tes seins de perle, tes bras clairs, ton corps nacré.

Et tu te pâmes dans les lueurs ! Dédaigneuse
Des amantes et des jeunes gens ! Ô baigneuse !
Toi, qui, dans la piscine, attends l'heure où soudain

Les bûchers s'allument, rouges, sur le ciel vide
Ta nudité s'enflamme et tu nages splendide
Dans la riche lumière impudique du bain !...

Bathing Wanton

The water is—amorously—stirred by vague Roses
Laughing among the moss and the pure marble,
For a body, irradiating the pure azure,
Has just plunged in, with ripple of happy waves !...

...Ah bather !...this is the secret of your laughter !...
With the caressing water your ripe desires are appeased,
You cherish the cool clarity and those flowers that kiss
Your breasts of pearl, your bright arms, your nacreous body.

And you swoon away in the gleams ! Disdainful
Of lovelorn girls and children ! O bather !
You who in the pool are awaiting the hour when sudden

The pyres blaze and redden on the empty sky,
Your nakedness flames and you swim resplendent
In the rich shameless radiance of the bath !

À Alcide Blavet

Tu rappelles ces grands enfants frais et naïfs
D'abeilles amoureux et de légers dytiques
Dont la flûte attirait aux lisières antiques
Les nymphes en amour qui s'enlaçaient aux ifs.

Tu leur ravis quelqu'un de ces hymnes furtifs
Sur leurs lèvres, mêlés au miel aromatique.
Mais tu surpris aussi le sourire érotique
Donc s'éclairait le bas de leurs masques pensifs !

...Et c'est pourquoi, mon tendre Alcide, quand tu chantes,
Sur tes lèvres souvent des lèvres de Bacchantes
Nous dérobent tes vers — pour ton baiser sucré.

La dryade que nul poète n'effarouche
A traversé, parfois, le soir, le bois sacré
Et de sa lèvre d'or, elle a scellé ta bouche !

To Alcide Blavet

You recall those great children, fresh, ingenuous
Lovers of the bees and light-winged water-beetles
Whose flute-playing would draw to the antic forest verge
The amorous nymphs who wove themselves about the yews.

You ravished one of those furtive hymns of theirs
On their very lips, mingled with aromatic honey.
But you also surprised the lascive smile
That lit up their pensive masks from beneath.

And that, tender Alcide, is why, when you sing,
Often the lips of Bacchants on your very lips
Rob us of your verses—for the sake of your dulcet kiss.

The dryad whom no poet can startle
Has sometimes of an evening traversed the sacred wood
And, with her golden lip, she has sealed your mouth !

Les Chats blancs

À Albert Dugrip

Dans l'or clair du soleil, étirant leurs vertèbres,
— Blancs comme neige — on voit des chats efféminés,
Closant leurs yeux jaloux des intimes ténèbres,
Dormir — dans la tiédeur des poils illuminés.

Leur fourrure a l'éclat des glaciers baignés d'aube.
Dessous elle, leur corps, frêle, nerveux et fin,
A des frissonnements de fille dans sa robe,
Et leur beauté s'affine en des langueurs sans fin !

Sans doute ! ils ont jadis animé de leur Âme
La chair d'un philosophe ou celle d'une femme,
Car, depuis, leur candeur éclatante et sans prix

Ayant l'orgueil confus d'une grande première
Les aristocratise en un calme mépris,
Indifférents à tout ce qui n'est pas *Lumière!*

White Cats

To Albert Dugrip

In the clear gold of sunlight, stretching their backs,
—White as snow—see the voluptuous cats,
Closing eyes jealous of their inner glooms,
Slumbering in the tepid warmth of their illumined fur.

Their coats have the dazzle of dawn-bathed glaciers.
Inside them, their bodies, frail, sinewy, and slender,
Feel the shiverings of a girl inside her dress,
And their beauty refines itself in endless languors.

No question but their Soul of old has animated
The flesh of a philosopher, or a woman's body,
For since then their dazzling and inestimable whiteness

Holding the mingled splendor of a grand premiere,
Ennobles them to a rank of calm contempt,
Indifferent to everything but *Light* itself!

Cimetière

Ô fleurs obscures des sépulcres, vos parfums
Montent vers le soleil immobile des tombes...
En moi, battent de l'aile, Éternelles colombes,
Les blancs désirs du calme où dorment les défunts.

Car les poètes morts ne soufflent les Paroles,
Les rêves plus subtils qui hantent les tombeaux,
Rêves sans fin ! lents et secrets, toujours plus beaux,
Encens des vagues Nuits souterraines et molles.

...Les funèbres jardins sont tendres, et les fleurs
Y sont fraîches de l'eau douloureuse des pleurs,
Et je sens que parmi vos corolles vermeilles,

Ô fleurs obscures ! fleurs de [mon] pressentiment,
Légères de la Vie, ivres confusément
Les âmes valsent comme un essaim blond d'abeilles.

Cemetery

Oh occult sepulchral blossoms, your perfumes
Are mounting to the motionless sun of the tombs.. . .
Within me beat their wings, Eternal doves,
White longings for the calm where the dead are sleeping.

For dead poets never breathe the Words,
The dreams finer-spun that haunt the tombs,
Dreams without end! Growing in beauty, secret and slow
Incense of the vague soft subterranean Nights.

. . .Funereal gardens are kind, and the flowers there
Fresh with the painful watering of tears,
And among your rosy corollas I can feel,

Oh occult flowers, flowers of premonition,
That souls disburdened of Life confusedly waltz
In a heady whirl like a blond swarm of bees.

Le Jeune Prêtre

Sous les calmes cyprès d'un jardin clérical
Va le jeune homme noir, aux yeux lents et magiques.
Lassé de l'exégèse et des chants liturgiques
Il savoure le bleu repos dominical.

L'air est plein de parfums et de cloches sonnantes !
Mais le séminariste évoque dans son cœur
Oublieux du latin murmuré dans le chœur
Un rêve de bataille et d'armes frissonnantes.

Et — se dressent ses mains faites pour l'ostensoir,
Cherchant un glaive lourd ! car il lui semble voir
Au couchant ruisseler le sang doré des anges !

Là-haut ! il veut nageant dans le Ciel clair et vert,
Parmi les Séraphins bardés de feux étranges,
Au son du cor, choquer du fer contre l'Enfer !...

The Young Priest

Under the calm cypresses of a clerical garden
Goes the black-clad youth, his eyes slow and magical.
Wearied with exegesis and liturgical chants
He savors the blue dominical quiet.

The air is filled with perfumes and pealing bells !
But forgetful of the murmured Latin in the choir,
The young seminarist arouses in his heart
A dream of battle and thrilling clash of arms.

And. . .his hands fashioned for the monstrance stiffen
And rise in search of a heavy brand ! For he seems to see
The glittering blood of angels streaming in the sunset !

There in the height, floating in the clear green Heaven,
Among the Seraphim armored with strange fires,
He longs, at the sound of horns, for the clash of steel with
    Hell !. . .

Viol

Bronze du musée secret

Dans le métal sonore et rare de Corinthe,
Un artiste ancien a figé savamment
Le païen rêve — si troublant et si charmant
D'une coupable et triste et trop exquise étreinte.

Belle et chaude ! — une Femme agace un mince enfant
Ignorant de l'Amour, qui repousse la lèvre
Et les tétins vers lui dardés, brûlants de fièvre
Et les regards chargés d'un désir triomphant...

...Millénaire ! le viol de bronze se consomme !
Le petit inquiet, sous le brasier charnel
Se tord et ne veut pas, horreur ! devenir homme...

Mais Elle le contient ! qui d'un geste éternel
Impose la splendeur de ses chairs odieuses
Et lui cherche le sexe avec des mains joyeuses !...

Rape

A Bronze in the Forbidden Museum

In the rare and resonant Corinthian metal
Cunningly an early artist has molded
The pagan dream—so troublous and beguiling—
Of a guilty, forlorn, and too exquisite embrace.

Warm and lovely !—a Woman entices a slip of a child
Ignorant of Love, repulsing the lips
And the breasts darted towards him, feverishly fiery,
And the looks charged with desire triumphant....

...Ten centuries old ! The rape in bronze is fulfilled !
The child alarmed under the fleshly brazier,
Writhes and rejects the horror of coming manhood....

But She holds him in ! She who thrusts with an ageless
    gesture
The splendor of her hateful flesh upon him,
As she gropes for his sex with joyous hands !...

Ensemble

À Pierre Louÿs

Je vous salue, ô frère exquis !...ô Mien !
Ensemble venons quand le jour mourra
Écouter le vieux chant grégorien !
Pénitente, une cloche tintera.

Comme un couvercle de tombeau, le soir
Bandera nos yeux, ouvrant notre cœur
Et nous marcherons, tenant l'encensoir
Dans la Nuit silencieuse du chœur.

Ô combien seuls devant Dieu ! combien seuls
Cherchant les purs et nocturnes linceuls
Où bruit la parole auguste d'or...

Marchons vers la Lampe des Bien-Aimés,
Prions, ô frère ! puis, les yeux fermés
Embrassons-nous devant le Saint Thrésor.

Together

To Pierre Louÿs

I greet you, oh exquisite brother!...Oh Mine!
Let us come together when day dies,
To listen to the ancient Gregorian chant!
A bell, penitent, will be pealing.

Like the lid of a tomb, evening
Will bind our eyes, laying open our heart
And we will walk, bearing the censer
In the silent Night of the choir.

Oh how lone before God! How alone
Seeking the pure nocturnal shrouds
Where rustles the venerable golden word....

Let us walk towards the Lamp of True Lovers,
Let us pray, oh brother! And then with eyes closed
Let us kiss before the Sacred Treasure.

Fleur mystique

Lys mystique ! Elle avait la ferveur des Élus !
Et Vierge ! Elle adorait les pieds calmes des Vierges ;
Dans l'étincellement des métaux et des cierges,
Sa voix douce tintait comme des Angélus.

Une couleur de lune ondulait sous son voile.
Et dans sa chair, semblaient fuir les reflets nacrés
Du petit jour, luisant sur les vases sacrés,
Aux messes du matin, vers la dernière étoile.

Ses yeux étaient plus clairs que des astres naissants !
Indicible parfum de cires et d'encens,
Son vêtement sentait l'antique sacristie !

Et c'est en la voyant que le regret me vint
De n'être pas le Christ de ce rêve divin,
Car mon visage pâle était comme une hostie !

354

Mystic Flower

Mystic lily! She had the fervor of the Blessed!
And Virgin she worshiped the calm feet of the Virgins;
Amid the glittering of metals and candles
Her sweet voice would ring like the Angelus.

A tint of moonlight wavered beneath her veil.
And the mother-of-pearl gleam of first light seemed
To vanish in her flesh, shining on the sacred vessels,
At morning mass, when the final star sets.

Her eyes were clearer than astral dawnings!
Inexpressible perfume of waxes and incense,
Her robe was redolent of the ancient sacristy!

And it was on seeing her that I felt a sadness
At not being the Christ of that divine dream,
For my face in its pallor was like the Host!

Merci

Comme pour prédire un sort pur
À qui des nudités s'amuse,
Penchant sa vérité camuse
Et sa barbe d'automne sur

L'ornemental pré qu'il effeuille
Un Faune, épars au calme esprit
Du paysage et qui sourit
De son ironie haute, cueille

La gerbe ! heureuse de se voir
Surprise au détour du dimanche
Pour, rieuse, odorante et blanche,
Être au gré de ce geste noir

Offerte en signe de malice
À qui s'amuse de Narcisse.

Thanks

As though to foretell a pure fate
For one who makes fun of nudities
Leaning his snub-nosed frankness
And his autumnal beard above

The decorative meadow he disleafs
A Faun, diffused in the calm mind
Of the landscape, smiling down
From his lofty irony

Culls the sheaf—happy to be
Surprised in the nook of Sunday—
As a token offering of malice

—Merry, scented and white—
At the beck of that black gesture
To one who mocks at Narcissus.

Ballet

Sur tes lèvres, sommeil d'or où l'ombreuse bouche
Bâille (pour mieux se taire à tout le bête azur),
Sens-tu, tel un vil astre indifférent, la mouche
Transparente tourner autour du mot très pur

Que tu ne diras pas — fleur, diamant ou pierre
Ou rose jeune encor dans un vierge jardin
Une nudité fraîche sous une paupière
Balancée, amusée hors du chaos mondain.

Cette minute ailée éparpille un sonore
Vol d'étincelles au vent solaire pour briller
Sur tes dents, sur tes hauts fruits de chair, sur l'aurore

Des cheveux où j'eus peur à la voir scintiller
Petit feu naturel d'un sidéral insecte
Né sous le souffle d'or qui tes songes humecte.

Ballet

On your lips, golden slumber where the shadowy mouth
Yawns (the better to be dumb to all the brute azure),
Can you feel—like a vile and trivial star—the fly
Transparent hovering round the pure pure word

You will not utter—flower, diamond, or stone,
Or rose still young in a virgin garden
A cool nudity under an eyelid,
Poised and amused outside the worldly chaos.

This winged minute scatters a sounding flight
Of sparkles in the solar wind to gleam
On your teeth, on your lifted fruits of flesh, on the dawn

Of the hair where I feared to see it scintillate
Tiny natural fire of a sidereal insect
Born under the golden breath moistening your dreams.

Intermède

Ô soirée à peine frivole
D'une mince lune sur l'eau
Qu'hallucine sans qu'il s'envole
Le noir silence d'un oiseau

La plume d'ombre un peu lointaine
Du cygne funèbre qui dort
Charmant tombeau sur la fontaine
Anciennement pleine d'or

Se mire à l'eau sainte et lucide
Qu'égratine un souffle enchanté
Frôlant un souvenir limpide
Dans son exil diamanté.

Le deuil d'une dame nocturne
Éprise de larmes, ce soir
Ne serait-ce la taciturne
Ténèbre où gît le cygne noir?

Naïve ! qui ne dissimule
Sous l'aile triste un doux éclair
De plume, érotique scrupule
Comme un jupon deviné clair.

Interlude

O evening barely frivolous
With a thin moon on the water
Which the dark silence of a bird
Transfixes without his taking wing

The rather remote and shaded plume
Of the funereal sleeping swan
Charming tomb over the pool
Lately brimming with gold

Is mirrored in the holy, lucid water
Grazed by an enchanted breath
Brushing on a clear memory
In its diamonded exile.

The mourning of a lady of night
In love with tears, this evening
Could it be the taciturn
Gloom where the dark swan is entombed?

Ingenuous! who cannot hide
Beneath the dull wing a soft flash
Of feather, erotic scruple
Like a glimpse of bright petticoat hem.

Vers pour Mme de R...

Plongerai-je l'éclair secret dedans? que n'ai-je
Rêvé de lourds baisers — marchant dans cette neige
Dont le vent d'or m'aère allégeant mon Été
De blanc crêpe et touchant de bulles ma peau d'ombre
Par cet intime jeu de s'y être jeté?

Ô mon front vois de l'onde accourir le pur nombre !

Lines for Madame de R...

Shall I plunge the secret lightning therein? What have I not
Dreamed in the way of burdened kisses—walking in this
    snow
Whose golden wind airs me, lightening my Summer
With a white veil, and touching my shadowed skin with
    bubbles
By way of that inward game of having dived in?

O my brow, see in pure number how the water advances!

Moi à Paris

Ô ! Tu diligemment vagues
Parmi ton semblable et tu
Exposes si n'extravagues
Et si même un pur mais tu

Son de flûte humaine émue
Dans la ville où tu t'en vas
Voir sur les ponts si remue
Moins d'ivresse que rêvas

Tu? jadis dans cette blême
Tête où s'esquive du feu
Née en solitaire emblème
Pour savoir si c'est un Dieu

Qui se mire les narines
Dans l'eau de gauche, vitrines !

Me in Paris

Ah, diligently you waft
Among your like and you
Expose to view unless you rave
And even if a pure yet mute

Sound of flute human and sad
In the city where you set off
To see if less than you dreamed
Of wildness stirs on the bridges?

As of old in that pallid
Head where fire dwindles away
Born as a solitary emblem
In order to know if that be a God

Who mirrors his own nostrils
In the left-bank water, shop-windows!

La Dormeuse II

Ma nuit, le tour dormant de ton flanc pur amène
Un tiède fragment d'épaule pleine, peu
Sur ma bouche, et buvant cette vivante, dieu
Je me tais sur ma rive opposée à l'humaine.

Toute d'ombre et d'instinct amassée à ma peine,
Chère cendre insensible aux fantômes du feu,
Tu me tiens à demi dans le pli de ton vœu
Ô toujours plus absente et toujours plus prochaine.

Et ce bras mollement à tes songes m'enchaîne
Dont je sens m'effleurer le fluide dessin
De fraîcheur descendue au velours d'une haleine

Jusqu'à la masse d'ambre et d'âme de ton sein
Où perdu que je suis comme dans une mère
Tu respires l'enfant de ma seule chimère.

Le Soir trop beau...

Le soir trop beau qui sur nos âmes tombe
Verse au néant un pouvoir sans retour.
Comme un grand roi dans la pourpre succombe,
Un jour se meurt. Un jour est mort. Un jour !
L'heure trop belle est une belle tombe
Pour ce jour mort et son pouvoir d'amour.

A Sleeping Girl II

My night, the sleeping contour of your side leads
To a warm stretch of ripe shoulder, scarcely
Touching my lips, and imbibing this feminine life, a god,
I am mute upon my shore facing the living one.

All shadow and instinct amassed for my pains,
Precious ash, unfeeling to the phantoms of fire,
You half hold me in the nook of your devotion,
Oh ever more remote and ever more close.

And this arm softly to your dreams enchains me
Whose fluid outline I can feel caressing me
With coolness falling on the velvet of a breath

To the animate, amber mass of your breasts
Where, sunk as I am as though within a mother,
You breathe the child of my sole chimera.

Too lovely this evening . . .

Too lovely this evening falls across our minds
Shedding a returnless power into nothingness.
A great king expiring in his purple,
A day dies. A day is dead. A day!
The hour too lovely is a lovely tomb
For this day dead with all its power for loving.

Il est vrai. Je suis sombre.

Il est vrai. Je suis sombre. Et misérablement
Las de moi-même, et las de ces aurores sombres
Où l'âme fume et songe et compulse ses ombres
...Je sens peser sur moi la fatigue d'un ange.

True, I am gloomy.

True, I am gloomy. And miserably
Tired of myself, tired of these gloomy dawns
When the soul smokes and dreams and sifts through its
      shadows.
. . . I feel the weariness of an angel weighing me down.

VERS DE CIRCONSTANCE

OCCASIONAL VERSE

Quatrain adressé à Tristan Derème

Tristan, votre cœur est de bronze.
Je compte plus de jours que de biens je n'acquis
Depuis le jour où je naquis
Trente octobre soixante et onze.

Vers pour Charles-Adolphe Cantacuzène

À qui par la grippe alité
Trouverait la saison méchante,
Charles Cantacuzène chante
Quelque rose réalité.

Il se trouve sans nul malaise
Jusque dans le Père Lachaise;
Et cette muse danserait

Dans les plus sombres atmosphères...
La mort même n'a de secret
Pour tel subtil chargé d'affaires.

Hypotypose

Kant accuse ici-bas une si fauve haine
(L'écho répond: Cantacuzène)
Qu'il est doux de se fondre à la fine syrinx,

Diplomate discret, mais fantasque larynx
Soufflant au frac brodé l'âme syracusaine
(L'écho redit: Cantacuzène).

Quatrain for Tristan Derème

Tristan, yours is a heart of bronze.
I reckon more days than goods I've won
Since the day when I was born
Thirtieth October, seventy and one.

Lines to Charles-Adolphe Cantacuzène

To one who is bedridden with the grippe
And finds the weather villainous,
Charles Cantacuzène intones
A certain rosy reality.

Never remotely ill at ease
Not even in Père-Lachaise;
That Muse of his would dance

In the gloomiest circumstance....
Death itself has no secrets
For a plenipotentiary so subtle.

Hypotyposis

Kant accuses here below so wild a hate
    (Echo answers: Cantacuzenus)
That makes it sweet to melt into the slender syrinx,

Tactful diplomat, but marvelous larynx
Filling the braided jacket with a Syracusan afflatus
    (Echo insists: Cantacuzenus).

373

Dédicace à Léon-Paul Fargue sur un exemplaire
de *La Jeune Parque*

Hèle-moi ce 3-mâts barque
Ébène et sombre pavois !
    «La Parque»
A rugi le porte-voix...

Sous la barre, il prend le largue
S'il cède au souffle savant
    Si Fargue
Me le campe au lit du vent !

To Léon-Paul Fargue, on a copy of
La Jeune Parque

Hail me that 3-mast boat
Ebony, and somber-flagged !
   "The Fate"
Roars the loud-hailer....

Under the tiller, she'll take the open
Sea if guided by the wise
   Breath of Fargue
To settle her in the breeze !

Pour André Gide

(Ambroise, au Jardin Botanique...)

Ambroise, au Jardin Botanique
Avec toi-même a devisé...
Alas ! quel broyeur mécanique
À nos moments pulvérisé !

Sur cette tombe inoffensive
(Il n'y avait personne dedans)
Nous rîmes ! — La rose gencive
Éclatait encore de dents !

Mais les Terrestres Nourritures
Le citron, les choses à l'ail
Les purges et les confitures
Ont eu raison du bel émail.

Finissons par la chose triste:
il me faut demain mercredi
Ouvrir largement au dentiste
Ma bouche qui l'avait prédit.

Le Temps est fait d'un tas de choses,
C'est un Océan qu'on a bu !
De mille merdes et de roses
Monte dans l'âme le rebut !

For André Gide

(Ambroise, in the Botanic Garden...)

Ambroise, in the Botanic Garden,
Chatted with yourself in person....
Hélas ! What mechanical grinder
Pulverized away our time !

On that inoffensive tombstone
(Nobody whatever inside)
We laughed !—The gingival rose
Was then still flashing with teeth.

But then the Fruits of the Earth,
Lemons, and garlic-flavored things,
Sweetmeats, and purgatives
Have taken their toll of the fine enamel.

Let's close on the sorrowful note:
Tomorrow Wednesday I must
Open wide to the dentist
A mouth that had foretold just this.

Time is made of so many things,
It's like an Ocean one has swallowed !
The refuse rises in the soul
From thousands of messes and roses !

À Gênes

Odoriférantes
Sentes où l'on sent
Tant d'herbes et cent
Drogues différentes,

Où, narine errante,
Tu fends les encens
Que cède aux passants
L'ombre incohérente...

Connais-tu ce coin?
— Je n'ai pas besoin
De pupille glauque!

Ni bruit ni couleur
Ne valent la rauque
Friture en chaleur.

Quatrain à Mlle Adrienne Monnier

D'autres préfèrent la prairie
Mais les plus sages vont nier
La rose, dans ta librairie
Ô Mademoiselle Monnier.

At Genoa

Odoriferous,
Note how one sniffs
All the herbs and a hundred
Drugs in variety,

Where, errant nostril,
You cleave the incense
The incoherent shade
Offers the passer-by.. . .

You know this corner?
—No need have I
Of a glaucous eye !

No noise, no tint
Can equal the shriek
Of hot fried fish.

Quatrain to Mlle Adrienne Monnier, 1917

Others may prefer the meadow
But the wisest will forego
The rose, in your bookshop, Oh
Mademoiselle Monnier.

Vers à Miss Natalie Clifford Barney

Quoi ! C'est le chemin des Vignes
Qu'à la faveur des hivers
Vous prenez pour fuir mes vers ?
Mais quoique de vous indignes

Les voici, chœur acharné
À chanter pour Miss Barney !

À la même, dans une lettre du 11 août, 19..

Toujours, même dans le Maine,
Elle est close dans son flacon
Cette Nathalie inhumaine...
(Qui considère *as a bad job*
De ne pas être ru' Jacob.)

Sonnet à Mme Lucien Muhlfeld

Vous qui logez à quelques pas
De ma littéraire cuisine,
Belle dame, bonne voisine,
Voici mes fruits qui ne sont pas

Dans la laque ni le lampas,
Ni de Boissier fruits de l'usine,
Mais ce sont fruits de Mnémosyne
Qui sait confire ses appas.

Verses for Miss Natalie Clifford Barney

What ! So you take the road of the Vines
Under cover of the winter
So as to escape my lines?
But unworthy of you though they are

Here's the rabidly obstinate choir
Set on singing for Miss Barney !

To the same, in a letter of August 11, 19..

As ever, even in Maine,
She is locked up in her flagon,
Nathalie the Inhumane....
(Who feels it *as a bad job*
To be away from rue Jacob.)

Sonnet to Mme Lucien Muhlfeld

You who dwell a few paces away
From my literary kitchen,
Lovely lady, kindly neighbor,
See my products, they are made

Neither of lacquer nor flowered silk,
Nor are they fruits of the Boissier factory,
But fruits they are of Mnemosyne
Who knows how to confect her charms.

Croquez, mordez les rimes qu'offre
Le sonnet ou bizarre coffre,
Non ouvré par les fils du Ciel;

Et choisissez dans une gangue
De mots collés selon leur miel
La noix fondante sur la langue !

Quatrain à Valery Larbaud

Ma soif n'est pas peu piquante,
Ô Viñes et V. Larbaud,
De boire le soleil beau
Vobiscum, en Alicante.

Dédicace à Anna de Noailles

Noailles, tout le feu qui n'est point dans ces vers,
C'est que vous l'avez pris pour votre seul usage;
Ces Charmes n'ont d'espoir, par vos mains entr'ouverts,
Que dans les chauds regards de votre clair visage.

Vers pour Mme M. B.

Sur cette page, afin d'y retenir
Un peu de moi qui deviens souvenir
Et tels propos dans l'heure consumée,
Voici ma main, qui parle par fumée...

Bite and crunch on the rhymes offered
By the sonnet, a curious box
Not laid open by Heaven's offspring;

And select within the matrix
Of words combined for their sweetness
The center melting on the tongue !

Quatrain, in reply to a postcard from Valery Larbaud, 1920

My thirst is not a little whetted,
O Viñes and V. Larbaud,
To quaff the lovely sun
With you in Alicante.

Dedicatory lines to Anna de Noailles on a copy of *Charmes*, 1922

Noailles, all the fire that is missing from these lines
Must have been captured by you for your sole use.
Opened by your hand, these Charms have no hope
But in the warm gaze of your clear countenance.

Album verse for Mme M. B.

On this page, that it may retain
A little of me becoming a memory
And certain sayings in the used-up hour,
See my hand, speaking through the smoke....

Souvenir de Marrault, septembre 1939

Quel souvenir fait à demi
D'inquiétudes et de charmes !
Tout pour le calme et pour l'Ami,
Mais le ciel roule des bruits d'armes...
Marrault, les bois, le salon clair,
Nos regards sur la paix dorée...

Mais au cœur la poigne de fer
Et dans l'âme l'ombre abhorrée.
Ô ce septembre auprès de vous,
Sur le bord bleu d'une ère noire,
Mélange étrange, amer et doux,
Chers habitants de ma mémoire !

P. V. ce jour de Noël 40.

A Memory of Marrault, September 1939

What a memory, half and half
Made up of disquiet and delight!
Wholly given to calm and Friendship,
But the sky rolls with sounds of arms....
Marrault, the woods, the shining room
Our gazing on that golden peace....

But in the heart a mailed fist
And in the soul the detested shadow,
Ah, that September by your side
On the blue edge of a black era,
A strange blend of sweet and bitter,
Dear denizens of my memory!

      P.V. this Christmas day, 1940

EDITOR'S NOTE
AND
A NOTE ON THE TRANSLATIONS

Editor's Note

THIS EDITION includes all of Valéry's poems except a few of the immature early pieces and some later light verse written as letters to friends, etc.

Valéry wrote the autobiographical fragment "Recollection" during the first World War with no thought that it might serve as an introduction to his poems. It was written, he said, as a buffer against despair—against "the extraordinary commotion of a world gone mad." It was taken from his volume *Mélange*, "a sort of album made up of various fragments and illustrated with his own engravings," published by Les Bibliophiles de l'Automobile Club de France, September 30, 1939.

The translator is David Paul, the English writer who has also translated Valéry's informal dialogue *Idée Fixe*, his essays on art *Degas, Manet, Morisot*, and has collaborated on other volumes of the Collected Works. "Hélène," "Naissance de Vénus," "Un feu distinct," "Baignée," "Au bois dormant," and "Profusion du soir" were published, with English translations by David Paul, in *The Southern Review*, Spring, 1970, by permission of Princeton University Press.

James R. Lawler, who selected and translated the excerpts from Valéry's Notebooks "On Poets and Poetry" and wrote the "Notes and Commentaries" on the French poems, is the Professor of French Studies at the University of Western Australia.   J. M.

A Note on the Translations

A TRANSLATION of a poem cannot simply be a reflex or a replica. It must in some sense be an attempt at re-creation. What was fashioned, found, built together in the terms of one language must, ideally, be unmade and then rebuilt, re-fashioned in the terms of another. Only the element of finding becomes a completely different problem in the second process: it becomes a question of search with a very specific end in view—a search for the as yet unknown equivalents for what is there, given, final in the original.

Ideally (again) the given poem must be known, assimilated to a degree where the translator can almost press it back to an area of feeling, of meaning—pre-articulate but urgent—insisting on expression and form in the language he is using. Such a process implies long acquaintance. On the other hand, if rarely, a particular poem may strike a translator as something *wanted*, by him, by his language. The sense of recognition may be instant, but even then, the most literal-seeming translation of a line can be the result—tortuous path to clearest view—of a long and roundabout process.

But the problem varies with any two languages, and with every individual poet. Presumably there can be no correspondence of verse-forms between Chinese and English. But French and English are neighbor languages, and pretty well every verse-form in French has a possible equivalent in

English. The form is not a container: it is integral to the meaning of a poem; a prose crib of a Villon ballade, or a Baudelaire sonnet, inevitably loses the poem, however literally it may retain the words. This is even more the case with Valéry. In his poetry, words, theme, meaning, are indissolubly bound up with sound and form, through whatever transformer it may have to pass. The process might be very different with, say, Verlaine—a sly opportunist of lilts, hints, grimaces, overtones, an artfully artless exploiter of music and moods. Valéry, much the more difficult poet, may also be more possible in terms of translation.

French and English may be neighbor languages; but to work between the two is to increase the sense of their difference. (And it is the beginning and end of pedantry, whatever its terms, to object that a translation does not *sound* like the original. It can only sound like English.) Among linguistic instruments French, it seems to me, is the violin. No other language surely, judged by sound alone, can match its *vibrato*, the dwelling quality of its pure or nasal sounds, the dilating, suspended, cantabile effect of its "line." English on the other hand is the keyboard instrument: more complex, impure, omnifarious. But the moment the question of *range* comes in... Yes, the literature of the keyboard instrument is that much richer in the work of the masters; and English poetry is a world, compared with the French territory— however seductive that territory may be. Consider the Protean qualities of English as compared with its neighbor. Contrast the Hebraic English of the Bible with the near-contemporary Latinity of Browne and Milton. Or, within the range of the Stuart Bible itself, how different the expressive language of the Song of Songs is from that of Job, or the Book of Kings. Whereas an up-to-date translation reduces all three to the same commonplace. It seems as though a live sense of the language must be a sense in depth. A tree can only go on growing from its roots. Further development can only come from a backward-seeming exploration. The religion of *now* may be very momentous, but the moment pronounced, the word is then....

With regard to the forms in which Valéry wrote: the capital problem is obviously the classic form of the French alexandrine; six-stress rhyming couplets, at any dramatic or narrative length, remain (until proved otherwise) impossible in English. But to use the accepted English equivalent, rhyming heroics or traditional blank verse, is also a kind of betrayal. And besides, one real function of a translation is to stretch, however slightly, the possibilities of the language it uses—for their own sake. It must be an attempt to see what the translator's language can be made to do; an appeal merely to accepted usage is a dead end. The first essay in English blank verse was, after all, a translation, a real if necessarily rough attempt to break new ground. It seems to me that the six-stress line has considerable further possibilities—provided any iambic regularity is broken up, and provided it can resort to a five-stress line at least as often and as readily as the Augustine rhymed couplet could rely on the occasional hexameter.

Perhaps the two languages differ most in the matter of rhyme. English rhymes are so often consonantal, hard; comparable rhymes in French—*sec, avec, choc, foc*—are so rare as to be only usable for special purposes: a staccato emphasis, irony, the grotesque, or a literal shock value, as at the end of "Le Cimetière marin." Add to this that the very nature of Valéry's poetry—the finality of the structure in which rhyme, form, meaning, tone are indissolubly one—rules out any manipulation for the sake of rhyme; and it seemed to me that the latter had to be sacrificed, wherever it did not simply occur of itself. By a careful avoidance of clashes, the completeness of rhyme may seem to be there when absent in fact. A sonnet can remain a sonnet without rhyme, provided the ear's expectations are not too aggressively interfered with. . . .

Otherwise, no claim is made that these are meant to be "free" translations. Freedom is about as delusive or question-begging an assertion in translation as it is in the writing of an original poem. And the separate art of imitation, from Dryden to Pound, is simply, at its best, another form of autonomy, with self-created but necessary rules. The Poundian method may have been very difficult to evolve. It is all too easy to imitate, in a manner which offers the user every kind of escape clause. And after all, it is hard to imagine that all the world's poets, outside the English language, wrote in the same fashion.

DAVID PAUL

ON POETS AND POETRY

from the

NOTEBOOKS

On Poets

I have known many poets. Only one was as he should be, or as I should wish him to be. The rest were stupid or dull, shiftless cowards in matters of the mind. Their vanity, their childishness, and their huge and disgusting reluctance to see facts clearly. Their superstitions, their self-importance, their terrible likeness to everyone else as soon as their work was done, their servile minds. All this has nothing to do with what is called literary talent, which exists in perfect accord with downright stupidity.   1:193

The poet's poem interests me less than the subtleties and enlightenment he acquires by way of his work. And that is why one must *work* at one's poem, that is, work at oneself.
                                                                                          5:26

While writing verse, I observe the *ideas* that come to me, and I separate the *poetic* ones from the rest; and among the others are some I try to make poetic.

Now a poetic idea is a precise ambiguity, presenting by way of a fragment at a given point the *resonance* of the whole being.

It is something that can in some way be expressed by *itself*, almost *A Thing*, almost an event.   5:637

The true poet does not know the exact meaning of what he

has just had the good luck to write. A moment later he is a mere reader.

He has just written non-sense: something that must not *present* but *receive* a meaning, and that is very different.

How can this paradoxical enterprise be conceived? To write something that restores what was not given. The verse is waiting for a meaning. *The verse is listening to its reader.*

And likewise, when I say that I look at my ideas, my images, I can just as well say that they look at me. Where is one to situate the self?   6:195

The poet's object—his desire—is the improbable (the discovery). He cannot set himself a precise *subject*. Treating a subject leads to artificial transformations.   6:652

I work on a stanza. Ten, twenty times I am not satisfied, yet by coming back to it repeatedly I am familiar not with my text but with its possibilities, its harmonies.

The initial idea, the words set down—all that is of no importance. And it is just this freedom which is poetry, and makes my presence a sort of plastic matter. To communicate finally the state of perfect relationship by way of a verbal system obtained by such freedom—or which *should be*, and which at least it necessarily suggests: this is the object of poetry.   6:761

The poet's function is to celebrate, at the same time as he demonstrates, that amazing invention, language.

Among animals that have the gift of speech, some are more gifted than others. Just think about this: language has made almost everything and, among other things, it has made the mind.   6:923

The finest poetry is not written under the impact of an emotion, but a long time after, in the presence of a mistress or during a quiet walk. And that is why poets seem to extract so many things from nothing. The "nothing" in question is related to men's average capacity for discovering the poetic substance in themselves.   7:82

The poet is a man who seeks the intelligible and imaginable system of words, of which a lucky accident of language would be part; such and such a word, or a harmony of words, such and such a syntactical movement, or beginning, hit on by chance.   7:149

The poem is not related to *truth*; but the poet's act, his plan, his work, the arrangement of his illogical fantasies, owe everything to *logic*, which has judged and judged well *in secret*.   7:154

To get poetry—you should have a very vague notion of the poem to be written, and the most precise possible idea of poetry itself.

This is the opposite principle from prose, but not exactly opposite. The thread of poetry is the voice. The thread of prose is variable: sometimes the voice (and all this word signifies).   7:402

Poet—your verbal materialism—

You can snub novelists, philosophers, everyone whose credulity makes him subservient to words; who *must* believe that his discourse is *real* by its color, and that it signifies some *reality*. But you are aware that the real substance of a discourse is words alone, and forms.   8:368

The poet has every chance of botching his poem. He succeeds only when he spends uncounted time. Every poet is prodigal of his time—not only working time but especially the time when he is not working. 8:895

The effect of rules is to increase *the degree of consciousness* in a man writing verse.

The measure of the increase depends on the number of independent conditions which the *unified* act must satisfy.

8:910

A poem with variants is a scandal in the eyes of most people. For me it is a virtue. Intelligence is defined by the number of variants. 9:49

The secret, embarrassing, and indefinite aim of the poet is to *compose*—that is to say, to reach the singing-speaking state which is poetry.

A thing is *poetic* when it makes us sing—touches directly the instrument of song. The effects are poetic when they act on our organism as a song. 9:514

The poet searches for the verse that suits his *voice.* 9:703

The writer—no, the poet—passes through a strange crisis when what he first thought of as himself, and more himself than himself—becomes the intermediary between himself and a vague public. 9:722

Feci quod potui cum conscientia id faciendi.

When circumstances brought me back to poetry, I acted in this spirit—which requires a new start, getting rid of inspiration, novelty, etc.—everything that vanishes when we bring in awareness of the self and of what we are doing.

10:162

At times I have called myself a *versifier* because the word is clear, and *poet* is not.

10:163

The greatness of poets is that they grasp with their words what they only glimpse with their minds.

10:205

Poetry alone is not enough for a mind of any power. That is why powerful minds who have been poets have tried to combine the movement of the mind with what it does when its movement stops—and what this implies.

10:728

What matters for poets is the energy of image-formation— the images themselves are of no interest; it is the sensation of a leap, a short cut, a surprise—of control over the universe of differences.

11:53

Of all occupations the poet's is perhaps the one in which the greatest impatience has an essential need of the greatest patience.

11:244

I am a coward when I think of the amount of work I require of myself in poetry. I demand too many conditions, and my scarecrow of perfection frightens me.

This is what happens when we make such a rigorous distinction between reader and writer.

11:445

Consciousness and the *state of song.*

Poetry. Can a concern for poetry be brought to a high degree of consciousness and precision, without a loss of confidence in the vagueness and the surrender to movement that seem necessary to the *state of song*?   11:502

To be a poet is to offer to an unknown public those models of movement that are supreme, or delightful, or strange, the contrary of normal states, and expressed in absolute purity, as clearly as the language will allow.   13:429

A professional poet is a man who sits down regularly at the table of his mind to try his luck.

It is a game of mixed chance. Cards are dealt, and the player calculates.

He plays against the common language.

A person plays against a brain, a semi-external being, against a wholly internal one. Against oneself.   14:207

While some poets (Rimbaud, etc.) have aimed at giving the impression of an extraordinary *state* (a *vision*—the reciprocal resonance of things—the desperate exploration of the senses and expression), others, and myself, have sought to communicate the idea of a "world," a system of things separate from the common world, but made up of the same elements —the connections alone being chosen, and the definitions.
15:248

Too poetic to be a poet. On the contrary the artifex enjoys *making* more than *feeling*. He *makes* poets more than he *is* a poet himself.   15:520

My "poetry" is a product very much influenced by hidden presences, invisible precepts, undeclared fields of positive or negative force. . . .   15:754

Why refuse the poet what you allow the least musician, or painter, to say nothing of the architect—the right to meditate on the relationship of the whole to the details? The composition of tones, of partial forms? Because the direct meaningful element of language, the "imaginary" element, its fiduciary aspect, has won the day.   16:37

For a poet, it is never a matter of saying *it is raining*. It's a matter of...making rain.   16:246

My work does not come from a need. It is *mental occupation* that for me is a *need* (beginning with excitement). What excites me excites me to do this very piece of work, and not to realize its *product* (unless the idea of the *product* is a *goal*, a condition of the work, but not the sole or essential one).

The work of art then, in my eyes, is an *activity*, while for most people it is the capital resource of the moment.

So, the *Magnum Opus* for me is the knowledge of work itself—transmutation—the *works* being local applications, particular problems. They are problems in which the characteristics of other people enter as indeterminate conditions—my notion of the effect of works on others.   16:744

To extract the poem from reflections on poetry, from a vivid notion of poetry—and not to discover poetry as the result of an incident that produces an effect, but to start from an effect and go toward incidents, making poetry first of all out of a knowledge of its nature and structure, and setting up the "*poetic phase*," *a priori*. That is my ideal as a poet.

Poetry until now has thought of itself as an accident. The subject or a certain detail is given—and this lights a match. The fire grows, and by its erratic flicker one sees the poetic universe. The flame leaps up, blazes, dies down. *People have believed that this capricious lighting was essential to vision.* But I believe the contrary. 17:870

Poetry: this point of departure comes to me: *Lointaine Moi* (*ou Toi*). It remains in the air. A good example, the waiting on the remainder, the complement; and from complement to complement, a more or less closed composition could be made. These four syllables can be the beginning of a line of eight or ten syllables, or some other. Now a general desire is always made up of a real part and a truly imaginary one. The eyes, for instance, possess, and the hands do not. We know that possession by the eyes is all-powerful with respect to the rest. The proverb: eyes bigger than the stomach. The mind constructs the whole from a given part. 18:5

My poems were born, or rather developed, or were elabo-rated, *in the presence* of a certain conception I had formed of language. 18:60

"Jeune Parque"
    I tried there to make "poetry" out of the living organism.
18:530

As a writer I dreamed only of *constructions*, and I abhorred the impulse to cover paper with a continuous production.
    However pressing and rich and happy this abundance, it fails to interest me. I see it as a linear formation that excludes all composition. I know that most people admire this and are intoxicated by it. But fires that are lit from summit to summit and die out never give me full pleasure.
    My desire would have been to write by treating all the

parts of a work almost simultaneously, and to bring them almost at the same time to their final state. As we paint on a wall. And with preparations, and whatever is needed to provide connections and relations from one end to the other. Not forgetting the conclusion when we write the beginning, etc.

And not leaving to chance the structure of the paragraphs and sentences—the *lengths* and complexities and contrasts of these forms as forms.

And—the capital consideration, the total *planned* length.

18:560

I differ from others (and quite precisely, from Mallarmé) on this point: that they confer on literature an "absolute" value, the value of a final aim, whereas I see in it nothing more than the development of powers of expression or the power of construction. But these values are means.

My aim is not literary. It is not to produce an effect on others so much as on myself—the *Self* in so far as it may be treated as a work...of the mind. Hence it follows that "Self" and "mind" are notations that may be opposed one to the other. The result is that nothing that comes into the mind is of any value except whatever increases the possession of precise acts and exhausts the general possibilities, *formulas* as boundaries, etc.

For example: I am not interested in writing verse without a view to its function, without imagining that this industry is an application of properties and powers, etc. The "Jeune Parque" was a complex problem. A physiology and a melody. 18:703

If being a "great poet" requires one to accept and cultivate in himself what I reject or restrain in myself, I agree not to be a "great poet," and I consider that this fair title neither pleases nor suits me. 19:59

History of the "Jeune Parque."

Curious example of a poem that was both undertaken by chance and pursued systematically.

If one turns his back on the aim of "self-expression" to pursue "effect upon," one introduces *procedures*, explicitly and imperiously, without reservations.

Then follows a series of problems of various kinds—the details, the whole—and finally: the problem of making it all seem natural.

(And finally: *to be a saint*—said Gracian.) 19:59

Poets have forgotten that they practice the craft of a singer. Some of them have taken it to be the craft of an orator—the rest, nothing. 19:124

Poetry: Inspiration, etc.

A fine line of poetry (or a fine image or idea) is a fruit plucked from the tree. But which tree?

This leads to the curious point of trying to *make* the tree whose fruit *would be* this fruit.

Finally, then, it is the fruit of two trees. One hidden, unknowable, which produced the fruit. The other, the work in which the fruit takes a more or less necessary place.

19:777

"Jeune Parque." Poetry led me to play the idiot, to appear to be prodigal of roses, because for me, what was truly *poetic* was called only by antipoetic names with scholarly or techni- cal echoes. Names for things of the mind are impossible—and

that is what I should have liked to "sing." I had great
difficulty in putting a few of them into verse.   20:543

Poet.

And as tears come into the eyes of a man who is moved, so
the divine and *more than exact* words of the poet.

As tears come from a point of life *deeper* than all freedom
and all control of one's act, so these discourses come as a
language that does not obey free thought, but rushes out.

20:678

(The "Jeune Parque" and I)—Every work I have composed,
except those too much dictated by circumstances, should
carry its *real title*, which would be for example: A study of the
transformations of an initial datum, which preserve certain
characteristics of that datum, and must satisfy certain condi-
tions.

The consideration of "external" effects plays a parti-
cular role—the importance of this role, and defining it, are
essential points. For external effects are *tests*, of resistance, etc.

21:146

Ego poeta.

They talk about inspiration; yet they think of it as a more
or less sustained impulse which "in reality" does not admit of
composition but lives in a happy sequence.

Whereas my "dream" as a poet would have been to
compose a discourse—a speech containing modulations and
internal relations in which the physical, psychological, and
conventional aspects of language could combine their
resources. With this or that division and change of tone
clearly defined.

But, in fact, *who* speaks in a poem? Mallarmé claimed it was language itself.

For me, it would be living and thinking *being* (a *contrast*), driving self-awareness to the capture of its sensibility— developing resonances, symmetries, etc. on the vocal cords. In sum, language coming from the voice rather than voice from the language. 22:435–6

I wanted to be a poet who was not naïve, that is to say, one who goes from what he wants to what he does. For the poet's wish is ill-defined, comprising on the one hand a subject or a particular object that excites him, and on the other hand the aim of producing an effect on a reader—all mingled, mingling with the idea of himself which he wants finally to give, with the idea of his present occupation and other people.

I was particularly concerned about what I *could do*, and the developments of this—in the domain of action as well, the most general type of action, trying to find what would make the most independent products. 22:436

In sum, Mallarmé and I have this in common—a poem is a problem. And this is very important. 23:149

What Mallarmé told me when he showed me the "Coup de dés"—that he planned to compose every year, on the same model, a work whose character was more intellectual than ordinary poetic expression allowed—made me think that in his own way he was running into a difficulty I knew very well (since I had given up poetry some four or five years previously, for that reason among others).

There comes a time when the possible themes and words

in French poetry are no longer enough to stimulate a mind gifted with a certain power of abstraction, and so the insoluble problem is put.

I approached this problem twenty years later with the "Jeune Parque."   23:152–3

Ego scriptor.

I cannot write as others do. Facility paralyzes me. I am frightfully sensitive to the arbitrary; and what might seem good if it had cost me dear, seems worthless when it springs from me of itself. I wait for something resembling both a natural formation due to intrinsic forces (crystals), and a very rare, improbable, exceptional formation. This is after all the case of a diamond.   23:153

There arose in me, about 1892, a certain scorn for poetry and poets, due to the intellectual weaknesses I found in most of them, even the most famous. I noted on the one hand that they lived on a capital of ideas that was miserably common and naïve (so that a poet of the year 1000 B.C. is still readable) and that they did not exercise all the powers of the mind; that they were ignorant of the *imaginative* developments we owe to the sciences, that is, to organized thought. Besides, their craft itself had made no advance in the way of perfection—that is, poetic continuity and composition—as music had done, with its technical progress from the sixteenth century to our time. A sentence from Poe's "Arnheim" had given me much to think about.   23:273

Mallarmé and I.

This morning, in the darkness of the hour and the particular brightness of that moment of waking, in the presence of the absence *of light*—I consider the difference between poems like "Hérodiade," "L'Après-midi d'un faune," and "La Jeune Parque." The last named would not have existed without the others, of course. But there is an interesting point concerning the different conditions.

While Mallarmé's two poems were written by weaving over the form with a subject whose plan is determined only by the need to be recognized, the poem does not lead to a deeper delving into the subject but treats it as a pretext or a condition equivalent at the most to its manner, which is incomparable and (in "L'Après-midi d'un faune") superior to any subject. "La Jeune Parque," which properly speaking has no subject, has its origin in the intention to define or display a knowledge of the living organism which it is not sufficient to recognize but must be learned. This, joined to the condition of form, gives the poem its very serious difficulties. It is not enough to explain the text; one must also explain the theme. My conviction was that no one would read it. That was between 1914 and 1917!

*   *   *

In short, my literary vice was to wish (being able to do nothing else) to put into a piece of work of normal type and design a particular way of seeing things and connections or definitions that came from my research into life, psychological functions, etc. Mallarmé was hardly concerned with anything but form. That concern dominated everything. The rest remained free. But I have never put together my system except in very small fragments.   24:117

Preface or conclusion to the course in Poetics—

"There is a poetry of the very things of the mind." That is what struck me as early as 1890 or so. Or rather I felt myself interested in these abstract things about 1892-3—in my own way, and as stimuli—(M. Teste).

It was a sensibilization, a poeticization.   25:460

I am much more an inventor of ideas or views than anything else. And that, at bottom, is what makes my poetry. It is not so much that I purposely put "ideas" into it. On the contrary, I do not want them there—for an idea that interests me seems to require quite a different treatment, suggesting another state and another possible composition, neither of them "poetic."

But as soon as I am launched on a form and a mode of song, I conceive the *future* of this seed of a poem as a problem, or rather a series of problems, and here ideas are introduced as solutions. A few words, like the arc of a curve, suggest themselves. It is a matter of tracing a whole curve that passes through fixed points—rhymes, etc. *Mignonne, allons voir si la rose...* And then? A movement begins back and forth between the dictionary of rhymes that is more or less in the mind, a growing *sense* and purpose, and the movement or rhythm.

The idea of the making of a poem or of works of art excites me, lifts me more than any particular work, and (*nota bene*) all the more as the act of imagination becomes more independent of the person and personality of the maker. It is not *someone* who makes. (The somnambulism of the thinking man—that is, someone who is transformed into maintaining a point of view.)   25:373

The poet, the maker of verse with fixed conventional conditions, is always uncertain whether he will be able to carry his work to its intended end.

He is a hunter and, I assume, a good marksman. But the bird may be absent from his sky, and he can also miss his mark.

The free poet always catches something—but at times it is a snail, at others a rat, at still others a hare.   26:163

If I think of myself as "a poet" I find that, since the age of twenty, a kind of instinct or ideal has possessed me more or less consciously, and rather *more* than *less*.

An intellectual tropism led me to try to *construct* poems, or compose them, according to an analysis of conditions which I found in the possible effect of language (exploited according to the modes of poetry) on someone, and this required an idea of that someone and his probable functioning.

Among those conditions were the impression to be made on memory, the continuous charm to be exercised by details, and the "truth," as naïve and surprising as possible, of the things signified. I do not like fantasy that changes people and things, but I prize the kind that multiplies the ways of seeing them. The sight of a face upside down changes nothing about it, yet makes it unrecognizable at very little cost, and so teaches us all the poverty inflicted upon us by the acquisitions of our minds.   27:166

As a poet I have sought to be a non-simulator. I mean: I wanted my research and my work as a maker of poems to be in agreement with my thought in general, my self-awareness, my reflections and analyses, the tastes of my mind. It was an experiment to be tried, to which I gave myself as a poet. It was a question of showing that the absence of mythology and vague ideas, of collusion with the impure and floating products of tradition, of mental lethargy and boasting or poetic mysticism, was compatible with the practice of art and the fabrication of effective works. I proceeded to an analysis of poetry as a pure and simple problem.   27:518

> Epitaph: *Poeta fui.*
> *Nunc poemata factus sum.*   28:354

Of all the writers and poets I have known or imagined by instinct (which reveals what is really valuable in X for Y and according to the nature of Y)—I find only Stéphane Mallarmé and myself, in diverse ways, who have isolated, laid bare, consecrated, kept, and worshiped in secret the abstract idol of the perfect self—that is, self-awareness, the heritage of Poe. By its radical use an inner equalization of everything is produced that corresponds, or can correspond, to that exhaustive rejection. It is the idol that demolishes all others, whose presence acts as a reflex and gives at least the illusion of the most complete generality.

Note that the practice of conscious verse-writing, which leads to maneuvering words and treating them as relative values, predisposes one to this and favors it. Such virtuosity is incompatible with common idolatries (those of the philosophers in particular), since the value of words resides no longer in themselves but in their placement (Boileau), and the word *if* is then worth as much as, and more than, the word *God*.

I noticed that the system presupposed by Mallarmé's art was more profound than any theory of literature and consisted in the secret of a universal attitude which could only be what I have said and which I possessed virtually within myself. The freedom which Mallarmé's versification and his obscurity presuppose, etc.

But this sort of enlightenment came to me above all from four lines of Poe—here and there. And I made myself rapidly stronger by a faith in my pure and implacable absolute, to the point of seeing myself soon as much more brutal even than Mallarmé (who at least held onto poetry) in the rigorous application of a principle of negation and the exercise of the power that results from it.

And I began to see only idolators and idolatries around me (1892). (M. Teste says: *What can a man...?*)

The blow struck everything the mind can solve in the mind and bring under the scorn with which it *must view* its own productions and fluctuations *in general*, and consequently everything that is language and *language alone*.

I then had to find what could *save* language....

I observed that, in the same way as purely abstract algebraic operations can in many cases give good results in physics, so verbal combinations used without respect to an initial idea to be expressed, but rather with a care for their own efficacy and with full liberty to change the initial idea, allowed one to form the most perfect poetic objects.

This state of mind made me avoid any influence of philosophers or others, except the authors I have named. (I mean, influence on my way of thinking.) In any case, I do not read philosophers for more than a few lines; they take too long and their abstract jargon seems to me inefficient (Spinoza: "essence," "existence"!) All this brings no power. And then all those questions of origin (of the world, language, life) are ridiculous. Look at them. They are naïve images.

Likewise the *historical* spirit! It's all idolatry. And logic, if you look at its definitions, deserves no confidence.

The illusion of generality has value only for the possibilities of thought; but not beyond that. There is no generality in the realm of particular cases. But people have believed that the notions extracted from it were its substance. For example, that the idea of order or law taken from an observation of phenomena was the generative *principle* of those phenomena.

29:536–8

On Poetry

Verse must have a magical character or it does not exist.

5:585

Poetry must convey the idea of a perfect thought. It is not a true thought. Poetry is to thought what a drawing is to the object—a convention that restores what, in the object, is briefly eternal.   5:871

Note: verse and great oratorical prose, which is so close to verse, are always associated with the sensation of effort, whether in breathing or articulation. The sensibility appropriate to these efforts gives this language its laws and creates measure, the contrasts of vowels or consonants. When the effort is reduced, words cease to be felt and no longer impose laws—just as acts and movements which do not imply effort are without rhythm. To march in step always consists of perceiving the effort of walking and emphasizing it.   5:633

The "meaning" of a poem, like that of an object, is the reader's business. *Quantum potes, tantum aude.*

The poet's business is to construct a sort of verbal body that has the solidity as well as the ambiguity of an object. Experience shows that an over-simple poem, for example an abstract one, is inadequate, and exhausted at first sight. It is no longer even a poem. The ability to be reread, savored again, depends on the number of meanings compatible with the text, and this number itself results from a clarity that imposes the obligation to interpret, and an indefiniteness that repels interpretation.

A memorable example: the mad abundance of meanings and counter-meanings that can be drawn from sacred books. The slightest evangelical gesture, an act in itself clear and precise, can have an infinite number of meanings (that gain nothing by being made more precise).   6:118

Proof: in practice the reader always breaks up long poems. Think of Poe.

The secret of great art is to put invisible chains on the patient....

The study, and quest of these chains, connections *hard to make implicit*, leads to the study of lateral psychological phenomena. Living beings, man or horse, are so admirable in their movement because skeletons, articulations, muscles are hidden and molded in the mass.   6:124

Poetry and industry. Would not the best verse be that in which utilization would be brought to its peak? In which production would not leave any remainder? In which, by chance, the words would all be in agreement with the resulting meaning, in which the necessary words, by their syntax and meaning, would be found to be sounds and images that increase the power of expression?   6:373

A fine line of poetry repeats itself spontaneously and remains somehow mingled with its meaning, half preferable to the meaning, and the meaning's endless origin.   6:687

The qualities that can be enunciated in a human voice are those that must be studied and communicated in poetry.

And the "magnetism" of the voice must be transposed into a mysterious and ultra-fine alliance of ideas and words.

The continuity of fine sound is essential.   6:732

Most men have such a vague idea of poetry that the very vagueness of their idea is for them the definition of poetry.

This definition by vagueness is not bad. It is worth more than any other except the true and precise one.

It is the labor of a lifetime to arrive at a precise idea of poetry. I agree that the game is not worth the candle.

6:775

Poetry is a quest for its own self.

It is perhaps the possession and, as it were, the science of causes that have music for their effect. (Listening to music produces causes for the effects experienced.)

It is that which causes the movement of the dance, the *élan*, the attitude, the meditation, the desire.

Poetry also engenders a continuum out of various juxtaposed objects. What music *tends* to form in order to justify these movements and halts, these pure purposes, this internal mimicry...is of the nature of poetry.

But it is only a tendency.   6:877

Poetry—The principle of the voice, i.e., the singing voice, as a condition, is to temper descriptions, etc., to paralyze non-vibrant things; or to oblige us to find first of all that vibration without which poetry cannot be. But all that vibrates is not good. Moreover, make no mistake: what I call *vibration* is only the obligation imposed by the text itself on the reader's voice, *independently of the meaning*, to resound, to hear itself, to notice relations and connections and contrasts in the quality of the tone or the articulation of the words.

7:125

One must say Poetry as one says Fencing, Dancing, Horsemanship, and the same goes for everything else that is a gamble.

Moreover this appraisal is much nobler, more accurate and more profound than that which makes of poetry an oracle. 7:399

Pure poetry does not ask any kind of credulity of its reader, and that is what makes it the supreme genre in literature (the most vulgar genre is narrative, fiction). Pure poetry must pay cash, and use only the absolute *reality* of the properties of language. 8:98

Poetry is the use of certain singular properties of language, a use that consists *in regenerating the meaning by the sign, and the sign by the meaning*. But this reciprocal quality is exceptional.

A poet is a man who is specially endowed to see this property, to be sensitive to it, and to produce it.

When a human mechanism functions as a poet, this suffices to create a *poetic* world.

It follows that no *meaning* exhausts the sign. The whole organism remains active. 8:681

In general, people try "to express their thoughts," that is, to pass from an *impure* form mixed with all the means of the mind, to a *pure* form, that is, merely verbal and organized, reduced to a system of acts or arranged contrasts.

But it is remarkable that the art of poetry leads one to envisage the pure forms themselves. 8:774

Think of what you need to please three million people. It is paradoxical that you need *less* than if you are to please a hundred.

I do not write for people who cannot give me an amount of time and attention comparable to that I give them.

10:163

I am not very confident about the future of poetry. Poetry is of the nature of song, and song is a thing destined to disappear.

Poetry results from a swelling, a tonalization of the articulate voice, in all its phonic, psychic, propulsive properties—and its modes result from a very subtle analysis of this voice and its effects. 10:858

Poetry is a formation by the body and mind in creative union of that which suits this union, and excites or reinforces it.

Poetic is everything that provokes, restores, this unitive state.

By the body I mean the expressive parts of the body and their movements. 11:289

The number of syllables or feet assigns an average time for the *aim* of the voice.

In every act there is a tension, a degree of forecast (forecast equals tension, concentration) that materializes the probable effort.

The creation of the state of springiness, of elastic restitution. 11:492

Poetry—Wave mechanics!

It is finally the use, the fact of following, etc., events of perception by their wave—to perceive the wave more than the body, the radiance engendered by passing from an impression to the atmosphere it creates. The use and combination of values of resonance, of harmonics and their relationships, to the detriment of the values of finite substitution.

12:275

Critics or admirers of my verse have not suspected that I subject poetry to certain conditions, and that the hidden conditions deny me many effects that people reproach me for not discovering, and that oblige me to impose difficulties on my readers.   12:291

Everything verbal is provisional. All language is a means. Poetry tries to make it an end.   12:673

Literature (poetry) embellishes by suddenly *abandoning* something, by leaving the earth to move in the atmosphere of language. The qualities of language that bind it to our immediate acts and designs and realizable exchanges are thus rejected. Clarity, precision, brevity (unrelated to speaking-time)—uniformity—in order to acquire or bring to their peak other qualities—excitement, free energy.   12:893

Since poetry demands a balance between sound and meaning, an equilibrium by counterbalance like that of the tightrope walker, poetry with a precipitate form, accelerated lyricism, is a solution, the simplest solution to this problem.

One seeks, in the dynamics of bodies in movement, the requisite average stability.   13:33

In truth poetry is only the sensuous aspect of language. The presence of a *sign*, and speculation upon it. A lucky expression. 13:345

The beauty of verse is in the pleasure of *giving it a meaning* to which *it* constrains us. 14:6

Poetry is nothing but a formation of words that have *resonance*. This quality is independent of any meaning. Its presence is manifest. We say: magic. The means of poetry aim to make such words artificially. But since it is very difficult to define what this resonance consists of, the means are gropingly created.

Such resonance is often individual. Moreover this is true of all the arts. 14:459

A poem, that is, a production of *extreme* expressions, of mad imaginings. The mind is wholly turned toward the outside and suspended from the (real) heart. 14:654

"Sesame." The *true* beginning of a poem (which is not at all necessarily the first line) must come to the author like a magic formula about which he does not as yet know all it will open up to him.

For indeed it opens up a dwelling-place, a cave and a labyrinth intimately felt and yet unknown. 15:301

Poetry is a dance. This is the analogical principle which must keep us from confusing poetry with prose.

Verse is a way of speaking as dance steps are a way of moving.

This dance feigns speech and *thought* (by metaphors). It is more or less *figurative*.

422

Stanzas and rhymes break the tendency to go *the shortest way*, to reach an end—that is to say, prose.   15:918

A poem must impose the perfection of a *complete* language, appear always as an exceptional creation; one need only take the contrary of *common* characteristics, the useful, vulgar, immediate characteristics of ordinary language, to divine meanings and to experience transpositions that announce the approach of *poetry*.   16:247

The effect of a fine verse is *like a pendulum*. It puts "the soul" in a state of oscillation between its form and its meaning.

The agreement of sound and sense is not conformity (which would be imitative harmony) but complementarity —*green* and *red* do not look alike. The soul, that is to say, expectation. Potentiality.   16:316

The "poetry" of a work results from the impression (re-ceived by someone) of a phase of true freedom—for true freedom is, by reason of this reciprocity, a "harmonic" state. There is an "illusion" (if not more than an illusion) of com-mensurability, of equivalence between heterogeneous and irreducible factors.   16:414

The sound of a meaning and the meaning of a sound. Poetry !
16:908

Poetry. The presence and intervention of *time* in formations. In the hemistichs: "Le vent se lève...il faut tenter de vivre!" the connection of the second to the first is like a *reflex*. One sensation suddenly stirs a whole attitude and energy, which requires a certain reaction time.

So, besides the basic rhythm, there is a "movement" which must be an *imitation* of *true intervals of time.* 17:310

I can no longer think about "Poetry," conceive poetry, judge it, except as a composition. And the composition I envisage is of essentially complex elements.

Determine these elements, define the "operations" (generally implicit, invisible) that combine them in brief psychological acts.

Try to form, from conceptions of wholes, the elements of the psycho-physical substance of works of art. 17:789

One can (for instance) use regular verse because everybody uses it.

One can on the contrary use it "in another spirit," as if one had invented it, as an originality.

It is only then that one sees its strangeness...and its justification. 17:852

Poetry consists of using words to produce in someone that which excludes the use, the possibility of using words.

It wants words to be at every moment the negation of speech. 18:38

The finest poetry always has the form of a monologue.

I tried in "La Jeune Parque" to bring to the state of monologue what seemed to me the substance of the living being, and the physiological life in so far as that life can perceive and express itself *poetically.*

While the *historical* element of a self generally plays the principal role, I preferred here, and elsewhere, its feeling of an eternal present. 18:533

The poet seeks the magical verse, whose *sense* will be mysterious to himself, and therefore of such a kind that *the verse will be preserved* and repeated.

If a verse produces an exact meaning, that is, one that can be translated by another expression, this meaning destroys it.

18:782

Poetry must provoke the state in which what it says— incidentally—is not *without reason, without value,* although having neither *reason* nor *value* as ordinary discourse, and relating to nothing that cannot be either neglected or expressed more directly.

20:721

Poetry is distinguished by the miraculous. This observation is worth what it is worth. But it is the truth. The quality untranslatable into prose.

21:873

The expression of wholly coherent ideas (that is to say, ideas which advance toward a *conclusion*) is almost forbidden in poetry, as the dancer is forbidden to walk purposefully to a point. For a conclusion is outside speech, and is a modifica- tion of the person to whom one speaks. Logic aims to con- strain this person to think about a point in conformity with another's thought.

22:23

I like a poem to rise of itself to Poetry by the sole virtue of its powers of organic development, and not by the movement of significant tone. *As a melody that is born of the voice.* I propose to define *Melody* by *Voice*—and voice by linear energy produced by the energy of *volume*. . . . The empty egg floating on a fountain shows the fluctuations in pressure. . . and, in sum, those of a *life*.

22:141

Poetry requires an organization of the individual that is extremely delicate in its construction if it is to reach the purity and truth of this production.

For it demands a very exact adjustment which by the nature of things is very unstable, since one must at every moment set language back on the right track.

Poetry is the locus of points equidistant between pure sensibility and pure intellect in the field of language.

22:213-14

Intellect and Poetry are only different moments, like seeing where one is going and going to that place, like rehearsing a play and playing it. The former tries, and establishes arguments; the other executes them. The whole question is to execute them without showing the endeavor.

They can be badly conceived, as when the language or matter of the poem is badly chosen for agreement. Then one has didacticism.

This agreement is that of language in as much as it imposes repetition, and not of language in as much as it is abolished and transformed into an idea: its "infinite" and its "finite"—its wave and its corpuscle.

Poetry demands that the form be preserved when it is consumed. The form is a system of acts of perception (voice, hearing) to which one must join all that gives a *sensible* value to the bringing together of words and to syntactical articulations, characters that are imperceptible, or disappear, in purely useful discourse but which in poetry and its annexes must have their function. It is evident that this function is to help to create and preserve or prolong the singing state; also to add to the meaningful effect. In poetry the importance or probable effect of the work is shared between form and meaning; the former being more active than the latter. 23:505–6

Poetry is recognizable (that is to say, defined) by the *abnormally frequent* presence (in discourse) of *products of the sensibility* (harmonics, figures, similitudes, antitheses, repetitions) and this frequency tends to cause the "text" to be conceived as doubly constituted: first, of a general *line* of meaning, *translatable*, susceptible of being represented in other terms; second, of a *band* of successive but cumulative effects, which on the contrary are *untranslatable*, constituting the form and tending to answer the questions they put in the first place. Thus qualities antithetical to those of pure meaning are introduced: for example, *repetition, which is the very negation of what is meaningful.* 23:594

Regular verse is the mode by which "form" has the greatest effect on the "subject." The *subject* in poetry is the most variable constituent of the productive act, whereas the contrary is true in the intellectual and practical domain.

There is navigation by sail and navigation by steam. The poet goes on a spree and proceeds by rule of thumb. This is so true that he is often forced to take a bearing, that is, to consider his divergence from the direct line that would lead to his first definite goal. 23:720

Poetry demands continual invention, just as it demands the full use or rejection of every single moment. The ball must not fall to the ground. 23:872

Poetry uses language in a way that is sufficient for understanding and more than sufficient for imagining, feeling.

Any variation of such expressions that tends to make understanding more complete and imagination or suggestion less powerful goes against "poetry."   24:384

Regular verse makes us feel at each instant the generality of a law of *verbal movement*, and its independence of the content, or rather its resumptions, its recovery in time.

*   *   *

The singing state is a state of reciprocal exchange between reception and production, energy and action, equivalences, freedom and constraint.

A process of balances that conserve energy. A phase.

The act arouses the energy it needs.   25:342

I cannot divorce my idea of poetry from that of *complete* formations—which are self-sufficient, whose sound and mental effects correspond to one another in a certain "infinite" way.

In such cases something is detached, like a fruit or a child, from its generation and from the potential that bathes the mind—and is opposed to the mutability of thoughts and the freedom of language as a function.

What has thus come forth and affirmed itself is no longer *someone*, but as it were the manifestation of intrinsic, impersonal properties of the complex function of *Language*—a rare production that occurs under conditions as rarely encountered as those that transform carbon into diamonds.

25:698

Those fools cannot stop treating poets as if poets *were* *saying* something !

The *meaning* of poems is only a quasi-necessity, not a *goal*. One must certainly breathe in order to notice a perfume, but breathing is not the *goal* of the composition of a perfume, any more than it is the goal of words. 25:727

Poetry aims to *express* by means of language precisely that which language is powerless to express. 25:840

A comprehensible but "beautiful" line of poetry is *beautiful by what is incomprehensible in it*. For example its *symmetry* of terms: Mallarmé's experiment, his rashness, lay in placing the incomprehensible in the *first period* without neglecting the *rest*—resonance, secondary harmonics.

The stimulus must therefore be situated in the incomprehensible.
26:524

Selected and translated by James Lawler

Notes and Commentaries

ALBUM DE VERS ANCIENS

THREE YEARS AFTER "La Jeune Parque," two years before *Charmes*, the *Album de vers anciens* appeared in 1920 with the imprint of the well-known Parisian literary figure and publisher Adrienne Monnier. The title was modest, underlining the fact that the works had been written long before, employed traditional meters, represented an earlier generation. At the same time Valéry made no pretense of having composed a book of poems with a coherent structure or dominant theme in the manner of Baudelaire; on the contrary, he offered a collection that bore "the condemnatory word 'album'" by which Mallarmé had described the volume of his own work published in 1887: "scraps... glued to pages...as for an assemblage of precious, or centuries-old, pieces of material." Valéry could well think that the name was appropriate to his purpose; nor would he have disowned the irony of its *fin-de-siècle* accent, for an age attuned to Dada.

On several occasions he had already attempted to select the best of his early poems and make them into a volume. But nothing came of it. About 1912, André Gide began to encourage him to gather his early poems and submit them to the recently founded publishing house, the Nouvelle Revue Française. When a copy was prepared for him with a view to forcing his hand, he was dismayed. But the more he looked at his poetry, typed out for him, the keener he became to correct what were for him glaring weaknesses: he felt "ill-defined desires to reinforce them, to renew their musical substance." He began to revise, and gradually conceived the idea of another poem to accompany them which would be "a kind of farewell to these adolescent games." "I call these poems exercises," he said, "for they do not represent my thoughts. They are not the expression of my principal interest. But on the other hand I esteem nothing more highly than gymnastics."

The edition of 1920 contains sixteen pieces, dated "1890–1900" on the title page. It includes this preliminary note:

Almost all these little poems—(or others they presuppose and resemble)—were published between 1890 and 1893, in a few reviews that have not survived.

La Conque, Le Centaure, La Syrinx, L'Ermitage, La Plume were once kind enough to accept these ventures, which led their author quite promptly to a lasting dissociation from poetry.

Two unfinished pieces, abandoned about the year 1899, have been added to them, as well as a page of prose that concerns the art of poetry but makes no claim whatsoever to instruct or to proscribe.

The 1926 edition incorporates four more titles, and the inclusion of "Les Vaines Danseuses" in 1931 brought the total number to twenty-one, forming a kind of diptych with the twenty-one poems of *Charmes*.

LA FILEUSE

"I have composed a line of verse in my sleep," Valéry wrote to André Gide in June, 1891; and he continued: "I shall submit it—probably quite alone—to *La Conque*." Nevertheless, a few days later, that initial line had become a poem of eighteen alexandrines arranged in *terza rima*, which grew to twenty-five by September of that year when "La Fileuse" first appeared in *La Conque*. It is possible that its origins can be traced to a painting by Courbet in the Musée de Mont-pellier entitled *La Fileuse endormie*. The epigraph is from the Sermon on the Mount: "Consider the lilies of the field, how they grow; they toil not, neither do they spin."

HÉLÈNE

One of the earliest poems of the *Album de vers anciens*, "Hélène" was originally published in the first number of the review *La Chimère* in August, 1891, under the title "Hélène la reine triste." It was signed "M. Doris" (a pseudonym Valéry used at the time) and bore an epigraph taken from his own "Vaines Danseuses": "To drink the frail water of lilies, where pure oblivion sleeps." Valéry included this poem with minor variants in the 1920 edition of the *Album*; in the meantime, however, it had played a vital role in his "second puberty" of 1912–13 when it served as a motif for what was to become the opening of "La Jeune Parque." In a draft headed "Hélène belle pour les autres—Hélène dorée" the first line conjures up a new Helen who looks into her mirror to discover the tears of self-consciousness, her fateful sensi-bility: "Qui pleure là...?"

ORPHÉE

Embodying one of Valéry's most characteristic themes, "Orphée" was written at Montpellier in 1891. It was first published in prose form at the end of his lyrical essay "Paradoxe sur l'architecte" in *L'Ermitage*, March, 1891, and appeared again the same year in *La Conque* as a sonnet. At the time of the composition of *Charmes* it was rehandled very considerably and incorporated in the second edition of the *Album de vers anciens* in 1926. The figure of Orpheus expresses an ideal act of construction that would marry music and architecture, advance from disorder to order and from the arbitrary to the necessary. On a page headed *Orphisme*, Valéry once wrote: "The poet recreates the world (like a Domain of Arnheim) by way of unique and various rhythms. He evokes the perfect Man dancing in a pure landscape and uttering magnificent words to a divine music."

NAISSANCE DE VÉNUS

The title of the original version as it appeared in the *Bulletin de l'Association générale des étudiants de Montpellier*, December 1, 1890, was "Celle qui sort de l'onde." Valéry was again at work on this sonnet in 1913 during his holidays at Perros-Guirec in Brittany, at a time when he was returning to the practice of poetry and beginning to compose "La Jeune Parque." In July of that year he wrote to his wife: "I have been trying out, on the threshold of sand or rocks, the lines: *Creuse, creuse, rumeur de soif....* And I am just about content with them." As the first tercet shows, he was seeking to equate the sonnet's language with the actual sound of the surf.

FÉERIE

"I should be tempted to advise poets to produce a number of variants on the same subject, in the manner of musicians. Nothing would seem to be more consistent with the idea I like to entertain of a poet and poetry." Valéry's conception of art as an "exercise" justifies the inclusion side by side of "Féerie" and "Même Féerie." The former is close to the original version written in August, 1890, and published in that year under the title "Blanc" in the December issue of *L'Ermitage*. Some twenty years later, it appeared under the title "Fée" in *Les Fêtes* of January, 1914. An early draft of "Fée" bears the dedication "À J. K. H.," recalling Valéry's affection for Joris-Karl Huysmans, whose *À Rebours* (Against the Grain)—"My Bible and my bedside book"—affected him strongly at the age of nineteen.

MÊME FÉERIE

In 1926, "Même Féerie" appeared in *Quelques vers anciens* under the title "Féerie (variante)" and again, the same year, in the second edition of the *Album*. Only four lines are identical.

BAIGNÉE

Between its publication in *La Syrinx* in August, 1892, and its inclusion in the *Album de vers anciens* almost thirty years later, "Baignée" underwent few changes. In this poem Valéry obviously recalls Mallarmé, and obliquely Baudelaire, in the images of hair and jewels and several other details; but the sensuality is of his own nature and force.

AU BOIS DORMANT

This sonnet originally appeared under the title "La Belle au bois dormant" in the little Montpellier review *La Cigale d'or* on June 15, 1891, where it was accompanied by a translation in Provençal. The final version in the *Album* brought many changes.

CÉSAR

"César" appeared first in 1926, in *Quelques vers anciens* and, the same year, in the second edition of the *Album*. Although it was extensively revised for the volume of *Charmes*, as the manuscripts indicate, it was no doubt conceived at an early date. It is related in theme to such works as *Monsieur Teste*, *Introduction à la Méthode de Léonard de Vinci* and "Air de Sémiramis," expressing "intoxication with one's own will, and strange excesses of self-consciousness." It is the emblem of *imperatoria brevitas*, to use Valéry's own phrase from one of the drafts.

LE BOIS AMICAL

Written in nine-syllable lines that show the influence of Verlaine, "Le Bois amical" appeared in *La Conque* in January, 1892. It bore a dedication to André Gide in the familiar form of address, but it had actually been written before their first meeting. "It is a vague suggestion of Friendship," Valéry commented. And in a letter to Gide he defined the meaning he ascribed to the word friendship: "A single sympathy exists, made necessary by superior laws; it is a chemical affinity, perhaps a correspondence to some marvelous unity." Only revisions in punctuation were made in "Le Bois amical" when it was brought into the *Album* in 1920.

LES VAINES DANSEUSES

This poem, not included in the *Album de vers anciens* until 1931, had first appeared in *La Conque* exactly forty years before. Valéry returned to it in the last decade of his life, altering it so radically that only three lines of the original version remain intact. He did away with the preciosity, pursued and deepened the tone, and composed some of the poem's most delicate lines.

> *Celles qui sont des fleurs de l'ombre sont venues,*
> *Troupe divine et douce errante sous les nues*
> *Qu'effleure ou crée un clin de lune. . . . Les voici*
> *Mélodieuses fuir dans le bois éclairci.*
> *De mauves et d'iris et de mourantes roses*
> *Sont les grâces de nuit sous leurs danses écloses*
> *Qui dispensent au vent le parfum de leur doigts.*
> *Elles se font azur et profondeur du bois*
> *Où de l'eau mince luit dans l'ombre, reposée*
> *Comme un pâle trésor d'éternelle rosée*
> *Dont un silence immense émane. . . . Les voici*
> *Mystérieuses fuir dans le bois éclairci.*
> *Furtives comme un vol de gracieux mensonges.*
> *Des calices fermées elles foulent les songes*
> *Et leurs bras délicats aux actes endormis*
> *Mêlent, comme en rêvant sous les myrtes amis,*
> *Les caresses de l'une à l'autre. . . . Mais certaine,*
> *Qui se défait du rythme et qui fuit la fontaine,*
> *Va, ravissant la soif du mystère accompli,*
> *Boire des lys l'eau frêle où dort le pur oubli.*

Those who are flowers of shade have come,
Divine and gentle troop wandering beneath the skies
Brushed or created by a glance of moonlight. . . . See how
Like melodies they flee into the clear wood.
Of mallow, and iris, and dying roses
Are the graces of night that blossom beneath their dance
Strewing on the wind the perfume of their fingers.
They change the azure and forest depths
Where a slender stream glimmers in the shade, resting
Like a pale treasury of eternal dew
Emanating an immense silence. . . . See how
Like mysteries they flee into the clear wood,
Furtive as a flight of gracious lies.
They tread on the musing of closed calices
And their delicate arms whose acts are asleep
As if dreaming beneath the friendly myrtles,

Mingle their caresses one with another.... Yet one,
Shedding the rhythm, turns from the fountain, runs,
Ravishing a thirst for mystery fulfilled,
To drink of the lilies' frail water where pure oblivion sleeps.

(*Translation by James Lawler*)

UN FEU DISTINCT...

First published in the *Album* in 1920, though one version, clearly not the original draft, is contained in a notebook of 1897 (*Cahiers* 1:202). There Valéry breaks with the atmosphere of legend and the Parnassian tone, to create a drama of sensibility. The image of fire had particular resonance for him at this period: "My only love was fire. I thought nothing could finally withstand my stare, my desire to see...." In the first manuscript of the poem he names someone "le feu Amour."

NARCISSE PARLE

In a letter to André Gide (February 15, 1891), Valéry said that he had written "Narcisse parle," a poem of 53 lines, in two days or six working hours, to meet a deadline set by Pierre Louÿs who was then launching his review *La Conque*. The poem appeared in the first issue, of March 15, 1891. Valéry here used the theme and many of the images of a sonnet he had written the previous September, which itself had been inspired by a conversation with Gide in the Montpellier Public Gardens near the tomb of Narcissa Young. In a lecture at Marseilles in 1941, Valéry said:

The Narcissus theme is a sort of poetic autobiography that requires some explanation.

At Montpellier there is a botanical garden where I used to go when I was about nineteen years old. In a somewhat hidden part of the garden there is a vault with a marble plaque bearing these words:

Placandis Narcissae manibus. That inscription made me dream, but here is a bit of its history: in 1820, at that spot a skeleton was found, and according to certain local traditions it was believed that it was the grave of the daughter of the English poet Young. She had died at Montpellier towards the end of the eighteenth century, and could not be buried in the cemetery because she was a Protestant. Her father was said to have buried her there one evening by moonlight. The dead girl's name was Narcissa.

For me the name of Narcissa suggested Narcissus. It was at this time that I wrote the first *Narcissus*, an irregular sonnet which became the origin of all the poems that followed from it.

On one manuscript Valéry wrote the words "Narcisse parle—*Narcissae placandis manibus*," suggesting the poem's close relation in his mind to the inscription on the tomb of Narcissa, and added the following verses, addressed no doubt to Pierre Louÿs:

> *La rime veut que je farcisse*
> *L'intérieur du sieur Narcisse*
> *De quelques vers je l'ai farci*
> *Tu les demandes: les voici.*

Valéry had expanded his early sonnet into an elegy of fifty-three lines, a lament managed with a control of language and tone that won the praise of his contemporaries.

"Fifty years later," Valéry said in his lecture at Marseilles, "that early *Narcisse* (i.e. "Narcisse parle") appears to me a specimen of what I should probably have accomplished in poetry if I had persevered, instead of taking my distance and following the formation of my mind along different lines. It remains for me an early effort, characteristic of my ideal and my technical capacity at the time." When he took it up again with a view to including it in the *Album de vers anciens*, it became a slightly longer poem of fifty-eight lines.

But in working at it he conceived the idea of a *new poem*: not a "pastoral symphony in the classical style," as he had dreamed in 1892, but a tragic monologue that would go beyond self-love to the tension of self-knowledge. This new poem grew into the "Fragments du Narcisse" of *Charmes*.

From sonnet to elegy, from symphony to soliloquy, and later to the libretto of *La Cantate du Narcisse*, in the end Valéry had treated the Narcissus motif in a variety of modes, constituting, as he said, "a kind of poetic autobiography."

ÉPISODE

The first version of these lines appeared in *La Syrinx* of January, 1892. It was rehandled in a series of manuscripts and was published twice before its inclusion in the *Album de vers anciens* in 1920. Toward the end of his life Valéry again took up the piece in an unpublished draft, revising details of phrasing and continuing the development briefly so as to make a fragment of twenty-seven lines in all, instead of the present nineteen and a quarter. The poem constitutes in fact anything but a normal "episode" for there is only a hint of action.

VUE

In a note to Julien Monod written in later life Valéry dated this poem "1891-92?". It was published for the first time, however, in *Le Centaure* in 1896 and would seem to have been directly inspired by Mallarmé's sonnet "Toute l'âme résumée..." (likewise Elizabethan and likewise heptasyllabic) which had appeared in the previous year. It is a controlled syntactical pattern, a single sentence whose resolution is held up, as so often in Mallarmé, by the resources of qualification and playfulness.

"Vue" was included in the first edition of the *Album de*

vers anciens with only minor changes of punctuation. Valéry might well have set alongside it a prose poem found on the original manuscript, which shows him interpreting the theme in another mode: " She ! The slight showing of moist teeth, many and white—like nerves on watch—the nostrils sleeping and yet naturally curious. The eye glides with the head nodding inward, projecting a wave-washed beach, a surface ready for storms—not of pure tears; nothing dry."

*

Julien P. Monod was Valéry's intimate friend, adviser, and benefactor, descendant of an old Swiss Protestant family. He made the only complete collection of Valéry's published work, which he named the *Valeryanum*. This collection is now in the Jacques Doucet library of the University of Paris.

VALVINS

One of twenty-three poems presented to Stéphane Mallarmé in 1897 by his friends, "Valvins" was published in *La Coupe* in February, 1898. It was originally arranged in the form of an Elizabethan sonnet, a further homage to Mallarmé who had adopted the pattern on several occasions. It uses language characteristic of Mallarmé's writings, reminiscences of such works as "L'Après-midi d'un faune," "L'Azur," and "Le Nénuphar blanc," and personal details associated with the village of Valvins in the Fontainebleau forest, where from 1874 until his death Mallarmé spent his summers, often boating on the Seine.

Two basic ideas of the Mallarméan aesthetic provide the framework of octave and sestet: the poet is one who explains the world, joyfully violates its mystery, "unknots the forest";

443

at the same time he tames chaos and obsessive solitude by the pure potentiality of expression, a blank page—like the white sail that contains all movement. "The piece is wholly yours, Valéry, abstractly rich and ardent," Mallarmé wrote in his letter of thanks.

ÉTÉ

"Été" first appeared with another poem, "Vue," under the title *Deux poèmes* in the little review *Le Centaure*, 1896. It was republished in the anthology *Poètes d'aujourd'hui* (1900) with a dedication to the Franco-American poet Francis Vielé-Griffin. Valéry included it in the first edition of *Album de vers anciens*, 1920.

In the 1942 edition of *Poésies* Valéry presented a new version of this poem. Instead of five stanzas "Été" was now composed of eleven, the six new stanzas being inserted between the first three and the final two. The added stanzas are these:

> *Aux cieux vainement tonne un éclat de matière,*
> *Embrase-t-il les mers, consume-t-il les monts,*
> *Verse-t-il à la vie un torrent de lumière*
> *Et fait-il dans les cœurs hennir tous les démons,*
>
> *Toi, sur le sable tendre où s'abandonne l'onde,*
> *Où sa puissance en pleurs perd tous ses diamants,*
> *Toi qu'assoupit l'ennui des merveilles du monde,*
> *Vierge sourde aux clameurs d'éternels éléments,*
>
> *Tu te fermes sur toi, serrant ta jeune gorge,*
> *Âme toute à l'amour de sa petite nuit,*
> *Car ses tumultes purs, cet astre fou qui forge*
> *L'or brut d'événements bêtes comme le bruit,*
>
> *Te font baiser les seins de ton être éphémère,*
> *Chérir ce peu de chair comme un jeune animal*
> *Et victime et dédain de la splendeur amère*
> *Choyer le doux orgueil de s'aimer comme un mal.*

Fille exposée aux dieux que l'Océan constelle
D'écume qu'il arrache aux miroirs du soleil,
Aux jeux universels tu préfères mortelle,
Toute d'ombre et d'amour, ton île de sommeil.

Cependant du haut ciel foudroyant l'heure humaine,
Monstre altéré de temps, immolant le futur,
Le Sacrificateur Soleil roule et ramène
Le jour après le jour sur les autels d'azur. . . .

Vainly in the heavens a burst of matter thunders;
If it lights fire to the seas, consumes the mountains,
Pours out a torrent of light upon life
And sets all the demons whinnying in our hearts,

You, on the tender sand where the wave surrenders,
Where its power of tears loses all its diamonds,
You, lulled by boredom with the world's wonders,
Virgin deaf to the clamors of eternal elements,

You close round yourself, hugging your young breast,
Soul possessed by love of its little night,
These pure disturbances, this mad star that forges
The raw gold of events as stupid as noise,

Make you kiss the breasts of your ephemeral being,
Cherish this bit of flesh like a young animal
Both victim and scorn of the bitter splendor,
And coddle the sweet pride of self-love like an evil.

Girl exposed to the gods, and starred with Ocean's
Foam that he steals from the mirrors of the sun,
You prefer to the world's games, mortal girl
All darkness and love, your island of sleep.

Meanwhile from heaven, shattering the human moment,
A monster thirsting for time, immolating the future,
The Sun, the Sacrificer, rolls on, bringing
Day after day upon the altar of azure. . . .

(Translation by James Lawler)

PROFUSION DU SOIR, POÈME ABANDONNÉ...

This poem, begun about 1899, was reworked in 1922 and included in the 1926 edition of *Album de vers anciens*. The word "abandoned" in the title may refer then specifically to the poem's history, as well as to the fact that no poem, in Valéry's eyes, could ever be finished, only abandoned. The many titles ("Infusion du soir," "Regard," "Facilité du soir," "Fantaisie du soir," "Regard du soir," "Ciel," "Breuvage") and the many manuscripts show Valéry's extended search for the form and language of the poem. A vision of the sun setting in a vast seascape composes an act of exalted contemplation. "Mon corps ne sait pas encore, et mon esprit ne me dit plus rien," Faust murmurs at a similar moment. "Seule, chante cette heure, la profusion du soir." ("But my body doesn't know yet, and my mind is dumb. There's nothing now but the richness of the evening, the song of sunset." Collected Works, 3, 61.)

In September, 1942, Claudel wrote from Brangues to say: "I did not know the fragment on the sunset which I find in the *Album de vers anciens*. It is admirable." Valéry was touched, and dedicated the poem to Claudel in the 1945 edition of *Poésies*.

ANNE

In its present form "Anne" is more than twice as long as the original version, which appeared in *La Plume* on December 1, 1900. The six quatrains, dated 1893, correspond to the first five and the last of the final text. Other versions were to follow: in 1912, the poem consisted of only five stanzas; of nine in 1920 (in the review *Les Écrits nouveaux* and Valéry's

Album de vers anciens), and finally, thirteen in the second edition of the *Album* published in 1926.

The poem as a whole is a controlled alliance of realism and abstraction, precision and passion, in three sections. The reader may be reminded of "La Jeune Parque." The manuscripts show that the two poems developed together, the hymn to Spring being sketched out on an old draft of "Anne" written on War Ministry paper, while one of the Parque's invocations to the self is found on the back of a typed version of the six stanzas that appeared in the *Album de vers anciens* of 1920.

AIR DE SÉMIRAMIS

In a corner of the original manuscript of "Air de Sémiramis" Valéry wrote: "I thought of this because of Dimier's article —on Degas, and against this painting." He was obviously referring to an appraisal by the well-known art critic, Louis Dimier, of Degas's 1861 canvas showing Semiramis at the founding of Babylon, now in the Jeu de Paume. It shows the queen in shining robes surrounded by her followers as she looks out from a high balcony upon the rising towers of her young city; behind her is a magnificent horse held by an attendant. She alone, and the horse that is the token of her power, are not distracted; they directly confront her domain.

Taking up this theme in the 1890s Valéry first traced out in a mixture of verse and prose the argument of the poem: "To my nostrils the whole of my empire is like an infinitely pervasive perfume that causes my lungs to open like inner wings. I inhale my power. My dominance lifts me to heaven"; likewise: "And at the height of my power, and my vision, like the bird on the cedar—I sing ! I can no longer speak. The dogs bark. A surge of pride, excitement, transcendence of the self—the highest summits of the voice"; and finally: "Semiramis is the soul of such a day."

One draft contains a long analysis of the erotic element and the loss of intellectual control, which Valéry reduced to three stanzas in the final version; still another combines French and English in its sub-title: "*Reine* of the Apes." The final version was first published under the title "Sémiramis (Fragment d'un très ancien poème)" in the review *Les Écrits nouveaux* in July, 1920. Valéry again returned to the theme in his play *Sémiramis* (1934).

l'amateur de poèmes

The *Album* closes on what was called by its first publisher "a curious literary document" (G. Walch in his *Anthologie des Poètes français contemporains*, 1906). Valéry wrote the piece at his personal request, says Walch, in order to explain himself and his art. According to Valéry, it is "a page of prose that concerns the art of poetry but makes no claim whatever to instruct or prescribe."

LA JEUNE PARQUE

ON NONE OF HIS OTHER WORKS did Valéry comment so fully as on "La Jeune Parque," which stands at the center of his career. Its composition occupied him from 1913 to 1917, and he judged the time well spent: "Those four years of toil taught me, I believe, many things which I did not in the least suspect. It seems to me that there is nothing so valuable for getting one's ideas clear as to write a long and obscure poem."

We can follow the making of this "exercise" (as he called it) in many ways: in the Notebooks, particularly volumes four, five, and six; in numerous letters; in the retrospective conversations with Frédéric Lefèvre published in 1926; and in two essays, "Memoirs of a Poem" and "The Prince and La Jeune Parque," collected in volume seven of this edition. One must also mention a study by Octave Nadal (*La Jeune Parque*, Le Club du Meilleur Livre, 1957) which contains the reproduction of many of the eight-hundred-odd pages of the poet's manuscripts, from his first jottings to the copy as it was sent to the printer.

The original scheme, however, was modest. In 1912 and early 1913, after Gide had encouraged him to collect his early verse, Valéry decided to write one last piece to be added to the collection: "I wanted to compose about forty lines of verse. To constrain myself to work, I decided to impose on these the strictest rules of so-called classical poetics." He would use alexandrines in rhyming couplets, respect the caesuras, and proscribe weak rhymes. At the same time he set himself a further goal: "I had the notion of some recitative after the manner of Gluck; almost a single long phrase, for contralto." The mention of a contralto voice brings to mind the warm resonance of the poem's monologue, which for its source goes back to an experience that served as a compelling model. "At a tender age," he observes in a notebook of the time just before "La Jeune Parque," "I perhaps heard a voice, a deeply moving contralto. That song must have put me in a state such as nothing had suggested to me before.... And I took it unknowingly as the measure of psychological states, and have striven all my life to make, find, think something that might directly revive in me, force from me— in accord with this *chance song*—the real, necessary, absolute thing for which from my childhood this *forgotten* song had prepared a niche."

That contralto voice came to be associated with the music of Gluck, whose *Orpheus* and *Alcestis* he especially admired: "I envied that line of melody." It presented an unfolding that was not gratuitous but (to use a favorite word of Valéry's) an organic modulation. Over the next four years Gluck was a capital point of artistic reference.

The drafts reveal the important role of phonetic and linguistic analysis in the poem's genesis. Repetitions, echoes, contrasts, symmetries, etymologies, were explored before the fable was fixed. "I started out," says Valéry, "from the language itself—first, to compose a fragment the size of a page; then, little by little, it swelled to its final dimensions." Proceeding from matter to meaning, Valéry noted with respect to the second section: "All the development that concerns the serpent came out of the rhyme *-ordre*." "The history of the whole poem," he said, "is summed up in this strange law: an artificial fabric that took on a kind of natural growth."

The first plan had to be abandoned as one passage led to another: "My divertimento was taking me where I had not thought to go." One factor which had a determining role in the composition was the outbreak of war in 1914. It was the Great War that led Marcel Proust to delay publication of the later parts of his novel and to spend four years enriching it; similarly, Valéry was to give himself to "La Jeune Parque": "I wrote it *sub signo Martis*. I wrote it in a state of anxiety, and half to combat that anxiety....I discovered then that the way to struggle against thinking about events...was to devote oneself to a difficult game; to create some infinite toil weighed down with conditions and clauses, wholly hedged about with strict observances." The poem became a task that allowed him to channel his energies. Yet he also felt the need to conceive it in more general terms: he was not only redeeming his own lost years, but working to "save" the French language. "At times I flattered myself by trying to make myself believe that I must at least work for our language since I could not fight for our soil; that I must raise a small, perhaps funereal monument to that language, made with the purest of its words and its noblest forms—a small dateless tomb, on the threatening shores of the Ocean of Gibberish." In 1917, when "La Jeune Parque" was completed, he named the artists who had been his familiar spirits: Virgil, Racine, Chénier, Baudelaire, Beethoven, Wagner, Euripides, Petrarch, Mallarmé, Rimbaud, Hugo, and one contemporary, Paul Claudel; in addition, he again underlined his debt to Gluck. If it is tempting, then, to try to define what "La Jeune Parque" variously owes to these writers and musicians, a statement from the same notebook suggests the way: "One may," Valéry observes, "consider the types of our poetry— Racine, Hugo, Baudelaire, etc.—as instruments, each more appropriate to certain effects, more adapted to certain requirements of the language, the rhythms, the images. It is not impossible to link these violins, these brasses and woodwinds to form an orchestra."

"The *subject* matters little," he said. "Commonplaces. True thought cannot be adapted to verse....Consider that the real subject of 'La Jeune Parque' is the painting of a sequence of psychological states and, in sum, the *transformation of a consciousness* in the course of a night." Again, "Imagine that you wake up in the middle of the night and that all your life revives and speaks to you. Sensuality, memories, landscapes, emotions, the feeling of your body, etc."

We note the not dissimilar plan of "Agathe," the prose poem begun in 1898 in which Valéry endeavored to project the ideas he had formulated in his research on time, memory, sensation, sleep. "La Jeune Parque" was further proof that he was no longer able to compose a poem on the pattern, and with the assumptions, of his writings of 1892. "In spite of myself I had to make a place for this new spirit (far-removed from poetry as it is generally conceived) in the work that my will has assigned to me. . . . What I wanted above all was to combine in a work the ideas I had formed about the living organism and its very functioning in so far as it thinks and feels. . . ." His project was not to write a vignette, but the complete portrayal of a sensibility. He created a fictional character who emerges from the Mediterranean myths, though not identified with any particular legend: she is Eve and Psyche and Helen and Pandora who, at a tragic conjuncture of the forces of her nature, is our destiny struggling with the inherent mystery of the mortal self. She feels the forces of love but this also, she well knows, implies death. She weeps, she would wish to die—and so succumbs to sleep. Her song begins again as dawn breaks. Beyond death, yet in full awareness of it, she offers herself to the fires of the sun.

The economy and originality of the poem become manifest when we look beyond the line of discourse to the form. "La Jeune Parque," as it was published in its final state at the end of April, 1917, consists of a series of verse-paragraphs of uneven lengths that make up altogether five hundred and twelve lines. They are arranged in fifteen main sections, some composed of more than one paragraph, as Valéry indicated by way of a table of contents in the editions of 1931 and 1938. "The transitions," he said, "cost me infinite pains."

It is clear that the structure would not have the balance of a poem like "Le Cimetière marin" in which the regular stanzaic composition allows an exact adjustment of the parts. On the other hand it has a necessity of its own, which may be described as musical. "You will note," Valéry writes, "that the divisions of the poem may recall those of a musical composition. The notion of the recitatives in lyric drama (for solo voices) pursued me." "La Jeune Parque" consists of a sequence of recitatives forming an opera.

Yet the parts have a further justification which corresponds to the basic metaphorical pattern as foreshadowed in the epigraph taken from Corneille's *Psyché*. The poem comprises a number of "coils" (*nœuds*) which form a sinuous emblem, an image of the sensibility. Valéry described the structure specifically in terms of the Serpent in a letter to Maurice Denis written before "La Jeune Parque" was published. It is, he said, "an infinitely extensible hydra, that may also be cut into parts—I do not say they would be so many living parts," a "serpent of trucks"—railway cars loaded with his personal "foibles." Its line of progression bends and turns on itself as body and mind measure out their fatal dilemma. At the heart of the poem then—both in form and meaning—is the Serpent: self-awareness making of the Parque its victim.

CHARMES

In a letter of 1922 to Jacques Doucet, Valéry described his volume *Charmes*, published the same year by the *N.R.F.*, as "a collection of prosodic experiments." The twenty-one poems it contains are remarkable for their rhythmical variety and their classical schemes of versification. In this regard, *Charmes* may be said to make a significant break with the *Album de vers anciens* and *La Jeune Parque*, bringing to an end the dominance of the alexandrine in Valéry's work and demonstrating his technical virtuosity.

Yet underlying this brilliant variety there is a unity of tone and purpose. The title itself conveys the author's ambition: *Charmes ou Poèmes*, and in the 1942 edition: *Charmes:* c'est-à-dire, *Poèmes.* With this Latinism and his designedly literal application of it, Valéry emphasizes that he is offering us poems that are poems, not fragments of the unconscious such as the Surrealists of post-war Paris were hoping to produce. More than this: his art seeks to engage both sensibility and intellect by going beyond the ordinary function of words, by weaving a complex spell in which natural objects are "enslaved as by a charm, to the whims, the wonders, the powers of language." The poem in its harmony of sound and sense would transform our image of reality.

The theme and the style had emerged as it were naturally from the long period of composition of "La Jeune Parque." Valéry observed to Alain in 1930: "*Charmes* was born (or were born) from the 'Parque.'" The seed of whole stanzas and sections of *Charmes* can be traced directly to the manuscripts of that poem.

It becomes clear when we study the manuscripts and the early editions that Valéry saw his poems and their diverse themes as constituting an organic whole, a meaningful order. How could he not have had in mind the project he had defined in 1920, in writing about another poet, his friend Lucien Fabre? On that occasion he said: "The most difficult and most enviable thing in our art" is to create "a system of poems forming a spiritual drama, a total drama played out between the forces of our being." In his notebooks, when he was planning the publication of *Charmes*, he made several different lists of poems, sketching out now a thematic development, now a musical one. In the process many titles were discarded, or reserved for *Pièces diverses*. Valéry finally adopted an alphabetical arrangement, but a plainly inconsistent one, for the original edition of 1922. In the two editions of 1926, the order had become almost definitive. The only change henceforth to be made was the relegation of "Air de Sémiramis" to *Album de vers anciens* (to which it belonged by its origins) and the placing of "Fragments du Narcisse" after "La Dormeuse." The collection now consisted of twenty-one poems, the same number as in the *Album de vers anciens*. "Aurore" and "Palme," two poems in the same form, open and close the sequence of *Charmes*.

AURORE

First published in the *Mercure de France* of October 16, 1917, "Aurore" is one of the poems Valéry wrote shortly after "La Jeune Parque": "I wrote 'Aurore' and 'Palme' at a single stretch. In the beginning they were one and the same poem. About May, 1917, with 'La Jeune Parque' finished, I found myself in a state of extreme virtuosity after four years given to difficult alexandrines. These short heptasyllables came forth so easily in the space of two or three weeks that I was almost...shocked!" But although they have identical forms and other elements in common, "Aurore" and "Palme" develop opposite attitudes. To open his book, Valéry chose the "slightly visionary" register (as he put it) of a masculine will that rejects sleep and discovers beyond reason an exultant language in the forest of the senses.

AU PLATANE

A direct line of descent can be traced from the Spring theme in "La Jeune Parque," through "Pour votre Hêtre 'Suprême'," to "Au platane," written for the most part in June 1918 at the Château de l'Isle-Manière near Avranches—"that rich region where tall trees grow like weeds." This poem gives the fullest representation in Valéry's poetry of the motif of the tree, which was for him from early youth an exemplary image of organic wholeness. "The tree," he writes in his twenty-fifth notebook, "is the poem of growth. The crescendo. To touch the extreme point of one's being, as the body extends itself from the tips of the toes to the *depths* of the fingertips." The first version, published in the small provincial review *Les Trois Roses* (Grenoble) of August-September, 1918, has only ten stanzas, but the elegy was later augmented and given new depth with a view to its inclusion in *Charmes*.

CANTIQUE DES COLONNES

The theme of this poem, the music of architecture, is one of the constants in Valéry's work. It had been developed in detail in 1891, in an article "Paradoxe sur l'Architecte"; he returned to it in "Cantique des colonnes," and again in his long Socratic dialogue, "Eupalinos, ou l'Architecte" (1924). (See Collected Works, 4.) Several years later he again used the theme in his verse ballet or "mélodrame," *Amphion*, presented with the music of Arthur Honegger at the Paris Opera in 1931.

It was with amused irony that Valéry allowed "Cantique des colonnes," a poem in praise of classical grace, to be published for the first time in André Breton's pre-Surrealist review *Littérature* in March, 1919.

L'ABEILLE

A feminine voice here develops a theme which Valéry found
latent, he tells us, in the rhyme "abeille–corbeille." He had
used it in "La Jeune Parque:"

> *Et roses! mon soupir vous soulève, vainqueur*
> *Hélas! des bras si doux qui ferment la corbeille. . . .*
> *Oh! parmi mes cheveux pèse d'un poids d'abeille*
> *Plongeant toujours plus ivre au baiser plus aigu,*
> *Le point délicieux de mon jour ambigu. . . .*

> And roses! the sigh I heave lifts you, vanquishing
> Alas, the arms so soft folded about your cradle. . . .
> Ah, through my hair weighs with a bee's weight,
> Plunging ever wilder to the sharpest kiss,
> The delectable glint of my ambiguous dawn. . . .

"L'Abeille" was first published in *La Nouvelle Revue
Française*, December, 1919.

POÉSIE

The only poem in *Charmes* whose title calls attention to
poetry itself, "Poésie" was probably written at about the
same time as "Aurore" and "Palme," although it did not
appear until 1921, in *La Revue de France* of July 15.

It is one of the few poems Valéry chose to record at the
Musée de la Parole; he also included it in his personal
anthology, *Morceaux choisis*.

LES PAS

A poem of mathematical balance in four octosyllabic
quatrains which first appeared in the *Feuillets d'art* of
November, 1921. Valéry had sketched its outline in a note-

book of 1917, and there the allegorical element was explicit. Yet he was to say much later of "Les Pas" that it was a "small, purely *sentimental* poem" (*Cahiers* 28:427).

LA CEINTURE

Valéry used the *quatorzain* on several occasions, especially in his work of the early 1890s, but he nowhere else followed the scheme he used in "La Ceinture," which conveys a feeling of tenuous continuity. Surprisingly, the first manuscript shows that the final couplet was conceived as a quatrain, designed to be followed by yet another. As Valéry finally came to write it, however, the poem fully exploits the resources of the form. "La Ceinture" was first published in *Les Écrits nouveaux* of March 3, 1922.

LA DORMEUSE

"La Dormeuse," as it was published in *Charmes*, is no doubt Valéry's most accomplished regular sonnet. It had first appeared in the review *L'Amour de l'art* in June, 1920. The several drafts show the care he had taken to reach a fullness of sound and suggestion in his opening: "Tu dors: le doux masque aspirant une fleur" / "Ton doux masque aspirant une invisible fleur" / "Ombre par le doux masque, aspirant une fleur...."

FRAGMENTS DU NARCISSE

The three sections that form the poem as we know it were brought together for the first time in the 1926 edition of *Charmes*, although they owed their origin to the treatment of the same theme in "Narcisse parle" thirty-five years before. Now, however, the points of reference, the formal requirements, the poetic ambition were more demanding: "...I had the idea of making a kind of counterpart to the severe and obscure 'Jeune Parque.' I chose my old theme of Narcissus—or rather the theme chose itself: it was appropriate to what I wanted to write, that is to say, a work almost the counterpart of 'La Jeune Parque' but much simpler in form, giving little difficulty of understanding, my efforts being devoted above all to the harmony of the language."

LA PYTHIE

Written for the most part near Avranches in 1918, "La Pythie" was published in *Les Écrits nouveaux* in February of the following year. It is surely Valéry's most dynamic poem and among his most ambitious. He saw it characteristically as a formal exercise, an attempt to develop the resources of the octosyllable in a personal way, in response to a discussion with Pierre Louÿs concerning its virtues. Yet the first line came to him like a magic formula: "The sonority composed itself," he wrote. We know that this first line, the fifth in the final version ("Pâle, profondément mordue"), attracted to itself the rest of the poem: "My fragment behaved as if it were alive; plunged into the (doubtless nutritive) milieu offered by my mind's expectancy and desire, it proliferated and engendered what it needed: a few lines above, and many below." The theme was the quest for a poetic language, the evolution of a cry into ordered discourse. "Creation requires a condition of initial chaos, as in *Genesis*," he remarked. In one of the earliest manuscripts of the poem, he wrote: "The logic of the Pythia: the path of the idea: using the body to form ideas." And again, many years later: "In 'La Parque' and 'La Pythie,' I believe I am the only poet who has made a sustained effort to trace a physiological feeling of conscious-ness; the functioning of the *body*, in so far as it is perceived by the *self*, serving as a continuous ground bass to the incidents or ideas."

LE SYLPHE

Valéry constructs a puzzle-poem around the familiar expres-sion "Ni vu ni connu," challenging the reader to find something, as in "hide and seek." The slightest of all the poems of *Charmes*, "Le Sylphe" appeared for the first time in *Intentions*, January, 1922.

L'INSINUANT

This short poem appeared in *Les Écrits nouveaux* of June, 1918 and was perhaps written at the same time as "Insinuant II," later included in *Pièces diverses*. See herein, p. 248.

LA FAUSSE MORTE

Like many of the poems of *Charmes*, "La Fausse Morte" first appeared in an ephemeral little magazine *L'Œil de bœuf*, April, 1921. Its theme is the art of feigning, as in "Le Sylphe" and "L'Insinuant," but here it is the poet who is misled.

ÉBAUCHE D'UN SERPENT

In a letter to Alain of January, 1930, Valéry gave a clear statement of his aim in this poem: "As for the 'Ébauche d'un serpent,' I do not know whether I told you that I intended it to be a burlesque monologue, that I thought of Beckmesser's role in the *Meistersinger*. All the very difficult work for this poem was concentrated on the *variations of tone*. I purposely exaggerated assonance and alliteration." Taking up a few lines from a draft of "La Jeune Parque," Valéry developed this "Satanic" hymn on the model of the love song made to a recipe by Wagner's ugly seducer. He brought great suppleness to his rhyme schemes (of which there are no less than ten), to his parodies (the Bible, Bossuet, scholastic theology), to his pleasantries, his ominous threats. Stylistically it is an extraordinary *tour de force*.

The original version of the "Serpent," only eleven stanzas, was severely criticized by Pierre Louÿs; but Valéry kept on, under such titles as "Chanson du serpent," "Fable," "La Fable du serpent: Souvenir de l'Éden," until he had written the third longest of his poems. "Ébauche d'un serpent" was first published in *La Nouvelle Revue Française* of July 1, 1921, in a version that concluded with the following lines:

> *Et parmi l'étincellement*
> *De sa queue éternellement*
> *Éternellement le bout mordre.*

This ending makes explicit the Gnostic theme of the *ouroboros*, the self-devouring serpent, a frequent image in the Notebooks. But the lines did not appear in the final text of *Charmes*.

LES GRENADES

This octosyllabic sonnet first appeared in *Rythme et Synthèse* of May, 1920. An invocation to the natural object, a pomegranate, opens into an analogy with the mind's possibilities (Valéry's "closed world of the possible") and the young poet's dream of himself.

LE VIN PERDU

The alternate rhymes and the tone of personal confession establish within the limits of a sonnet a movement like that of a narrative ballad. The poet describes how he made a libation to nothingness, the ultimate effect being the poet's surprise. The central metaphor suggests ancient rites, particularly the Eucharist; it also recalls a page from Henri Poincaré's *La Valeur de la science* illustrating Carnot's principle by the diffusion of wine in water. Valéry in his Notebooks used the figure to represent the workings of the subconscious: "I was diffused, near and far, in your substance...," says the Idea, "like a drop of wine in a cask of clear water."

The poem first appeared in *Les Feuilles libres* of February, 1922.

INTÉRIEUR

Published in *La Vie* of March, 1921, "Intérieur" originally formed part of a much longer poem. Gradually two poems emerged from the one; from "L'Heure et la Femme," Valéry obtained "Heure" and "Intérieur." "Heure" was later included in *Pièces diverses*.

In "Intérieur," a woman takes the place of nature and represents in the universe of the abstract mind *"everything that may be alive yet foreign"* (*Cahiers* 14:329). And in the closing line the poet turns an expected flash of irony on himself.

LE CIMETIÈRE MARIN

Valéry on several occasions—in his talks with Frédéric Lefèvre, in his essay "Concerning *Le Cimetière marin*," and in his Notebooks—described how his best known poem was written. He tells us that it came to him first of all as "a naked rhythm," "pure and simple percussion," a shape that demanded to be filled, drawing to itself words to accompany and confirm it. The process seemed automatic, he says, as when a photographic plate is put into a developing bath and an image appears: "I saw certain verbal elements appearing as on a rhythmic apparatus which perhaps acted as a developer." The syllables and words composed a line of poetry "impossible to modify" and, as it were, a "potential definition of the poem." The line was decasyllabic, and Valéry felt that this rather unusual rhythm was a challenge: "The demon of generalization prompted me to try raising this Ten to the power of Twelve," i.e., his decasyllable should have no less force than the alexandrine. He decided that it should be a long poem arranged with respect to the total effect to be obtained. "In *Le Cimetière marin,*" he said, "I remember shaping and placing stanzas as one does masses of color." The poem was to consist of a considerable number of stanzas (twenty-four), whose metrical pattern he would establish with care. His rhyme scheme enabled him to rule out any narrative element that might be suggested by alternate rhymes, in favor of the precise containment of a couplet followed by a quatrain of envelope rhymes, while the feminine rhymes in lines 1, 2, 4, 5 have two strong notes of resolution in lines 3 and 6. This form was coupled to a system of alliteration, well marked caesuras, strong rhymes, giving each stanza a coherence of its own.

The theme is an elegiac meditation in the presence of sea, sun, and sky, much as Valéry had experienced them at Sète in his childhood and early adolescence: "Nothing formed and impregnated me more, or taught me better." His poem then, in one regard, is extremely personal: its décor is a remembered one, its themes those he associates with that scene. But the elements also constitute for him a setting which suggests the source of all meditation, the potential harmony, the density and completeness of thought in itself, so that he could say without self-contradiction that he had written "as personal, yet as universal a monologue as [he] could compose."

In his essay on this poem Valéry wrote:

I said that the 'Cimetière marin' first came into my head in the form of a composition in stanzas of six lines, of ten syllables each. This decision enabled me fairly easily to distribute through my work the perceptible, affective, and abstract content it needed so as to suggest a meditation by a particular self, translated into the universe of poetry.

The need to produce contrasts, and to maintain a kind of balance between the different moments of that *self*, led me (for example) to introduce at one point a certain touch of philosophy. The lines in which the famous arguments of Zeno appear (though animated, mixed, swept away in a burst of dialectic, like a whole rigging by a sudden gust of wind) have the role of offsetting by a metaphysical tonality the sensual and 'too human' part of the preceding stanzas; also, they define more precisely the *person who is speaking*, a lover of abstractions....I have misused these few images from Zeno to express a reaction against the length and intensity of a meditation that makes us too cruelly aware of the gap between *being* and *knowing*, which comes from our consciousness of consciousness....

But I meant to borrow only a little of the *color* of philosophy.

To a lady who once questioned Valéry about the origins of the "Cimetière marin," he gave this account: "A melancholy insomnia gave birth to the first word; a leaking faucet was responsible for the second. I had the title; all that was left to write was the poem."

ODE SECRÈTE

In 1930 Valéry wrote to Alain, whose *Commentaires de «Charmes»* had just been published: "I am surprised that you like 'Ode secrète,' which I thought I alone could like a little....It is a kind of illegitimate child—of unknown parents—hence the title."

The poem was written in 1918 at the end of the First World War, when Valéry's principal poems were already finished. The victory he celebrates here is perhaps triple. Peace has come, the poet can rest, and the poetic forms he has created out of his own imagination, like the monsters and gods which primitive man imposed on the stars and the shapeless void, are fixed and perhaps immortal. The manuscripts of the poem offer many variants, one of the most interesting being the first version of the last stanza: "Seuls ces feux qui furent les yeux...," which recalls by its rhythm and language the change that Ariel celebrates: "Those are pearls that were his eyes / Nothing of him that doth fade...."

"Ode secrète" was first published in *Littérature* in February, 1920.

LE RAMEUR

Valéry's song of the will was begun in 1918 in Paris, completed the following July in Brittany, and published the same year in the December first issue of the *Mercure de France*. ("Visibly, too visibly, an exercise on, or against, certain difficulties," he wrote to his wife.) A passage from his Notebooks (*Cahiers* 5:586) illuminates the poem: "Man works against time, against his own life to attain something. He carries on a hidden labor with an intensity that quickly becomes unbearable. He must either stop or die, but not go on struggling, conceiving, sustaining. For he oversteps the amount of *beyond time* allotted to him, when he solidifies in this way. That is how the soul is detached from the body by separation from the *medium*."

PALME

This poem first appeared in *La Nouvelle Revue Française* of June 1, 1919. It reproduces the form of "Aurore," and serves in this way to frame the collection of *Charmes*.

In "Palme" Valéry approaches the Christian genre of the parable (the title of one draft reads: "Parabole de la palme"). In the opening stanza an angel brings a gift of milk and bread to the poet's table, revealing in an ordinary act this angel's share of human nature.

The poem is dedicated to "Jeannie," Madame Paul Valéry.

PIÈCES DIVERSES DE TOUTE ÉPOQUE

IN THE 1942 EDITION of *Poésies* Valéry brought together for the first time twelve of his smaller compositions under the heading above—"a few brief poems of diverse vintage and rather different forms," as he put it in a preliminary note. The majority had not appeared previously although four of them were included in *Mélange* in 1939, while "La Caresse" had already figured in the review *Les Écrits nouveaux* as far back as 1918. Valéry clearly thought of them as providing a complement to the other sections of his volume.

That selection of twelve *Pièces diverses* has here been enlarged to eighteen by the addition of "Le Sonnet d'Irène," "Pour votre Hêtre 'Suprême'," "À cet éventail," and three poems under the heading *Petites Choses*.

NEIGE

Originally published in *Mélange* in 1939, the opening poem of *Pièces diverses* is wholly personal in tone: the poet wakes to the sounds and the scene of new-fallen snow. More than half a dozen drafts of the poem are extant, several of them in typed form, showing the plan, later abandoned, to include it among the poems of *Charmes*.

SINISTRE

First published in *Mélange* in 1939 and described in the preface as having been written almost fifty years before, "Sinistre" appeared a second time in a warfront journal, *La Tranche de culasse* (April 2, 1940), where it was subtitled "vers de jeunesse."

This poem may well have been conceived in the 1890's; it is possible that it was "composed" in 1909, as Valéry told Julien Monod. Valéry's notebooks contain an epigraph found also on a draft of "Sinistre": "Erat navis in medio mari" (Mark 7:47): "And when even was come, the ship was in the midst of the sea, and he alone on the land...." It seems likely as well, that Edgar Allan Poe's narrative of the whaler "Grampus" (the storm that shakes the vessel after the mutiny, the vision of the ghost ship) was present in Valéry's thoughts; one manuscript carries the words "Gordon Pym." But one manuscript in particular bearing the precise date

"4–5 octobre 17," indicates the importance the poem had for Valéry when, at the height of his literary powers, he was working on the collection of *Charmes*.

COLLOQUE

"My 'inspiration'," Valéry observed in one of his notebooks, "proceeds...rather by way of musical forms." The remark finds its illustration in these few lines written as a diptych in which one voice depends on the echo it provokes. Originally called "Les Deux Flûtes" and subtitled "Romance: deux voix," it is dated 1920 in the proofs, which also contain the following comment (later suppressed): "Pièce ancienne, composée pour être mise en musique" ("An old poem, composed to be set to music"). It was first published in *La Nouvelle Revue Française*, June 1, 1939.

LA DISTRAITE

Though first published in 1939 in *Mélange*, "La Distraite" had been composed in 1917 and considered for possible inclusion in *Charmes*.

Who is Laura? The manuscripts make it clear that the feminine presence was in fact "Jeannie," Madame Valéry: "Daigne, Jeanne, très beau regard qui ne regarde pas..."

There were two distinct phases in the composition: Valéry first adopted the discursive manner of a lover's invitation to his mistress to walk with him; he later elaborated a single sentence of eight alexandrines, using details from previous drafts.

L'INSINUANT II

This is a companion piece to the pentasyllabic "L'Insinuant" included in *Charmes* in 1922. See herein, p. 180.

HEURE

"Day's end is woman," Valéry writes in *Mélange*. If dawn stirred his characteristic will to recompose the world, sunset brought him tenderness and abundance.

Written in 1917, "Heure" was among the first of Valéry's poems to be listed for inclusion in *Charmes*, yet it was published for the first time twenty-five years later in *Pièces diverses*. The form is close to the traditional rondeau, containing a refrain and only two rhymes. As one manuscript indicates, it is a "romance."

L'OISEAU CRUEL

The manuscript is dated 1935. As far back as the second notebook (1900–02), Valéry wrote: "Sur l'arbre de chair chante le minime oiseau spirituel, comme l'oiseau qui chante depuis l'éternité, inconscient, et étant conscience." ("On the tree of flesh the minute bird of the spirit is singing, like the bird singing from eternity, unconscious, being consciousness itself.")

L'AURORE

This poem, written probably in the mid-thirties, made its first appearance in the 1942 edition of *Poésies*.

ÉQUINOXE

This elegy was begun at the time of *Charmes*, and was included in some of the first plans for the collected poems; but it underwent many changes and over the years grew from the narrow span of five quatrains to the twelve stanzas of the definitive version, published in 1942. The earliest title was "Station," then "Pause." The word "Équinoxe," however, evokes more precisely the tenuous equilibrium which the poem develops between summer and autumn, past and present, life and death.

LA CARESSE

This brief song was the first of the poems of *Pièces diverses* to be published, in the review *Les Écrits nouveaux* of June, 1918. The heptasyllabic metre recalls three other poems of *Charmes* composed after the completion of "La Jeune Parque": "Aurore," "Poésie," and "Palme." All were written at about the same time.

CHANSON À PART

The original manuscript is dated July 3, 1938, which makes "Chanson à part" one of the last lyrics Valéry published. One might say that it stands as a kind of testament—rapid, unpretentious. The language is spare, the twenty-four rhymes all masculine. More clearly than any other of Valéry's collected poems, this inner dialogue has the tone of the man himself.

LE PHILOSOPHE ET LA JEUNE PARQUE

In one of his notebooks for 1935 Valéry made this brief note while on a visit to Zurich: "Parque raconte au Phil. son histoire naïve. Mais le P. pense en prose." ("The Parque tells the Philosopher her naïve story. But the Philosopher thinks in prose"). These words were the seed of his poem composed a few months later.

The "Philosopher" had a name: he was Alain, who had written his *Commentaires de "Charmes"* in 1930 and was now, six years later, on the point of publishing his remarks on "La Jeune Parque," with Valéry's poem as a prologue.

LE SONNET D'IRÈNE

This *sonnet galant* in the baroque style was published in *Mélange* in 1939. To all appearances it is a stylistic exercise with archaic spelling, a fictitious date (originally 1685, then 1655, MD CLIV, then 1644), and an abstract tone. Yet in fact it is a highly personal expression. "Ambroise," Valéry's middle name which he often used in his youth, perhaps takes on here its full meaning of "immortal," and "saint" its meaning of a being self-possessed.

POUR VOTRE HÊTRE «SUPRÊME»

These lines were sent as a gift to Madeleine Gide on All Souls' Day, 1917. The first draft had been written earlier that same year, in July, when Valéry was spending some weeks at Gides' property at Cuverville in Normandy, where he began writing an ode inspired by one of the five beeches there which he called (or was it a pun the Gides themselves had invented?) the "Hêtre 'Suprême'". In the sixth Notebook, part of which was written during this period, he jotted down the beginnings of a poem. Yet the adequate expression had still to be found. As Valéry wrote to Gide on July 27, the tree would one day speak of its own accord, at another time and place.

Three months later, on November 2, in Paris, he composed a short poem dedicated to Madame Gide. It was originally intended, he told Gide, as an intimate song: "But it was All Souls' Day," he said, "and despite the author's intention, the song grew serious; the intimate tone just kept it from turning into a lament."

À CET ÉVENTAIL

This poem signals its Mallarméan theme by adopting the *quatorzain*. It was not published by Valéry, but reproduced by Pierre Humbourg in *Vendémiaire* of April 8, 1936, in an article entitled "Du Vachette à l'Académie." The poem was written on a fan belonging to Mme Gabrielle Fontainas-Hérold.

AU-DESSOUS D'UN PORTRAIT

These four alexandrines originally appeared in Franz Rauhut's study *Paul Valéry, Geist und Mythos* (Munich, Max Huebner Verlag, 1930), and were later included by Valéry himself in *Mélange*.

SUR UN ÉVENTAIL

Several of the later Symbolists adopted the theme of the fan by way of an indirect tribute to Mallarmé, who called it "this isolator, whose mobile virtue is to renew our state of unawareness in our causeless delight." This poem was first published in *Mélange* in 1939.

À JUAN RAMÓN JIMÉNEZ

Juan Ramón Jiménez (1881–1958), the Spanish poet and Nobel prize-winner (1956), wrote a tribute to Valéry entitled "6 rosas con silencio" which appeared in the *Hommage des écrivains étrangers à Paul Valéry* (Bussum, Stols, 1927). Valéry's poem to Jiménez, written three years before, was published there in facsimile.

DOUZE POÈMES

Twelve Poems, copied from the manuscripts in Valéry's study, were brought together in 1959 by Octave Nadal in a de luxe edition issued by the "Bibliophiles du Palais" and reprinted shortly afterwards in the *Mercure de France*. Though few, these poems made a considerable contribution to our knowledge of Valéry's range. By internal and external evidence approximate dates can be assigned to them, from an early *quatorzain* to the late "Odelette nocturne," along with a series of compositions from the early 1920s. They display a wide variety of tones and forms, and a lyricism of personal feeling which Valéry had, no doubt, been unwilling to expose to the reading public during his lifetime.

LA JEUNE FILLE

In five octosyllabic quatrains with alternate rhymes the naïve voice of an absent girl speaks in the mind of the man who loves her. The phrase *éphémère fiancée* may recall the words of Narcisse speaking to his own image: "Éphémère immortel."

ABEILLE SPIRITUELLE

Several titles were proposed for these lines ("Ambroise," "Ambroisie," "Abeille") before the final one was chosen. The poet here used the decasyllabic quatrains he had adopted in "Sinistre."

BÉATRICE

The name is found repeatedly in Valéry's notebooks of the early twenties. This octosyllabic sonnet is an image of love's fragility.

LE PHILOSOPHE

Probably written at the same time as "Béatrice," "Le Philosophe" has the same form, the octosyllabic sonnet, but is written in a lighter vein. The poem is a kind of allegory of conscious thought and its chastening effect on feeling.

À CHAQUE DOIGT

Valéry here uses the Elizabethan sonnet, or quatorzain, with an amusing lightness. The transparent images and their negative evocation turn emphatic at the end, with bagpipe and goat in a couplet rhyme—Mallarmé would have called it the "comet's tail."

T'ÉVANOUIR

Very little seems to be known about the origins of "T'éva-nouir." The closest parallel to it in Valéry's work is "Vue" (in *Album de vers anciens*) which was doubtless written about the same time.

À LA VITRE D'HIVER

Despite its conventional form, "À la vitre d'hiver" is among Valéry's most moving poems. We recognize a "meta-physical" voice, abstract and impassioned, that goes to the end of its despair. This poem with its austere energy in the exploration of grief would seem to have been composed in the early 1920s.

À DES DIVINITÉS CACHÉES

The title is something of a puzzle, and like "Ode secrète" aims to provoke attention. Valéry adopts the unusual form of four ten-line stanzas of hexasyllables that convey an agitated movement and correspond to the insistent use of apostrophe and command. The diction is exalted, taking its key perhaps from classical invocation, calling on ancient gods and goddesses, and including a grammatical gender that bears the distinctive mark of the seventeenth century ("Les beaux insultes").

ODELETTE NOCTURNE

A reproduction of the manuscript of these lines appeared in *Plaisir de France* in December, 1965, under the title "La Poésie est passée à Béduer." Composed in the last years of the poet's life, this "odelette" of eight pentasyllabic quatrains expresses the tenuous communion between two lovers who are apart.

"Béduer," a château in the Loire Valley, is the property of Mme Jean Voilier.

FRAGMENT

This piece, undated and incomplete, raises more questions than it answers. One would like to know the nature of the two syllables missing in the first line, and the conclusion contained in the missing tercet. We are struck by the severity of several lines (in particular line 7) which recalls certain baroque sonnets of the early seventeenth century.

SILENCE

In the discussion of "Fragments du Narcisse" it was noted that Valéry long played with the project of completing that poem in a different way. The unfinished sequence to which the title "Silence" has been given could well have found a place in it, having been almost certainly composed in the 1920s with this in view.

AUX VIEUX LIVRES

The last poem of the twelve is one of the most carefully developed. Written at the time of *Charmes*, it was considered for inclusion in that collection, although the metrical pattern is identical with that of "Au platane": in both cases quatrains of alternating alexandrines and hexasyllables constitute the pattern of an ironic elegy.

The poem has the same bitter note as Valéry's essay of the same period, "The Crisis of the Mind" (1919): "We later civilizations...we too now know that we are mortal....

The circumstances that could send the works of Keats and Baudelaire to join the works of Menander are no longer inconceivable; they are in the newspapers."

UNCOLLECTED POEMS

DESPITE THE APPEARANCE OF *Douze Poèmes*, it is clear that a good sheaf of Valéry's uncollected verse has still to be published. Some of it, such as the *Carmina eroticissima* and *Corona*, dates from the middle and late periods of his life; but the larger part consists of the works written before his arrival in Paris, which allow us to trace his intellectual and stylistic evolution from 1884, when he began to write in earnest. In the first notebook devoted to poetry he is already experimenting with metres. He imitates Victor Hugo in his manner and choice of subjects, yet also writes a parody on a Hugo poem: "Non, le bachot n'est à personne…" (Hugo: "Non, l'avenir n'est à personne…"); he adopts the accent of Lamartine, to whom he was not noticeably tender later on, and imitates other Romantic poets of languor and fragility.

But at the same time he turns to Latin verse, or to the *Chanson de Roland*. Medieval images and turns of phrase predominate in several poems of 1886, his fifteenth year, opening the way to his reading, in the late 1880s, the Symbolists and Poe. In 1889, in a lecture "On Literary Technique," he formulates his aesthetic theory in these terms: "And we love the art of this time, complicated and *artificial*, over-vibrant, over-tense, over-musical, the more so as it grows more mysterious, more restricted, more inaccessible to the crowd. What does it matter that it is closed to the majority of men, that its ultimate expression remains the luxury of a happy few, provided it reaches the highest degree of splendor and purity among the few righteous whose divine kingdom it is." The adolescent who wrote these lines was obviously ready to work out the consequences of Mallarmé's achievement.

The poems included here represent a choice of Valéry's production between 1886 and the early 1890s. They include a sonnet, "La Dormeuse II," no doubt written much later, which captures an essential motif of his poetry.

TESTAMENT DE VÉNITIENNE

This poem was written in February 1887, when its author was fifteen. Published by Octave Nadal in his edition of the *Correspondence Paul Valéry–Gustave Fourment* (1957), it develops the romantic topic of beauty in death. Valéry had no doubt read Banville, but his plaint owes most to Victor Hugo, of whom he was to write in 1890: "I began at the age of fourteen with the *Orientales*; I continued with *Notre-Dame*, which plunged me into the Gothic ecstasy from which I have not yet fully emerged."

PESSIMISME D'UNE HEURE

Theme, imagery and tone are here patently modelled on the "Spleen" poems of *Les Fleurs du mal*. This poem, written September 27, 1887, was published more than sixty-five years later, by Henri Mondor in *Le Figaro littéraire* of September 11, 1954.

SOLITUDE

Also published by Henri Mondor alongside "Pessimisme d'une heure" in *Le Figaro littéraire* of September 11, 1954,

"Solitude" had been written in the summer of 1887. Its Baudelairian intensity and its angelism already point to 1892 and the "night in Genoa."

LA VOIX DES CHOSES

These decasyllables offer a very young poet's formula for writing verse. They bear the date November 24, 1887, and were sent to a friend of his own age, Gustave Fourment. They are an improvisation on the romantic attitude to poetic creation conceived by Victor Hugo, who held that the poet must become "the sonorous echo" of the universe.

RÊVE

No doubt the first of Valéry's poems to be published, "Rêve" appeared in *La Petite Revue maritime* of Marseilles, dated August 15, 1889. A manuscript note indicates that it was written on February 11 of that year. Like so many of his early compositions, it expresses an adolescent flight into a world of immensity, night, solitude, and sensuous pleasure. The influence of two literary masters is apparent in the style: Hugo and, to a lesser extent, Baudelaire.

REPAS

The date of composition is September 30, 1889, but the poem was first published by P. O. Walzer in *La Poésie de Valéry* (1953). It is a regular octosyllabic sonnet whose theme and tone recall Hugo, although the form is Parnassian. Valéry was not yet eighteen.

L'ÉGLISE

In the first numbers of the review *La Conque* which appeared in 1891, Valéry announced the forthcoming publication of a collection of verse entitled *Carmen mysticum*, later to be called *Chorus mysticus*. It was a project he had often discussed with Pierre Louÿs, and he had composed a number of poems which would have formed the nucleus. One of the earliest of these liturgical pieces is "L'Église," written on October 3, 1889, and published by Octave Nadal. Its theme is the exaltation of religion as art: "He adores the religion that makes beauty one of its dogmas, and Art the most magnificent of its apostles," he said to Pierre Louÿs in 1890; "he worships above all his own Catholicism—somewhat Spanish, very Wagnerian and Gothic."

LA MER

In a letter of October 24, 1889, Gustave Fourment wrote a detailed critical commentary on these lines, written October 10, 1889, which Valéry was never to publish. They were revealed by Octave Nadal in the *Correspondence Valéry–Fourment*. The influence of Heredia and the Parnassians is strong here.

POUR LA NUIT

First published in *La Revue indépendante* of October 1890, but dated January 10, 1889, in a manuscript sent to Pierre Louÿs, "Pour la nuit" was hailed by Valéry's Parnassian friends. Louÿs wrote: "Be thou condemned to have it as thy *Vase brisé, Midi*, or Arvers' *Sonnet*"—that is, as closely linked with Valéry's name as these poems of Sully Prudhomme, Leconte de Lisle, and Félix Arvers were with theirs. The style is characteristic of the young Valéry: "We chose vocabulary that was imposingly vague, always 'recherché'," Valéry wrote of the Symbolist poets. "Nothing," he told Pierre Louÿs in August 1890, "—nothing but vision, mirage in an old mirror, moon reflected in water, can attract or hold me."

CONSEIL D'AMI

First published shortly after Valéry's death (in the *Nouvelles littéraires* of July 26, 1945), this sonnet shows the influence of Joris-Karl Huysmans on the young Valéry. "Huysmans is the present-day author with whom my soul is most at ease," he had written to his friend Albert Dugrip at the end of 1889. "I am forever rereading *À Rebours*; it is my Bible and my bedside book. Nothing stronger has been written in these last twenty years."

TU SAIS?...

First published in *Les Nouvelles littéraires* of May 1, 1952, this poem had been written May 5, 1890, for Valéry's close friend and critic of his early verse, Gustave Fourment. It is one of three sonnets composed in 1890 on the theme of mystical friendship. The others are "Le Bois amical" dedicated to André Gide, and "Ensemble" dedicated to Pierre Louÿs.

SUR L'EAU

These lines, published for the first time in Walzer's *La Poésie de Valéry* (1953), were almost certainly written in the course of 1890. They are close to the previous poem "Tu sais?..." At the furthest extreme from "Le Rameur" of *Charmes*, this poem evokes a liquid and lulling movement and the mere idea of flight.

LA SUAVE AGONIE

"The gift of subtle analysis, with a music adequate to it—this you certainly possess, and it is everything...." Such was Mallarmé's comment on the two poems Valéry had sent him from Montpellier in October, 1890. One was "Le Jeune Prêtre," the other "La Suave Agonie," both dated July 13, 1890, and later to appear in *La Conque* (June, 1891). More clearly than any other of his poems of that time, "La Suave Agonie" shows traits derived more or less directly from Verlaine's *Romances sans paroles* and *Sagesse*.

LUXURIEUSE AU BAIN

"Here, as usual, are a few lines of verse," Valéry wrote to Pierre Louÿs on September 26, 1890; and he continued: "I am afraid they are obscure." The first of the two sonnets he had sent was "Luxurieuse au bain," dated July 23, 1890, in which a close reading of Mallarmé is apparent. It is a kind of first study for "Baignée" and "Épisode" of the *Album de vers anciens*.

À ALCIDE BLAVET

A classmate of Gustave Fourment at the Montpellier *lycée*, Alcide Blavet published numerous poems in French and Provençal. He was secretary of the local review *La Cigale d'or*, to which Valéry himself in 1891 contributed "La Belle au bois dormant" (later "Au bois dormant," in *Album de vers anciens*). The sonnet here dedicated to Blavet is regular and resonant in the manner of Heredia. It is dated December 7, 1890.

LES CHATS BLANCS

The manuscript is dated September 26, 1890, but the poem was not published until 1953, in Walzer's *La Poésie de Valéry*. Valéry had sent his sonnet, just written, to Gustave Fourment, who criticized it for the inconsistency of its images. He did not refer to the obvious model Valéry had found in Baudelaire's "Les Chats."

CIMETIÈRE

An undated sonnet written no doubt in 1890 and revealed in Walzer's *La Poésie de Valéry* (1953), this poem takes a Mediterranean graveyard for its theme. Its relation to "Le Cimetière marin" is indicated in the figure of the immobile sun that stands over the scene in both poems, and even more pointedly perhaps in the rhymes, *tombes/colombes* and *fleurs/pleurs*, found in both. Valéry thought of sending "Cimetière" with his first letter to Mallarmé in October, 1890, but finally considered it "too awkward and too incomplete."

LE JEUNE PRÊTRE

In his first letter to Mallarmé (October, 1890), Valéry, "a young man lost in the depths of the provinces...," enclosed "Le Jeune Prêtre" with "La Suave Agonie." The former of these, published two months later in *La Plume* (Paris), which awarded it an "honorable mention" in its sonnet competition, reflected the young man's liking for liturgical themes, resonant epithets, unusual inversions, and dramatic contrast. This poem was intended moreover to illustrate the Parnassian technique he had formulated in his letter: "To describe himself in a few words," he wrote to Mallarmé, "he must affirm that he prefers short poems, concentrated toward a final brilliance, whose rhythms are like the marmoreal steps of the altar crowned by the last line!"

VIOL

This poem was submitted in 1890 to *La Plume* as an entry in that review's sonnet competition. It was published in the issue of November 15, 1890, but won neither a prize nor an honorable mention. "Viol" could well figure alongside Mallarme's "Une négresse par le démon secouée..." and other poems of the *Parnasse satyrique*.

ENSEMBLE

In 1890 Valéry wrote three quite different expressions of his fable of friendship. This sonnet, dedicated to Pierre Louÿs, appeared with "Le Bois amical" in *La Conque* (January 1892), but was not afterwards republished. It uses the liturgical imagery found in the Valéry-Louÿs correspondence of that time, echoing the same dream of a night of mystical communion.

FLEUR MYSTIQUE

This sonnet was published in the *Bulletin de l'Association générale des étudiants de Montpellier* of January 1, 1891. It is a heady mixture of the sensuous and the mythical, not without bathos. It foreshadows the *gaucherie* of his love for Madame de R. the following year, which finally provoked his abrupt re-appraisal of himself (the crisis in Genoa, November, 1892). For the moment however his inspiration and accent are Pre-Raphaelite. "One must perhaps write vaporous things, as fine and light as purple smoke, which suggest everything and say nothing precisely, but have wings," he wrote in November, 1890.

MERCI

"Merci" was sent to Gustave Fourment in April, 1892, apparently in answer to his friend's comments on "Narcisse parle"; it was published by Octave Nadal in his edition of the *Correspondence Valéry-Fourment*. The tone is "high irony," as the poet thanks his friend, in one sentence of involuted but impeccable syntax.

BALLET

Once more the measure of Mallarmé's influence on Valéry's early poems is shown in this sonnet, which later inspired "Baignée" (the last two lines reproduce the same rhymes) and the future portraits of sleeping women such as "Anne" and "La Dormeuse." It was written in 1892, but published posthumously in Henri Mondor's *Les Premiers Temps d'une amitié* (1947). It shows the extent of Valéry's break with his former styles.

INTERMÈDE

This poem appeared in *L'Ermitage* in September, 1892, just before Valéry came to live in Paris. The inspiration—even to the absence of punctuation—is Mallarméan: it is a salon piece whose "precious" imagery and manner are not unworthy of comparison with the "Éventail de Mademoiselle Mallarmé." All is touched by untragic death; it is a magical shadow, not vague but crystalline, like the reflected image of the star. The poet hints at the presence of mourning, but there is no anguish, for a flash of soft brightness implies the playfulness of love.

VERS POUR MME DE R. . . .

This fragment dated 1892 would seem to have been written shortly after Valéry's arrival in Paris at the end of November. It expresses an aspect of the desperate passion he conceived for the young Catalan woman whom he glimpsed in Montpellier but never met. The helplessness he felt—"having on one occasion stupidly skirted the abyss"—fired his resolve during the "crisis in Genoa" to go to the opposite pole of detachment and analysis.

MOI À PARIS

Octave Nadal dates the composition of this Elizabethan sonnet as "about 1894." It is once more a pastiche of Mallarméan style with its circumlocutions, its precious syntax, its wit. Valéry writes of the pleasure of a provincial newly come to Paris who compares the reality with what he had dreamed: he wonders, listens, looks as he strolls, and imagines for a moment that a God is mirrored in the shop-windows facing the Seine.

LA DORMEUSE II

Published for the first time in the *Mercure de France* of November, 1959, this sonnet is one of several variations on the theme of the Sleeping Beauty that Valéry wrote between "La Fileuse" (1891) and the final version of "Été" (1942).

The drafts contain a close analysis of the thought and structure to be developed: thus the pattern is outlined in precise terms ("1. Toi—Exposition; 2. Moi—Lucide; 3. Chant; 4. Descente"); similarly, the argument of the tercets ("Et ce bras qui m'enchaîne à ton songe, au plus profond de ton songe, et ce songe s'enchaîne aux ombres"). The poem is of special interest in that the poet is an actor in the scene and not a detached observer (the original manuscript bears his wife's name "Jeannie," the last tercet reading: "Et toute une ténèbre écoutant le génie / Tranquille de mon cœur... / Délicieusement renfermant ma Jeannie").

LE SOIR TROP BEAU...

This poem was published by Julien Monod in *Regard sur Paul Valéry* (1947), with the note that it was found by chance "on the back of an envelope" and probably dates from 1922.

IL EST VRAI. JE SUIS SOMBRE

These four lines have a tone of personal suffering heard nowhere else in Valéry's verse. They were published by Octave Nadal in his "Note to Twelve Poems."

THE FOLLOWING brief notes on the never very serious "occasional" poems of Valéry's later years will serve to identify the recipients. Some of these trifles accompanied copies of his own works. Or, as in the case of the first of the two poems to Gide and those to Charles-Adolphe Cantacuzène, they were acknowledgments of copies received. Others are in the nature of visiting cards, or album verse.

Tristan Derème was the pseudonym of Philippe Huc (1889–1941) who wrote much verse, notably *La Verdure dorée* (1922). Like Valéry he was born in the south of France. The quatrain was reproduced by Berne-Joffroy in *Présence de Valéry* (Plon, 1944).

Charles-Adolphe Cantacuzène, whose work on its first appearance was hailed by Mallarmé, wrote many books of verse. In 1926 he published *Identités versicolores: Les Phosphores mordorés* (Perrin). The two short pieces by Valéry were reproduced in the *Mercure de France* (April 15, 1926) in an announcement of the book's publication. The first had been written in 1918, the second in 1916, to celebrate a previous volume by the same author, *Hypotyposes*. ("Hypotyposis" is the rhetorical term for a vivid description of a scene, event, or situation.)

Léon-Paul Fargue (1876–1947), a bohemian poet and prolific author—Valéry once called him "the prince of metaphors"—gave a reading of "La Jeune Parque" at the home of Arthur Fontaine on April 29, 1917, to celebrate the publication of that work. Valéry's brief poem was written to mark the occasion.

The two poems to *André Gide* were sent in a letter of October 1917, the first acknowledging a copy of *Les Nourritures terrestres*, reissued by the *N.R.F.* twenty-five years after its first publication. The poem refers to their meetings long ago in the Botanical Gardens at Montpellier, beside the "empty tomb," supposedly that of Narcissa Young. The second poem, the sonnet "À Gênes," is followed by the facetious inscription, "Cy finissent les œuvres de Messer Paolo Ambrogio Currente-Calamo." Both poems first appeared in 1955, in the *Correspondence André Gide–Paul Valéry*.

Adrienne Monnier presided for many years over her famous bookshop in Paris, in the rue de l'Odéon, where she regularly invited poets to read their work to groups of friends. Valéry was often there, reading the poems of *Charmes*, or the prose of "Eupalinos, ou l'Architecte." His quatrain addressed to her was published in a volume of posthumous tributes, *Paul Valéry Vivant* (Cahiers du Sud, 1946).

Her contemporary, *Natalie Clifford Barney*, American-born but long resident in Paris and well known in literary circles, has written several books, including *Pensées d'une Amazone* (1920), *Aventure de l'esprit* (1929) in which Valéry's short poems appeared, and *Traits et Portraits* (1963).

Madame Lucien Muhlfeld, Valéry's "neighbor," lived in the rue Georges-Ville, next to the rue de Villejust where Valéry lived (now renamed rue Paul Valéry). He was at one time an habitué of her salon, and the sonnet was sent to her as a New Year greeting in January, 1918. Having recopied the poem for Gide, he commented: "I assure you it isn't as bad as all that. The ending will probably make your teeth hurt. With a little more work we'd have brought it off."

The well-known writer *Valery Larbaud* (1881–1957) is perhaps best remembered for his novel *A. O. Barnabooth* (1913). Other works of his include *Fermina Marquez* (1911), *Amants, Heureux Amants...* (1923), and a *Journal* (1955). He collaborated with Stuart Gilbert on the translation of James Joyce's *Ulysses* into French. Shortly after the appearance of "La Jeune Parque," Larbaud wrote to Valéry about the warmth with which his poem had been received in Spain. He later devoted a short monograph to his friend, *Paul Valéry et la Méditerranée* (1926), in which the quatrain, probably written in January, 1920, was published.

Anna de Noailles (1876–1933) was not only a famous and

prolific poet, author of many volumes of verse including *Le Cœur innombrable* (1901), and *Les Forces éternelles* (1920). The Comtesse de Noailles was also a social and literary celebrity, friend of Proust, Barrès, and many other well-known figures of her day. Valéry's homage was inscribed in a copy of *Charmes* which he sent to her in 1922. It was Henri Mondor who published the homage in *Le Figaro littéraire*, April 25, 1953, in an article devoted to Anna de Noailles.

The Album Verse for *Mme M. B.* (Marcelle Ballard) was written in Marseilles and is dated May 26, 1938. The album leaf, with a drawing by Valéry of his own left hand holding a cigarette, is reproduced in *Paul Valéry Vivant* (1946).

Valéry spent the summer of 1939 at Marrault, as the guest of *Louis Pasteur Vallery-Radot* (1886–1970), a distinguished physician, man of letters, and member of the French Academy, a grandson of Louis Pasteur. This short poem was sent to Madame Pasteur Vallery-Radot, with an unfinished watercolor on which Valéry wrote: "Dear friend, the verses are worthless. The watercolor is wretched. They are made for each other. But my heart is in them. It wishes you both all one can wish for such dear and true friends."

This colophon was chosen from a number of drawings by Paul Valéry of his favorite device.